DOING
QUALITATIVE
RESEARCH

RESEARCH METHODS FOR PRIMARY CARE

Series Board of Editors

The goal of RESEARCH METHODS FOR PRIMARY CARE is to address important topics meeting the needs of the growing number of primary care researchers. Purposely following a sequence from general principles to specific techniques, implementation strategies, and dissemination, the series volumes each examine a particular aspect of primary care research, emphasizing actually conducting research in the real world. The well-known contributors bring an international, multidisciplinary perspective to the volumes, enhancing their usefulness to primary care researchers.

Volumes in the series:

1. **Primary Care Research: Traditional and Innovative Approaches**
   Edited by Peter G. Norton, Moira Stewart, Fred Tudiver, Martin J. Bass, and Earl V. Dunn

2. **Tools for Primary Care Research**
   Edited by Moira Stewart, Fred Tudiver, Martin J. Bass, Earl V. Dunn, and Peter G. Norton

3. **Doing Qualitative Research: Multiple Strategies**
   Edited by Benjamin F. Crabtree and William L. Miller

Forthcoming titles in the series include:

4. **Assessing Interventions: Tradition and Innovative Methods**
   Edited by Fred Tudiver, Martin J. Bass, Earl V. Dunn, Peter G. Norton, and Moira Stewart

5. **Strategies for Implementing Research in the Primary Care Practice Setting**
   Edited by Martin J. Bass, Earl V. Dunn, Peter G. Norton, Moira Stewart, and Fred Tudiver

6. **Ways to Disseminate Research Findings and Have an Impact on Practice**
   Edited by Earl V. Dunn, Peter G. Norton, Moira Stewart, Fred Tudiver, and Martin J. Bass

DOING QUALITATIVE RESEARCH

EDITED BY
BENJAMIN F. CRABTREE
WILLIAM L. MILLER

Research Methods
for Primary Care
Volume 3

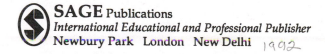
SAGE Publications
International Educational and Professional Publisher
Newbury Park London New Delhi

1992

For information address:

SAGE Publications, Inc.
2455 Teller Road
Newbury Park, California 91320

SAGE Publications Ltd.
6 Bonhill Street
London EC2A 4PU
United Kingdom

SAGE Publications India Pvt. Ltd.
M-32 Market
Greater Kailash I
New Delhi 110 048 India

Printed in the United States of America

Library of Congress Cataloging-in-Publication Data

Main entry under title:

Doing qualitative research: multiple strategies / edited by Benjamin
  F. Crabtree, William L. Miller.
        p.   cm. —(Research methods for primary care ; v. 3)
  Includes bibliographical references and index.
  ISBN 0-8039-4311-3 (hc). —ISBN 0-8039-4312-1 (pb)
    1. Family medicine—Research—Methodology. 2. Social medicine
—Research—Methodology.   3. Social Sciences—Research—Methodology.
I. Crabtree, Benjamin F.   II. Miller, William L. (William Lloyd),
1949- . III. Series.
    [DNLM: 1. Primary Health Care.   2. Research—methods.   W 84.6
D657]
R853.S64D65   1992
362.1'072—dc20
DNLM/DLC
                                                            92-7998

92 93 94 95 1 2 3 4 5 6 7 8 9 10 11

Sage Production Editor: Diane S. Foster

Contents

Series Editors' Introduction

This book is Volume 3 in the series on Research Methods for Primary Care. Each volume of this series has its own distinct content. Volume 1 contains principles and guidelines for both quantitative and qualitative designs. Volume 2 is primarily a "how to" guide for selected quantitative and qualitative approaches. Volume 3 focuses on qualitative research in primary care and as such is a very valuable resource.

With the growing recognition that primary care practitioners need knowledge of such issues as patients' experience, the nature of healing, and interpersonal processes comes the realization that qualitative methods are the methods of choice for many aspects of primary care research. Each chapter in this volume is a detailed account of one aspect of qualitative research. Together these chapters create a book of broad scope and wide relevance. The volume editors, Benjamin Crabtree and William Miller, have done primary care research a great service by providing in one volume a smorgasbord of qualitative approaches, thereby dispelling the misunderstanding that only one qualitative design or approach exists. As well, the volume contains invaluable chapters on particular research methods, such as sampling, interviewing, and computer management of text data. Chapter 1 is a gold mine all by itself in that it contains a taxonomy of research approaches, allowing the reader to put qualitative studies into a framework. Further, Chapter 1 presents a glossary of terms for those readers who are not yet familiar with the language of qualitative research.

As well as fulfilling its general goal to stimulate further interest in qualitative approaches and to prepare the reader for doing this type of research in primary care, this volume presents examples of studies that shed light on three important questions: How can health-seeking behavior be understood? How do primary health care providers become what they are? What goes on when primary health care seekers encounter clinical providers?

This book's usefulness is without question. First, it provides the potential investigator with practical chapters that will help him or her make decisions about the nuts-and-bolts issues in research. It will move the discipline forward by providing tangible support to the research endeavor. Second, the book identifies authors in the primary care discipline who can serve as mentors for the next generation of qualitative investigators. Those of us who teach research methods have been waiting too long for a volume like this to recommend to our students. Welcome to the new age of primary care research.

Moira Stewart
Peter G. Norton
Fred Tudiver
Martin J. Bass
Earl V. Dunn

Foreword

This book represents a remarkable step forward in the ability of primary care investigators to explore vital research issues related to their disciplines. During the 1950s and 1960s the general practice of medicine and the personal relationships and sense of caring that it imbued were fast becoming extinct in the United States. At the same time, general practice was becoming the cornerstone of health systems in most other developed countries. Its downfall in the United States in part was due to the scientific climate created by the national medical research enterprise. Successful medical researchers during this era were skilled in quantitative approaches and basic laboratory techniques. The vanquishing of disease was envisioned as occurring due to new knowledge regarding basic biological processes and the resultant development of specific therapies. Indeed during this era medical research made major headway in understanding the pathophysiology of disease and in developing therapies. The potential contribution to health of human interactions and the meaning of events in the lives of individuals who became patients was minimized, however, as not relevant to modern scientific medicine.

During the same era the United States public was increasingly distressed by the dearth of physicians able to administer comprehensively to the effects of illness on their lives and their families. As a result the specialty of family practice was created. In many ways it was an anomalous medical specialty. Other medical specialties have come into being due to the advancement of medical science in response to human need. For example the subspecialty of thoracic surgery developed due to advancements in general surgery, and the subspecialty of cardiovascular surgery developed out of advancements in thoracic surgery. Family medicine developed in response to human need without the intervening development of a scientific base.

During its early years, family medicine academicians were primarily consumed by the need to develop educational programs and the model practices on which they depend. Consequently research was not a major focus of many academic units. Few departments had chairpersons who championed the need for family medicine to develop its research base, and therefore supported family physicians intensely committed to the developing new knowledge relevant to daily family practice. Most of the investigators who were active had little previous research training and became self-taught researchers within a biologically reductionistic and quantitative medical research environment.

In the early to mid-1970s the computer was a relatively new research tool that dramatically increased the quantitative abilities of medical investigators. It was ideally suited to answering the quantitative questions of key interest to family physicians at the time. These included describing the age, sex, and morbidity characteristics of family practice and the relationships among these characteristics. Landmark studies such as the Virginia Morbidity Report, which involved over 200,000 diagnostic encounters, would have been impossible without the computer. Many family medicine academic units developed in close association with community medicine departments and the epidemiologic traditions carried by their faculty. The epidemiologic approach became a very valuable part of the family medicine research methods base, one that was well suited to the computerized morbidity registry capabilities developing concurrently.

Paralleling these research developments, early on, family medicine academicians also helped pioneer the introduction of social sciences into the medical curriculum. Sociological and anthropological insights into the functioning of individuals and families and their relationships to larger communities were seen as relevant and valuable components of the knowledge base of family practice. On occasion sociologists and psychologists conducted research using the family practice setting, but such investigations generally were separate and apart from that conducted by family medicine investigators.

During the 1980s, research by family medicine investigators began to flourish. The initial emphasis on development of the discipline's educational and practice bases paid off. Family medicine increasingly was accepted as an equal departmental peer within academic structures. At the same time, society began recognizing the limitations of reductionistic and quantitative scientific frameworks.

A new generation has joined the ranks of family medicine investigators. Many of these individuals are well trained and highly skilled in epidemiologic and other quantitative methods. This is leading to effective application of these research approaches to answer questions of relevance to the care rendered by family physicians and other primary care specialists. These skills have allowed family physicians to begin to compete successfully for federal and foundation support of major research projects. These skilled investigators also are identifying the limitations of such approaches to answer the full spectrum of questions relevant to practice. As a result, investigators are exploring other research traditions in their search for methods that complement their quantitative skills and broaden their ability to investigate the uncertainties of family practice.

It was within this context that Ben Crabtree and Will Miller began examining the application of anthropologic and other qualitative research methods to family medicine questions during the late 1980s. In visiting with them at the University of Connecticut, it was clear that they were developing, with active support from their chair, David Schmidt, M.D., M.P.H., a comprehensive understanding of the field of qualitative research and its applicability to family medicine and primary care. In this undertaking they were joined by other pioneers, including many of the authors of chapters in this book. Their search was for a set of research methods that would bring a sense of context and the importance of personal and cultural values and meanings as components of the human condition to join the quantitative research approaches.

This book is not about replacing quantitative methods in family practice and primary care research with qualitative methods. Rather it is about adding qualitative techniques as complementary methods. In this vein, it is important to note that Ben Crabtree is an accomplished quantitative researcher. He is as comfortable discussing the fine points of constructing a logistic regression model or time series model as he is with the qualitative approaches he helps present in this book.

With active support from the North American Primary Care Research Group (NAPCRG), Ben Crabtree and Will Miller formed an interest group in 1987 that quickly became, with the additional leadership of Tony Kuzel, a joint NAPCRG-Society of Teachers of Family

Medicine (STFM) interest group. In 1988 they initiated a newsletter, *The Interpreter*, that quickly became a major networking tool among family medicine qualitative investigators.

In 1989 we first explored the possibility of a workshop on qualitative methods to be held immediately prior to the 19th annual NAPCRG meeting in Quebec. Our initial aspirations were for a meeting that might attract as many as 30 or 40 individuals. Sage graciously agreed to consider publishing the presentations from this workshop as part of its Foundations of Primary Care Research Series. With exceptional support from Michael Labreque and the Laval University, Ben Crabtree and Will Miller proceeded with planning the workshop. When it finally was held, on May 22, 1989, more than 130 individuals took part, and another 30 had to be turned away due to inadequate space. Qualitative research clearly had come of age within the family medicine research arena.

This book reflects the proceedings of this event. Qualitative research is perceived as working in tandem with the quantitative survey and experimental approaches as discussed in Chapter 1. For some areas of investigation, qualitative research may proceed and identify the important questions and approaches for subsequent quantitative research. At other times, qualitative research will be critical to broadening the understanding of insights contributed by quantitative research. In many instances the two will work together to advance the understanding of primary care and its increasing contribution to health. This book provides invaluable insights into the application of qualitative techniques to the practice and research of primary health care.

Larry Culpepper, M.D., M.P.H.
NAPCRG President, 1989-1991
Associate Professor of Family Medicine
Brown University

Introduction

Puzzles abound at each moment of every day in community primary health care settings around the globe. A flustered young nurse practitioner ponders, "Why does this 80-year-old woman with hip pain for 6 years insist on seeing me now?" Another elderly patient suffering with hip pain stares incredulously at her new family physician and wonders, "How did this doctor learn to practice?" Both patient and provider worry and search for ways to discover, "What is going on here? How can I explain it?" These common primary care questions call for new research approaches. This book introduces research methods useful for exploring these kinds of questions.

How can health-seeking behavior be understood? Ben Crabtree and Will Miller (Chapter 5) explores this question in an elderly community and describe how to use codebooks to analyze participant observation field notes. Using focus groups and codebooks, David Morgan (Chapter 12) investigates the health-seeking decisions of caregivers for a family member with Alzheimer's disease. Tony Kuzel (Chapter 2) illustrates his discussion of qualitative sampling strategies with a study designed to understand why particular doctors seem to attract particular patients.

How do primary health care providers become what they are? Miguel Bedolla (Chapter 9) presents a historical approach to this question with a special focus on the emergence of family medicine as a specialty. Ritch Addison (Chapter 6) and Steve Bogdewic (Chapter 3) describe studies of the residency training experience of family physicians, using participant observation and key informant interviews and "cut-and-paste" type interpretive analytic techniques.

Valerie Gilchrist (Chapter 4) elaborates on key informant interviewing, and Al Reid (Chapter 7) describes how to use word processing software in the management of this kind of qualitative data.

What goes on when primary health care seekers encounter clinical providers? Moira Stewart (Chapter 8) explores the use of audiotapes and videotapes as a means of analyzing such encounters. Dennis Willms, Nancy Arbuthnot Johnson, and Norman White (Chapter 11) describe the use of depth interviews and analysis codebooks in the investigation of health promotion activities of family physicians. Finally Howard Brody (Chapter 10) demonstrates the use of philosophic inquiry to help understand the placebo effect and informed consent.

The overall goals of this book are to stimulate further interest in qualitative primary care research and to prepare readers for doing this type of inquiry. The intent is to expand existing research approaches and not to replace them. One specific goal of Chapter 1 is to provide a taxonomic foundation for understanding why particular research designs are selected. Primary care research asks questions at multiple system levels: from global, to community, to family, to individual, to organ, to cell, and to recursive interaction between and among these levels. The complex substance of primary care research is multilayered, configurational, holistic, particularistic, probabilistic, often ambiguous, and wonderfully mysterious. Primary care's significance connects at the macrolevel with generalizations about health and healing and at the microlevel with specific primary health care activities revealing their interpretive uncertainties and value-based decisions. Given these substances and significances and the range of primary care research, a multimethod approach is called for (Brewer & Hunter, 1989; Coward, 1990; Houts, Cook, & Shadish, 1986; Light & Pillemer, 1982; McWhinney, 1991; Stange & Zyzanski, 1989; Tudiver, et al., 1991). Primary care providers blend their intersubjective, longitudinal understandings of patients with their experimentally based knowledge of pathophysiology and their statistical understanding of risks and benefits. So too do primary care researchers need to use a multimethod approach.

The dynamics of the qualitative research process are illustrated in Figure I.1. Two features distinguish this process from traditional epidemiologic research design. First, no prepackaged designs exist from which to choose. Rather, multiple, specific sampling, data collection, data management, and data analysis options exist from which to select. Almost any mix and match is possible and depends on the

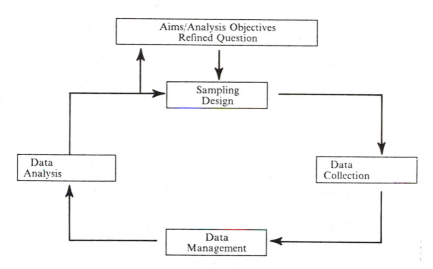

Figure I.1. The Iterative Qualitative Research Process

aims, objectives, and research question. The second distinguishing feature is the recursive, cyclical nature of the process. Collection and analysis usually occur concurrently. Initial analysis often changes sampling strategies and collection methods. Qualitative data management methods must be flexible enough to allow for these ongoing adjustments.

The organization of this book follows the structure of the above qualitative research process. Chapter 1 overviews how to decide what methods to use based on aims, objectives, questions, and paradigms. Chapters 2, 3, and 4 explore in more detail the discovery strategies of sampling, participant observation, and key informant interviewing. Depth interviews and focus group interviews have been described previously in the second volume of this series (Miller & Crabtree, 1992; Morgan, 1992). Chapters 5 through 10 reveal the specifics of doing different types of qualitative analysis, with Chapter 7 detailing one approach to computer management of text data. Chapters 11 and 12 put the whole process together by stepping through the design decisions involved in two completed qualitative investigations. Chapter 13 is more reflective and views the preceding chapters from the perspectives of academia, epidemiology, and journal editing.

Readers of literature on qualitative research may be confused by disciplinary and tradition-based jargon. This literature often seems especially dense to epidemiologically trained researchers. Terms such as *hermeneutic, constructionist, semiotic,* and *axial coding* can be confusing and mystifying. This book will intentionally attempt to avoid jargon in an effort to display and make accessible the existing panorama of qualitative methods. The appendix following Chapter 1 serves as a glossary and reference for those readers seeking more detail on particular methods and terminology.

Although no chapter on writing up qualitative research is included in this series (see Richardson, 1990; Wolcott, 1990), the authors in this book all effectively model the essential ingredients. These gifted researchers, many of whom are also clinicians, define their topic; reveal themselves and the context of their discussion; define the key themes and processes; provide thick, interesting descriptive examples; and share their excitement of discovery.

William L. Miller
Benjamin F. Crabtree

PART I

Overview of Qualitative Research Methods

1 Primary Care Research: A Multimethod Typology and Qualitative Road Map

WILLIAM L. MILLER
BENJAMIN F. CRABTREE

Welcome to the excitement, diversity, and possibilities of primary care research. Welcome to a journey of adventure. This chapter presents a road map of research methods to facilitate the development of a multimethod approach to this adventure. Five styles of inquiry are identified and described briefly. Research aims and analysis objectives are then matched with these styles. The research styles are also connected with three different paradigms. This information is used to describe the process of choosing an appropriate method for a particular research interest. This chapter elaborates a typology of qualitative methods and overviews how to develop appropriate qualitative designs.

A Multimethod Research Typology

Doing research is in many ways like taking a descriptive and explanatory snapshot of reality. For each particular photograph, the investigator must decide what kind of camera, what scene on which to focus, through which filter, and with what intent. At least five styles of inquiry are distinguishable, based on the primary camera, focus,

Table 1.1 Characteristics of Different Research Styles

| Characteristics of Style | Research Styles | | | | |
	Experiment	Survey	Documentary-Historical	Field	Philosophy
Camera	Laboratory	Instrument	Multimethod	Researcher	Thinker
Scene of Focus	Casual hypothesis	Probability sample	Artifacts	Human field	Ideal concept
Filter	Qualitative	Quantitative	Qualitative/ quantitative	Qualitative	Logic
Intent	Test casual hypothesis	Generalize to population	Description/ explanation/ prediction of nonreactive data	Holistic, realistic description/ explanation	Establish underlying principles

filter, and intent: experimental, survey, documentary-historical, field, and philosophic (see Table 1.1).

Experimental research creates study designs that test carefully constructed causal hypotheses. The laboratory is the camera used to focus the experiment's lens on the causal hypothesis. The laboratory, whether in a building, in the field of human activity, or in a computer simulation, is where the variable of interest is actively and measurably manipulated in tightly controlled conditions. The researcher doing the experiment wears quantitative filters that selectively gaze with accurate, measurable precision. The experimental style includes the many types of experimental designs and randomized controlled trial designs.

The **survey** style of inquiry, on the other hand, focuses on a representative probability sample from a defined population by means of a research instrument, such as a structured interview, rating scale, or questionnaire, with the intent of generalizing the resultant descriptions and/or associations to the larger population. *Survey* is used here in the broad sense intended by the social science traditions (Babbie, 1979; Last, 1983; Lin, 1976). The epidemiologist's understanding of *survey* as cross-sectional research (Mausner & Kramer, 1985) is understood here as one example of a more encompassing "survey" research style. As with the experimental style, the filter and form of expression are quantitative and statistical with emphasis on validity and reliability. Unlike the experimental style, survey research involves *passive manipulation* of the variable of interest. The observational designs of epidemiology, such as cohort, cross-sectional, and case-control, are examples of the survey style. Other survey designs include: descriptive surveys; correlational, longitudinal, and comparative survey designs; time series designs; theory-testing correlational surveys; ex post facto designs; and quasi- experimental designs. Burkett (1990) and Marvel, Staehling, and Hendricks (1991) have presented useful typologies for organizing the survey and experimental styles of research.

The common denominator of the **documentary-historical** style is a focus on artifacts. This style is an eclectic assortment of cameras and filters. The researcher using this style gazes at an artifact through the camera and filter most appropriate for the intent. The artifacts can be archives, literature, medical records, instruments, art, clothes, or data tapes from someone else's research. Examples of documentary-historical research include literature review, artifact analysis, chart audits, archive analysis, historical research, secondary analysis, and meta-analysis.

The **field** researcher is directly and personally engaged in an interpretive focus on the human field of activity with the goal of generating holistic and realistic descriptions and/or explanations. The field is viewed through the experientially engaged and perceptually limited lens of the researcher using a qualitative filter. Field research is often called *qualitative research*. Unlike the previously discussed research styles, field research has no prepackaged research designs. Rather, specific data collection methods, sampling procedures, and analysis styles are used to create unique, question-specific designs that evolve throughout the research process. These qualitative or field designs take the form of either a case study or a topical study. Case studies (Merriam, 1988; Yin, 1989) examine most or all the potential aspects of a particular distinctly bounded unit or case (or series of cases). A case may be an individual, a family, a community health center, a nursing home, or an organization. Topical studies investigate only one or a few selected spheres of activity within a less distinctly bounded field, such as a study of the meaning of pain for selected persons in a community.

Last is **philosophic** inquiry, which often serves as a generator and clarifier for the other research styles. The philosophical inquirer uses analytic skills as a thinker to examine an idea or concept through the filter of logic in order to move toward clarity and the illumination of background conditions.

RESEARCH AIMS

The choice of research style for a particular project depends on the overarching aim of the research, the specific analysis objective and its associated research question, the preferred paradigm, the degree of desired research control, the level of investigator intervention, the available resources, the time frame, and aesthetics (Brewer & Hunter, 1989; Diers, 1979). Scientific inquiry has at least five aims: identification, description, explanation-generation, explanation-testing, and control. The first three of these comprise what is often termed *exploratory research*. Qualitative methods usually are used for identification, description, and explanation-generation; whereas, quantitative methods are used most commonly for explanation-testing and control. These general guidelines have many exceptions, depending on the specific analysis objective (see Table 1.2).

The aim of *identification* is one of the most neglected aspects of scientific inquiry. All too often, investigators create concepts based on some "gut" feeling, their own reasoning, or the literature. They then produce measurement instruments that reify the concept, giving the appearance it really exists "out there." The result may be research that is powerful (minimal Type 2 error) and minimizes false positives (Type 1 error) but also may be solving the wrong problem (Type 3 error) or solving a problem not worth solving (Type 4 error). Qualitative field research, the documentary-historical style, and philosophical inquiry are ideally suited for the essential task of identification.

At least three types of *description* are distinguishable: qualitative, quantitative, and normative. Qualitative description, using qualitative methods, explores the meanings, variations, and perceptual experiences of phenomena. Quantitative description, based in descriptive statistics, refers to the distribution, frequency, prevalence, incidence, and size of one or more phenomena. Normative description seeks to establish the norms and value of phenomena (O'Connor, 1990). The choice of quantitative or qualitative methods depends on whether the norms of interest are numerical or textual.

Explanation-generation/Association can have at least three analytic objectives: interpretive explanation-generation, statistical explanation-

Table 1.2 Research Aims, Analysis Objectives, Research Questions and Appropriate Research Styles

Aim	Analysis Objective	Research Question	Research Style
Identification	Identify/Name	What is this? Who is that? What is important here?	Field Doc-Hist Philos
Description	Qualitative Description	What is going on here? What is the nature of the phenomenon? What are the dimensions of the concept? What variations exist? What meanings/practices occur in lived experience?	Field Doc-Hist Philos
	Quantitative Description	How many? How much? How often? What size? How is the phenomenon distributed over space?	Survey
	Normative Description	What is the value of a phenomenon?	Field Doc-Hist Survey Philos
Explanation Generation/ Association	Interpretive Explanation Generation	What is happening here? What patterns exist? How do phenomena differ and relate to each other? How does it work? How did something occur/happen?	Field Doc-Hist
	Statistical Explanation Generation	What are the measurable associations between phenomena? Does variable x relate to other variables? Why does it work? Why did something occur?	Doc-Hist Survey
	Deductive Explanation	Given these premises, then ____?	Philos
Explanation Testing/ Prediction	Causal Confirmation	What will happen if ____? If ____ then ____? Does one variable cause the other?	Exper
	Theory Testing	Is the original theory correct? Does the original theory fit other circumstances? Are there additional categories or relationships?	Field Doc-Hist Survey Exper
Prescription/ Control	Prescription Testing	Is ____ more effective than ____? Does ____ have greater efficacy than ____?	Exper (RCT)
	Evaluation	How can I make "x" happen? What difference does this program/intervention make?	Field Survey

generation, and deductive explanation. Some research seeks to discover relationships, associations, and patterns based on personal experience of the phenomena under question. This interpretive explanation-generation is best achieved using research styles with a qualitative filter, such as field and documentary-historical styles.

When concepts already have been identified, described, and interpretively defined, another objective is to explore possible statistical relationships, using quantitatively based styles of research. Another analytic objective is to deductively generate explanations from a set of given premises. This purpose is best met using philosophic inquiry.

Explanation-testing/Prediction includes both objectives of confirming causality and testing theory. One form of causal confirmation is to establish predictability; another is to demonstrate causality definitively, using experimental research design. Another analysis objective is to test explanatory theory by evaluating it in different contexts. The research style used to meet this objective depends on the type of explanation being tested.

Prescription/Control is an important aim for most primary care researchers—the testing and/or evaluation of some interventional strategy. One analysis objective is to test a prescription in such a way that either its efficacy or its effectiveness can be generalized to other similar situations. This is the *raison d'être* for the randomized control trial (RCT). At other times the analysis objective is to evaluate an intervention in a specific context with no immediate expectation for generalization. Qualitative evaluation strategies are especially useful for this purpose (Patton, 1990).

PARADIGMS

A paradigm represents a patterned set of assumptions concerning reality (ontology), knowledge of that reality (epistemology), and the particular ways for knowing about that reality (methodology) (Guba, 1990). These assumptions and the ways for knowing are untested givens and determine how one engages and comes to understand the world. Each investigator must decide what assumptions are acceptable and appropriate for the topic of interest and then use methods consistent with the selected paradigm. At least three paradigms exist (Habermas, 1968).

First is that knowledge that helps us maintain physical life, our labor and technology. This is most commonly represented by positivism and the biomedical model. Wet lab science and quantitative methods primarily inform this knowledge, referred to here as *materialistic inquiry*. This paradigm can be metaphorically understood as "Jacob's Ladder" (Figure 1.1). The materialist inquirer values progress, stresses the primacy of method, seeks an ultimate truth—a natural

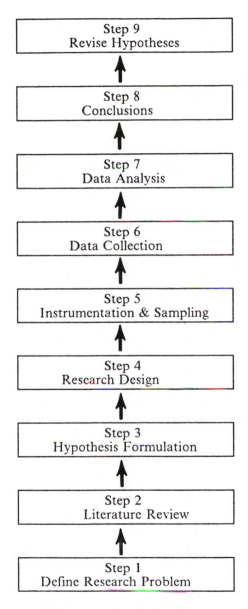

Figure 1.1. Jacob's Ladder of Materialistic Inquiry

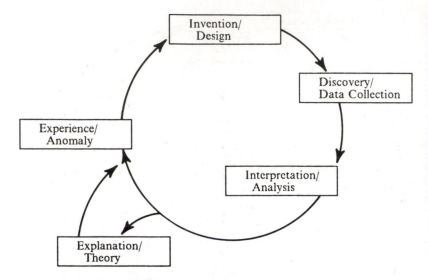

Figure 1.2. Shiva's Circle of Constructivist Inquiry

law—of reality and is grounded in Western, monotheistic tradition. Materialistic inquiry is best for social engineering. If one wants to understand the molecular genetics of hyperlipidemia or to develop a new drug, then this is the paradigm of choice. The materialist inquirer climbs a linear ladder to an ultimate objective truth.

A second paradigm is based on the knowledge that helps us maintain cultural life, our symbolic communication and meaning, and is referred to here as *constructivist inquiry*. This paradigm also has been called *naturalistic inquiry* (Kuzel, 1986) and *hermeneutics* (Gadamer, 1976; Guba & Lincoln, 1989). *Constructivism* is the term because it is human constructions being studied and because it is constructions the researcher is creating. Qualitative methods generally inform this knowledge, which can be depicted by the metaphor of "Shiva's Circle" (Figure 1.2). Shiva is the androgynous Hindu Lord of the Dance and of Death. A constructivist inquirer enters an interpretive circle and must be faithful to the performance or subject, must be both apart from and part of the dance, and must always be rooted to the context. No ultimate truth exists; context-bound constructions are all part of the larger universe of stories. Constructivist inquiry is best for storytelling. If one wants to understand how

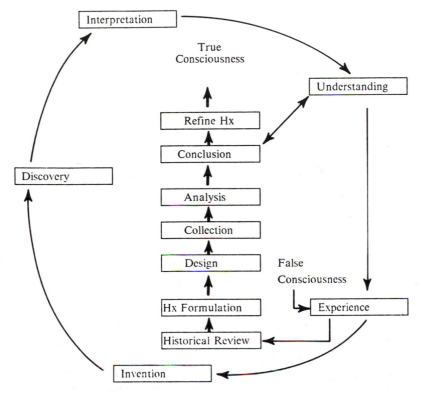

Figure 1.3. Gobal Eye of Critical/Ecological Inquiry

patients and providers experience pain or being informed their
cholesterol is high, then this is the paradigm of choice. The constructivist inquirer enters into Shiva's Circle, performing an ongoing
iterative dance of discovery and interpretation.

A third knowledge, which helps us maintain our social life, focuses on the reality of domination, distribution of power, and associated inequalities (Bateson, 1979; Fay, 1987). It is referred to here as
critical/ecological inquiry. This is the "global eye" that critically looks
in at both dancers and ladder climbers and gazes at the systemic
effects (Figure 1.3). The critical/ecological inquirer seeks to move
from the false consciousness of present experience and ideology to
a more empowered and emancipated consciousness by reducing

the illusions through the processes of historical review and the juxta-positioning of materialistic and interpretive inquiry. Critical/ecological inquiry is best for political engagement and the study of systems.

CHOOSING A RESEARCH STYLE

The determination and articulation of the research aim, analysis objective, specific research question, and appropriate mode of engagement all shape the choice of research style. Additional factors also may influence this decision and include time frame, degree of desired researcher control, and aesthetics. For example, historical and retrospective designs are better for investigating past events. The experimental style of research is suitable if the researcher desires a high degree of control over the variables of interest. Aesthetics plays a role in the sense that each researcher possesses a unique set of skills, gifts, and sensibilities that resonate better with certain styles of inquiry and/or paradigms. Research is a way to celebrate these differences. Three examples from upcoming chapters illustrate the process of choosing a research style.

Ben Crabtree's and Will Miller's aim (Chapter 5) is to identify and describe a particular aspect of illness behaviors in the elderly. They want to know: What do elderly persons do when they recognize illness? What is this phenomenon of illness behavior? What is important here? and What is going on here? They are particularly interested in questions of meaning and culture that call for constructivist inquiry. The field research style is their choice for meeting the analysis objectives of identification and qualitative description.

Ritch Addison (Chapter 6) wants to describe phenomena, promote understanding, and generate explanations. He seeks to understand, How did something happen? specifically, How did individuals become family doctors? Since the type of explanation is interpretive and his inquiry is also about culture and symbolic communication, constructivist (hermeneutic) field research is the choice.

David Morgan (Chapter 12) has two sets of questions but one major aim. He wants to interpretively explore, What is happening here? and What pattern exists? vis-à-vis caregiver decisions to institutionalize a family member with Alzheimer's disease and to seek expert diagnosis. He also wants to generate explanations about How does it work? and How do those decisions come about? He seeks interpretive explanation-generation. He, too, engages the research through constructivist eyes since his questions concern meaning and symbolic communication. His aim is best addressed with the field research style using qualitative methods. The choice of research designs for these three field or qualitative research projects is described later in the chapter. First, we will present a typology of qualitative methods.

Qualitative Methods: A Primary Care Road Map

The quest for a useful organizational map of qualitative methods is not unlike the quest for the Holy Grail. The methods derive from multiple disciplines and from at least 20 or more diverse traditions, each with its own particular language. Despite this tangled web, at least two paths to organizing qualitative methods are discernible. One approach, presented in the appendix at the end of this chapter, organizes qualitative methods on the basis of disciplinary traditions. The resulting typology enables the investigator to know "who to call" at their nearby university for methods advice. The approach in the remainder of this chapter focuses on specific methods of data collection and on styles of analysis and offers a pragmatic perspective on how to design a qualitative or field research project.

The field research style seeks "truth from the natives in their habitat by *looking* and *listening*" (Peacock, 1986, p. 49). This simple statement captures the essence of a pragmatic typology of qualitative methods. Field data are collected by *observation, interviews,* or the *mechanical recording* of conversation and/or behavior. The analysis of the resulting textual data is a subjective/objective dance toward contextual truth with four prototypical analysis styles to choose from. These analytic styles range on a continuum from objective and more standardized to subjective and more interpretive. The four styles are referred to here as *quasi-statistical, template, editing,* and *immersion/ crystallization*. A field research design begins with specific sampling strategies, data collection techniques, and an analysis style chosen to maximize initial understanding of the research question and its aims and objectives. The analysis of this first phase of the research guides future decisions concerning sampling, collection, and analysis. This evolving iterative process of collection-analysis-collection is central to the field research process. A basic understanding of the data collection techniques, the analysis styles, information-rich sampling, and iterative procedures enables one to design and implement a qualitative study around a primary care research question.

DATA COLLECTION

Table 1.3 lists qualitative data collection techniques. *Observation* is the most available but probably the most time intensive and demanding of the collection techniques. Two continua exist for understanding types of observation. One refers to the degree of researcher participation in the scene being observed. The other refers to the degree of structure in the observations themselves (Patton, 1990). The observer is always a participant in the observation, but a great difference exists between being a quiet note-taker staying in the background as much as possible (e.g., in the corner of a pharmacy) and keeping notes as a primary care provider during the course of one's duties.

The other continuum for understanding observation types refers to the degree of structure in the observations themselves. Any scientific observer must have a familiarity with the setting, participants, and activities, along with a set of questions concerning these prior to initiating observation. Contrast the situations of (a) the researcher who observes a family's first two days home with a newborn in order to examine how the family members interact and adapt, with (b) the researcher who visits the home with a checklist of mother-infant bonding behaviors. In either case, observation data are usually collected in the form of field notes but can also consist of maps and scales.

The research question and goal determine which type of observation is most appropriate. If the goal is to understand the experience of becoming a physician (as in Chapter 3), *unstructured participant observation* is highly desirable. If, on the other hand, the goal is to evaluate the hypothetical rules for being a "good intern," then *structured participant observation* facilitates the investigator's acting on the rules and observing what happens. The investigator may, however, only wish to see whether residents do physical exams the way attending physicians think they should. *Structured background observation*, using a rating scale, is suitable for this question. If the goal is to understand how nurses and resident physicians communicate with each other about patients in pain, *unstructured background obser-*

Table 1.3 Qualitative Data-Collection Techniques

OBSERVATION
Unstructured
Structured (Direct)
Mapping
Category systems
Check lists
Rating scales
Participant
RECORDINGS
Audio
Visual
A/V
INTERVIEWING
Unstructured
Everyday conversation
Key informant/Elite
Semistructured (Interview guide)
Depth/Focused
Individual (Long interview)
Group (Focus groups)
Life history (Biography)
Critical incidents techniques
Free listing
Ethnoscience interview
Structured (Interview schedule)
Pile sorts/Triad comparisons (Q sorts)
Rank order methods
Paired comparisons
Balanced incomplete block design
Diagram directed techniques
Genogram
Life space
Surveys/Questionnaires/Tests

vation is an acceptable initial approach since less is known about this question and no preexisting "expert" consensus exists.

Recordings of conversations and events are becoming technically easier and more common with the advance of recording technology. The decision on whether to use an audio recorder or a video recorder depends on the question of interest and the unit of analysis (see Chapter 8).

Types of *interviewing* are distinguished by exploring three dimensions which answer the questions "Who?" "How?" and "About what?" *Who* refers to whether one interviews an individual or a group.

The difference appears obvious, but it is often ignored in ways similar to the ecological fallacy in statistics. When a group of family practice residents is informally interviewed as a group in an on-call room, or when a group of caregivers is sampled for a focus group interview, the unit of analysis is the group (see Chapter 12). These data are not equivalent to individual interviews with the same residents or the same caregivers. Whom one interviews depends on the answer to the question, Who do I want to make inferences about—individuals or groups? Individual interviews often provide more depth about a topic, whereas group interviews frequently generate greater breadth of information.

The second dimension, *How,* refers to the degree of structure in the interview process (see Table 1.3). As with observation, no interview is completely unstructured, but three levels of structure can be delineated usefully (Bernard, 1988). *Unstructured interviewing* is equivalent to guided everyday conversation and is often part of participant observation, particularly in the form of key informant interviews (see Chapter 4). Key informants provide expert, inside information. The researcher has one or more topic areas that are probed whenever the opportunity arises during a given period of observation. *Semistructured interviews* are guided, concentrated, focused, and open-ended communication events that are co-created by the investigator and interviewee(s) and occur outside the stream of everyday life. The questions, probes, and prompts are written in the form of a flexible interview guide. *Structured interviews,* on the other hand, are more like spoken questionnaires with a rigidly structured interview schedule directing the interview. Structured interviews are best when sufficient trustworthy information already exists on which to develop the interview schedule.

Which type of structured or semistructured interview is selected for a particular project depends on *what* information is sought. *Depth interviews* intensively plumb a particular topic (McCracken, 1988). *Life histories* reveal personal biography (Denzin, 1989b; Watson & Watson-Franke, 1985), and *projective techniques* expose the shadows of personality (Pelto & Pelto, 1978). The terms and meanings of words and actions and the rules governing them are elicited through *free listings* and an *"ethnoscience interview"* (Spradley, 1979). *Pile sorts* and *rank order methods* are structured techniques for further clarifying cognitive and decision-making activity underlying human choices (Weller & Romney, 1988). The *structured diagram-directed techniques* are goal specific and include some primary care examples such as the genogram (McGoldrick & Gerson, 1985), life space drawings (Blake & Bertuso, 1988), and family circles (Thrower, Bruce, & Walton, 1982).

The decision to observe, record, and/or interview is often more complex than usually recognized. Behavior and conversations are best recorded; activities of daily living are best observed; and stories and cognitive maps are best obtained through interview. After these basic generalizations, the decision-making process becomes less obvious. A critical question guiding one to the most appropriate selection is, How is the topic in question usually shared in the culture or group of interest? (Briggs, 1986). For example, suppose our general topic of research interest concerns how particular health care providers learn the identity characteristics and style of their particular specialty. Surgeons often share this information in the operating room or in the trauma room in an apprentice-type interaction; therefore, participant observation as an apprentice is a preferred data collection technique. Obstetricians frequently share information in the form of "near disaster" and "dramatic save" stories while sitting and waiting in the delivery room lounge. Recording of these stories, if possible, is optimal. Many nurses and family physicians eagerly share information in the form of explanatory talk. Whenever two or more gather, they usually seize the opportunity to share experiences, puzzlements, insights, and frustrations. Interviewing works well with family doctors and nurses.

DATA ANALYSIS

Although nearly as many analysis strategies exist as qualitative researchers, these strategies derive from four idealized analytic patterns and fall along a continuum. At one extreme are analytic techniques that are more objective (separate the researcher from the object of research), scientific (valid, reliable, reproducible, accurate, and systematic), general (lawlike regularities), technical (procedural, mechanical), and standardized (measurable, verifiable). *Quasi-statistical* is the name given here to analysis techniques sharing these features. At the other extreme are those analytic techniques that are subjective (emerge from the researcher), intuitive (experiential insight), particular (personal, context-dependent), existential (concerned with everyday existence), interpretive (related to meaning), and generative. *Immersion/crystallization* analysis is the label given here

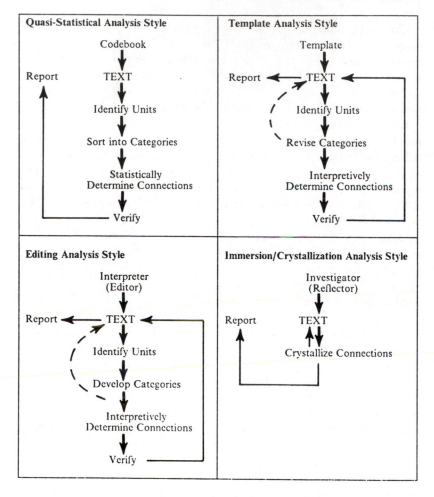

Figure 1.4. Diagrammatic Representation of Different Analysis Styles

to those approaches demonstrating these traits in the extreme. *Editing* (more subjective, cut-and-paste-like) and *template* (less subjective, codebook-based) styles are in the middle of the continuum and are the most commonly used. Table 1.1A in the appendix lists the four analysis styles with their associated research traditions and/or specific analytic techniques. All four styles are illustrated in Figure 1.4.

Quasi-statistical includes several approaches, one of which is basic or manifest content analysis (Weber, 1985). The content analyst reads the text searching either for "words" (often using a word search computer program) or for semantic units or themes based on a codebook. The words and/or themes are then sorted into categories and manipulated statistically; hence, the name *quasi-statistical analysis*.

Immersion/crystallization consists of the analyst's prolonged immersion into and experience of the text and then emerging, after concerned reflection, with an intuitive crystallization of the text. This cycle of immersion and crystallization is repeated until the reported interpretation is reached. The heuristic research of Moustakas (1990) and Kotarba's (1983) existential truth analysis are examples. The penetrating and revealing insights of Howard Stein (1990), well known to family physicians, are also examples of this style of analysis. The stories and case report insights of patients, nurses, and practicing primary care physicians are a variation of this analysis style and often serve as starting points for new directions in research or further enlightening of previous studies (Miller & Crabtree, 1990).

Template analytic techniques all share the use of a template or analysis guide, which is applied to the text being analyzed. The basic pattern or template underlying all the template analytic styles is distinguished from the codebook of quasi-statistics in that the template is more open-ended and undergoes revision after encountering the text. In addition the generation of themes, patterns, and interrelationships is an interpretive rather than a statistical process. The template derives from theory, research tradition, preexisting knowledge, and/or a summary reading of the text. Templates can be codebooks developed prior to data collection, as in the approach of Miles and Huberman (1984), or created after data collection has begun, as in ethnographic content analysis (Altheide, 1987) (see Chapter 5). Templates can also be a theoretical, behavioral, or linguistic structure. Whatever the template, it is applied to the text with the intent of identifying the meaningful units or parts. The units are behavior or language units such as words, phrases, utterances, and folk terms. If the text reveals inadequacies in the template, modifications and revisions are made and the text is reexamined. The interaction of text and template may involve several iterations and include the collection of more data until no new revisions are identified. The analysis then proceeds to an interpretive phase in which the units are connected into an explanatory framework consistent with the text. It is these final connections that form the reported outcomes.

Codebook-based template analysis usually uses tables and matrices (Miles & Huberman, 1984) to facilitate the generation and verification of connections. The structure-based approaches apply either interactional structures (e.g., sociolinguistics) (McLaughlin, 1984) or logical, semantic, or sequential structures (e.g., ethnoscience, ethology) to the identified units (see Appendix). For example, Spradley (1979), an ethnoscientist, would read text looking for how "term X is like term Y." "Is like" is the semantic structure applied to the identified terms.

The editing style moves analysis closer to the subjective/interpretive side of the analysis continuum. This style is termed *editing* because the interpreter enters the text much like an editor searching for meaningful segments, cutting, pasting, and rearranging until the reduced summary reveals the interpretive truth in the text. The interpreter engages the text naively, without a template. The researcher attempts to identify and separate from preconceptions prior to reading the data. The interpreter searches for meaningful units or segments of text that both stand on their own and relate to the purpose of the study. Once identified, these units are sorted and organized into categories or codes. The interpreter then explores the categories and determines the patterns and themes that connect them. It is often necessary to collect more data during this phase to evaluate the emergent hypotheses. After this step, the editing style is similar to template analysis (refer to Figure 1.4). The grounded theory approach of Glaser and Strauss (1967), popular with qualitative nurse researchers (Chenitz & Swanson, 1986), and McCracken's Long Interview analysis (1988) are examples of the editing analysis style. Ritch Addison (Chapter 6) and Dennis Willms, Nancy Arbuthnot Johnson, and Norman White (Chapter 11) illustrate the editing style in more detail.

The initial choice of analysis style depends, for the most part, on the research question and goal, on what is already known about the topic of interest, and on the data collection techniques used. When the goal is subjective understanding, exploration, and/or generation of new insights/hypotheses and when scant knowledge already exists, the more interpretive styles are preferable.

It is essential in concluding this section on data analysis to reiterate the iterative process of qualitative research design. Data analysis begins shortly after the first data are collected. This analysis creates new understandings, generates changes in the research question, and uncovers new anomalies. The result is often a change in the sampling strategy, new collection tools, and thus changes in the analysis style. This recursive cycle continues until understanding is complete enough and/or no disconfirming data are discovered.

Summary

The introduction in this book opened with three primary care puzzles: the health-seeking process, health care provider socialization, and client-provider encounters. This chapter's journey toward puzzle solving began by constructing a road map or typology of research styles based on aims, objectives, questions, and paradigms. At this first fork in the road, field research was selected as the preferred strategy for investigating these particular puzzles. Then we explored the maze of qualitative methods used in field research by viewing them through our eyes as doers of primary care qualitative research. The design options for data collection and analysis were identified. The remainder of this book describes these options in more detail, and each author explains his or her design decisions. Three of these decision pathways are now briefly described to illustrate how the qualitative methods' typology is implemented.

Crabtree and Miller (Chapter 5) want to understand how elderly people, within the context of their everyday life, decide to visit a doctor. They recognize that they need to understand their everyday life and to learn how health is incorporated into an elderly person's biography. Thus they choose unstructured participant observation and focused life-history interviews for data collection. Since much field research-based theory about health-seeking behavior already exists, and since the data are observational, a template analysis is used to analyze the participation observation field notes. Within this format, the particular choice of ethnographic content analysis is primarily an aesthetic one derived from their training as anthropologists.

Ritch Addison (Chapter 6) seeks to understand the experience of family physician training; to do so he actively enters the world of residency as a participant observer. He also uses key informant interviews since he found that family physicians share so much of their experience as talk. Addison wants to reveal the subjective complexity, interrelatedness, and depth of the residency training experience; he chooses a combination of immersion/crystallization and editing analysis styles. His specific selection of hermeneutic analysis is also an aesthetic one reflecting previous training and experience in psychology.

David Morgan (Chapter 12) wants to know how caregivers, as a group, make and accept decisions concerning institutional placement and whether to seek expert diagnosis. Suspecting the groups he is studying share this information as talk, he selects semistructured focus groups as the initial data collection tool. This research topic already has a substantial theoretical base, so he selects a template analysis style. The specifics of his analysis reveal his sociology background.

The road traveled in this chapter has prepared the reader for the new research adventures ahead. For pedagogical purposes, this chapter's discussion has separated the different research methods, including dividing qualitative from quantitative. In practice we believe the various methods complement each other, and their integration is encouraged. Expand your research perspectives and join the search. Welcome to the exhilarating adventure of doing qualitative primary care research.

Appendix: From Whence It Came: Qualitative Research Traditions

Each of the human science disciplines has several qualitative research traditions that have developed over the past century. For example, anthropology has ethnoscience and ethnography, sociology has symbolic interactionism and grounded theory, and psychology has hermeneutics and ecological psychology. Other disciplines, particularly education, nursing, and marketing, have borrowed liberally from these traditions and have fostered their own traditions. One unfortunate consequence has been a proliferation of conceptual jargon and difficult reading for those outside the particular tradition. This appendix serves as a brief summary reference for many of these qualitative traditions. The goal is to help the reader identify which tradition(s) and possible consultant(s) are pertinent to their research.

Table 1.4 identifies the major research traditions as they relate to the analysis styles discussed earlier in this chapter. Also included in this table are specific techniques such as *basic content analysis* (e.g., Berelson, 1971; Weber, 1985), a quasi-statistical analytic technique shared by many traditions; *ethnographic content analysis* (Altheide, 1987), derived from the qualitative tradition in sociology and nearly

Table 1.4 Qualitative Analysis Styles, Associated Research Traditions and Techniques

Quasi-statistical
  Basic content analysis

Templates
  Codebook-based
    A priori
      Qualitative positivism
    A posteriori
      Enthnographic content analysis
  Structure-based
    Ethlology
    Kinesics/Proxemics
    Disclosure analysis
    Ethnography of communication
    Ethnoscience

Editing
  Phenomenology
  Hermeneutics
  Ethnomethodolody
  Symbolic interactionism
  Grounded theory
  Ethnography
  Ecologiacal psychology
  Concept book approach

Immersion/Crystallization
  Heruistic research

identical to the codebook approach used by Crabtree and Miller in Chapter 5; and the *concept book approach* to content analysis (Mostyn, 1985), emerging from psychology and more like the editing approach described by Addison in Chapter 6. The a priori codebook analysis techniques elaborately presented by educational researchers Miles and Huberman (1984) are labeled *qualitative positivism* by us but are referred to by Tesch (1990) as *transcendental realism.*

Once an investigator decides field research and qualitative methods are best suited for the question of interest, the next step is to decide what aspect of human life is of primary concern. The focus can be the individual as a person with a biography created over time, or behavior and events, or social life, or culture, or communication, or intentionally lived experience, or it can be specific processes and practices such as caring, consuming, managing, teaching, and evaluating. Table 1.5 outlines how these units or domains of human life relate

Table 1.5 Domains of Study and Qualitative Research Traditions

Domain	Research Tradition

Lived Experience ("lifeworld")
    Intention of actor as individual
    Actors as access to social context
	Psychology
	Phenomenology
	Hermeneutics
	(Interpretive interactionism)

Individual As person with biography	Psychology & Anthropology Life history (Interpretive biography)

Behavior/Events
    Over time & in context
    Related to environment
	Psychology
	Ethology
	Ecological psychology

Social World
    How individuals achieve shared
      agreement
    How humans create and interact in a
      symbolic environment
    General relations among social
      categories and properties
	Sociology
	Ethnomethodology
	
	Symbolic interactions
	(Semiotics)
	Grounded theory

Culture
    As holistic whole
    As symbolic world
    As cognitive map of social organizations
      shared meanings, and semantic rules
	Anthropology
	Ethnography
	Symbolic anthropology
	Ethnoscience
	(Cognitive anthropology)

Communication/Talk
    Forms and mechanisms of actual
      conversation
    Forms and mechanisms of nonverbal
      communication
    Patterns and rules of communication
	Sociolinguistics
	Conversation analysis
	(Discourse analysis)
	Kinesics/Proxemics
	
	Ethnography of communication

Practice and Process
    Caring
    Teaching and Learning
    Managing/consuming
    Evaluation
	Applied Professions
	Nursing research
	Educational research
	Organizational/market research
	Evaluation research

to the different traditions of qualitative research. The boundaries between these traditions are often quite blurred. For example, symbolic anthropology borrows heavily from phenomenology, hermeneutics, and symbolic interactionism. A brief overview of each of the qualitative research traditions is now possible.

Phenomenology seeks to understand the lived experience of individuals and their intentions within their "lifeworld." It answers the question, What is it like to have a certain experience? To accomplish this, investigators must "bracket" their own preconceptions and enter into the individual's lifeworld and use the self as an experiencing interpreter. Paradigm cases and theories are frequently identified, and the experience is presented as descriptive narrative. Exemplars of this approach, begun by Edmund Husserl (1931), include Giorgi (1970), Colaizzi (1978), and Van Kaam (1969). Phenomenology has gained popularity among a number of nursing researchers (Bargagliotti, 1983; Oiler, 1982).

Hermeneutics is a movement beyond phenomenology in that the goal of hermeneutic research is to use the interpretation of lived experience to better understand the political, historical, and sociocultural context in which it occurs. Hermeneutics (see Chapter 6) also requires the investigator to enter an interpretive circle of intentional action (Allen & Jenson, 1990). Originating in the interpretation of Biblical text and developed for social science by such philosophers as Heidegger (1927/1962), Gadamer (1976), and Ricoeur (1981), hermeneutics as a methodology is well described by Packer and Addison (1989) and also by Denzin (1989a), who refers to it as *interpretive interactionism.*

The *life history* tradition borrows from both of the above and from ethnography with its use of key informant interviewing. Life histories provide rich narratives and portraits of an individual's life story, including its turning points and core themes. Watson and Watson-Franke (1985) and Denzin (1989b) explicate the process of doing a life history, also called *interpretive biography.*

Human ethology purports to be the biology of human behavior. Methodologically, ethology is an observational study of human or animal behavior over time in its natural context. Building from the work of animal ethologists Lorenz (1966) and Tinbergen (1951), human ethologists now attempt to discover the universal grammar structuring human behavior and interactions. They use video recordings to categorize form-constant behavioral sequences called *fixed action patterns* and to decipher learned behavior patterns. The goal is a theory of human behavior constructed from the rules governing the organization of the behavior patterns, often conceptually mapped as an ethogram. Eibl-Eibesfeldt (1989) has written a superb text describing the methodology, theory, and findings of human ethology research. *Proxemics,* the study of the symbolic use of space, including the concept of personal space (Hall, 1974), and *kinesics,* the study of body movement (Birdwhistell, 1970), are branches of ethology that overlap with sociolinguistics and anthropology.

Ecological psychology also focuses on behavior, but here the purpose is to discover the influence of environment on behavior. Whereas ethologists focus on the behavior itself, ecological psychologists, following the work of Barker (1968), focus and record both the "behavioral episode" and the surroundings in which the stream of behavior occurs. The goal is to develop principles and laws that explain the interdependence of the two. Descriptive statistics are used frequently, along with text analysis.

Heuristic research, as defined by Clark Moustakas (1990), derives from the phenomenological tradition in psychology and places a special emphasis on self-reflection in the research experience. The heuristic inquirer uses intensive inner searching and empathic immersion in others' experiences to reach a narrative portrayal of the phenomena in question.

Garfinkel (1967) presented *ethnomethodology* in 1967. He and subsequent ethnomethodologists, such as Mehan and Wood (1975), seek to understand how people make sense of the most common everyday occurrences. They wonder, How is it that people all know and come to agree that the act of holding a hand means one thing in the doctor's office and something else in the park? A common methodologic technique, the "incongruity procedure," consists of "breaking the rules" and then observing how people attempt to correct the damage done. The ethics of such research remains controversial.

Symbolic interactionists owe their ancestry to Weber (1968) and their contemporary tradition to the "Chicago School" of sociology (Thomas, 1983). This tradition is also concerned with how people make sense of social interactions, but the emphasis is on how the interactions are interpreted as symbols by the participants. The goal is to explicate the meaning of a word, action, or sign and to develop principles of symbolic interaction. *Semiotics,* the study of signs and their significations, is a commonly used tool by symbolic interactionists (Manning, 1987). The study by Becker, Geer, Hughes, and Strauss (1961) of medical students is an early example of the symbolic interactionist approach. Blumer (1969) provides an excellent source on symbolic interaction theory.

Grounded theory, a research tradition worked out by Glaser and Strauss (1967), has made major contributions to both the medical sociology and the nursing literature. One key to its popularity is the detailed descriptions of the methodology provided by Glaser and Strauss and their students. With philosophical roots in phenomenology, grounded theory searches to identify the core social psychological and/or social structural process within a given social scene. The goal is to develop classifications and theory grounded in the particular social scene investigated. *Grounded* means "based on and connected to the context-dependent observations and perceptions of the social scene." The researcher constantly and recursively compares research interpretations in the form of "memos" against the data, a process termed the *constant comparative method.*

Ethnography is one of the oldest field research traditions and the keystone of anthropology. The goal is to tell the whole story of a defined group's daily life, to identify the meanings, patterns, and passions of a bounded cultural group. Given such a holistic task, ethnographers use multiple methods over an extended period of time while immersed in the everyday life of the culture being studied. Murdock's *Outline of Cultural Materials* (Murdock et al., 1950) is a commonly used guide and codebook for this research. Goetz and LeCompte (1984) describe the use of ethnography in education. Helpful general references include Pelto and Pelto (1978), Hammersley and Atkinson (1983), and Fetterman (1989). All ethnographers work from the same technique tool kit, but their interpretive foci often differ substantially. Some ethnographers see the culture through materialistic eyes (positivism) wearing the glasses of neoevolutionism (White, 1959) or cultural ecology (Harris, 1966). Others see through glasses of neofunctionalism (Gluckman, 1963) or neo-Marxism (Singer, 1989) and perceive culture as a source of conflict and power struggles. A third group of ethnographers emphasizes the ideological aspects of culture rather than the materialistic and conflict-based perspectives. This group includes structuralism (Levi-Strauss, 1963), ethnoscience (see below), and symbolic anthropology (see below) and views culture as a system of shared symbols and meanings (much like the symbolic interactionists in sociology).

Ethnoscience, also called *cognitive anthropology,* represents a blending of the ethnographic and linguistic traditions within the discipline of anthropology. The original goal was to learn a culture's "emic" constructs or the meaning of things and events as understood by the members of the culture. This goal has translated into methods and studies that seek to map the cognitive world of a culture, the semantic rules and shared meanings governing conduct. The results are classifications and rules, often presented in the form of taxonomic trees or semantic network diagrams. The methods of ethnoscience, such as componential analysis, pile sorts, and multidimensional scaling, are especially suited for term identification and for decision modeling. Detailed descriptions of these techniques are found in Spradley

(1979), Werner and Schoepfle (1987a), Weller and Romney (1988), and Gladwin (1989).

Whereas ethnoscientists rely primarily on participants' statements about symbolic meaning, *symbolic anthropologists* go beyond the statements to examine how myths, rituals, and other cultural events are actually used in the everyday context of social and cultural life. The goal is to reveal the shared cultural categories and plans that enable people to communicate and to meet their needs. The outcomes are "thick descriptions" of cultural events (Geertz, 1973) and paradigm cases and/or the important cultural themes underlying and revealed by the event or ritual (Turner, 1969). These themes often are depicted in taxonomic grids (Douglas, 1982).

Sociolinguistics is home to both *discourse* or *conversation analysis* and the *ethnography of communication*. Both seek to understand the rules or structure of communication. Discourse analysts focus directly on conversation itself, using transcripts of naturally occurring conversations, such as those between doctor and patient (see Cassell, 1985; Mishler, 1984), to uncover a portrait of the forms, mechanisms, and rules guiding the conversation. Stubbs (1983), Van Dijk (1985), and Moerman (1988) provide good descriptions of the technique.

Ethnographers of communication, led by Hymes (Gumperz & Hymes, 1972), focus as much on the context of the conversation as on the conversation itself. They want to know not only the rules of communication but also the larger cultural patterns of communication which are often depicted graphically.

PART II

Discovery:
Data Collection Strategies

2   Sampling in Qualitative Inquiry

ANTON J. KUZEL

The Question

Dr. Yvonna Marshall is one of six family physicians in a group practice providing primary health care to about 12,000 patients in a Midwestern town of 60,000. Having joined the group 6 months earlier, she notices a clear difference in the kinds of patients her colleagues see. This difference is most apparent to her in those situations in which she is providing care for one of her colleagues' patients, such as on-call or when covering the practice of a vacationing partner. In particular, Dr. Marshall notices that two of her colleagues seem to have a much higher proportion of alcoholics in their practices than the remaining three. She wonders about this apparent difference.

One of her partners, Dr. Able, seems to Dr. Marshall to have many patients with sleep disorders, chronic stress, or anxiety disorders, most of whom are chronic users of prescription sedative-hypnotic or anxiolytic medications. Dr. Marshall notes in the charts of some of these patients that Dr. Able advises them to "cut back" on their drinking, particularly while taking the prescription drugs, and that for a few of these Dr. Able writes "heavy drinker" on the problem list in their charts. Dr. Marshall tends to get phone calls from some of Dr. Able's

AUTHOR'S NOTE: I want to thank my colleagues in the Department of Family Practice at the Medical College of Virginia, Paul Munson and Robert Williams, as well as the editors of this book, for their insightful comments and suggestions.

patients on the weekends she is on call; they request refills of their medication.

Another colleague, Dr. Baker, cares for patients whose medical problems seem fairly typical for the group practice, in most respects. Dr. Marshall notes, however, "alcoholism" or "alcoholism—in recovery" on several of Dr. Baker's patients' charts in the course of seeing them for unrelated acute illnesses. She does not see this diagnosis as commonly in the charts of her other partners' patients. Dr. Marshall also has never refilled a prescription for a benzodiazepine for any of Dr. Baker's patients (alcoholic or otherwise). She remembers one of his "recovering" patients contacting her one weekend on call, stating that she (the patient) had a "slip." She told Dr. Marshall that she had contacted her sponsor and was going to an AA meeting that evening. The patient thought Dr. Baker would want to be told about this on Monday.

This series of experiences while covering the patients of Drs. Able and Baker intrigues Dr. Marshall. Having graduated from a residency that supported her interest in research, she decides to investigate this interesting phenomenon systematically. She recognizes that how she frames the question or problem will influence how she designs and carries out this inquiry (Kuzel, 1986; Lincoln & Guba, 1985). After considering several options, Dr. Marshall decides on the following two questions:

1. How can I demonstrate to myself and to my colleagues that these apparent differences in proportions of "problem drinkers" in otherwise similar practices are "real"?
2. Assuming that the differences are real, how did this come about?

What to Sample

Before continuing the story of Dr. Marshall's research project and the way it can illustrate issues of sampling, I wish to propose certain definitions and ways of thinking about sampling.

What do I/we mean when we talk about "sampling" in both traditional, quantitative inquiry, and qualitative inquiry? More specifically, what does the procedure of sampling look like in both forms of inquiry? What is the underlying purpose in both cases?

Patton (1990) states, "Qualitative inquiry typically focuses in depth on relatively small samples, even single cases ($n = 1$), selected *purposefully*. Quantitative methods typically depend on larger samples selected randomly" (p. 169). These tendencies result from the underlying purpose of sampling in the two traditions of inquiry. In quantitative research, one's sample should be representative of some larger population to which one hopes to generalize the research findings. In qualitative inquiry, sampling is driven by the desire to illuminate the questions under study and to increase the scope or range of data exposed—to uncover multiple realities. It allows for development of theory that takes into account local conditions (Bogdan & Biklen, 1982; Glaser & Strauss, 1967; Guba & Lincoln, 1989; Lincoln & Guba, 1985; Patton, 1980, 1990). *Quantitative sampling* concerns itself with *representativeness*, and *qualitative sampling* with *information-richness* (Patton, 1990).

Theory development and verification in these two traditions also shape the process of sampling. In conventional epidemiologic inquiry, one begins with a priori theory that is relatively fixed (i.e., one has an explanation for something that is to be tested). This explanation is purported to hold in some universe that must be defined clearly. Theory is tested in the context of a random sample (to avoid investigator bias), using large enough numbers of subjects to demonstrate statistical significance (Guba & Lincoln, 1989). Qualitative inquiry, on the other hand, starts with a priori theory or understanding which is flexible (Glaser & Strauss, 1967; Lincoln & Guba, 1985). The initial question or problem allows for preliminary decisions about the boundary of the investigation. The investigator concerns herself with questions like: Which data sources are information-rich? Whom should I talk to, or what should I look at first? As theory develops, additional questions arise: Which data sources may confirm my understanding? Challenge my understanding? Enrich my understanding? (Glaser & Strauss, 1967; Guba & Lincoln, 1989; Lincoln & Guba, 1985; Marshall & Rossman, 1989; Patton, 1990). Both forms of inquiry begin with some sort of prior understanding or theory about the subject of study—no investigator is a *tabula rasa* (Kuzel, 1986). They differ in that quantitative inquiry usually starts with theory that is closed and needs to be proven or disproved. Qualitative inquiry generally begins with theory or understanding that is to be modified and confirmed in the context of the study.

The nature of the question/problem/event of interest allows one to make a judgment about what form of inquiry—quantitative or qualitative—is best suited for the investigation (Guba & Lincoln, 1989; Kuzel, 1986; Lincoln & Guba, 1985; Patton, 1980, 1990). In addition the *choice* of the subject of interest not only fashions the form of inquiry but also sets limits on the scope of the investigation (Lincoln & Guba, 1985). Problem boundaries are shaped by determining "what it is you want to be able to say something about at the end of the study" (Patton 1980, p. 100). This initial boundary of the problem may also be thought of as a sampling frame, and it may be defined further by considering what to sample. The "what" may include events, places, persons, artifacts, activity, and time (W. L. Miller, personal communication, Nov. 28, 1990).

To illustrate the practical implications of these ideas, I return to Dr. Marshall and her two questions. The first of these, How can I demonstrate to myself and to my colleagues that these apparent differences in proportions of "problem drinkers" in otherwise similar practices are "real"? requires confirmation that her colleagues do have similar practices and some convincing evidence that the proportions of problem drinkers (at least as she has experienced it in cross-coverage) are different.

She recognizes that her first question seeks *verification* of an apparent difference in proportion of a certain kind of medical problem in otherwise similar practices. This recognition suggests that she employ strategies from quantitative inquiry to pursue an answer. Dr. Marshall starts by defining the population she will study. She decides on all patients who have visited the practice since she joined the group 6 months ago. All patient encounters are recorded in a computerized data base that includes information on patient demographics, date of visit, primary physician, physician provider at time of visit, diagnoses, and procedures performed. This data base allows her to define subgroups from this initial population: those patients who identify Dr. Able as their primary physician, and those who name Dr. Baker. Dr. Marshall decides that to demonstrate similarity between these subgroups and the practice as a whole, she will look for like distributions of demographic characteristics within those groups. She reasons that since the distribution of diagnoses in each group may be tied to the distribution of alcoholism or problem drinking, it would not serve her purpose to look for similarity between these groups' medical diagnoses. Rather she must use a "marker" such as "alcoholism," "problem drinker," or "heavy drinker," as noted on the billing form and/or within the medical record.

Dr. Marshall's deliberations depict both a strength and a limitation of sampling in the quantitative tradition. Her strategy will allow her to determine the distribution of certain attributes of interest, but she will need additional information from her colleagues, perhaps obtained through qualitative interviews, to help her define what she is looking for in the study groups and how she will go about doing that. As Morse (1986) points out, "A primary limitation of probability sampling is that it cannot be used to obtain information about the *meaning* of a construct" (p. 182).

Dr. Marshall has another reason to involve her colleagues in her research project. The process she employs must not only convince her of the believability of the results, it must also convince her partners. She therefore decides to begin her colleagues' participation in her research project by describing to them the phenomenon that intrigues her and obtaining from them advice about how to answer convincingly her first question. In so doing, Dr. Marshall is guided by her question in choosing her method of inquiry, including site selection and sampling strategy (Marshall & Rossman, 1989).

Before beginning this dialogue, she considers how to start the discussion and what form it may take. "Who among my colleagues should I talk to, and who should be first? Should I talk to them individually, as a group, or both?" She recognizes the possibility that her interest will be interpreted as evaluation of her colleagues' practices (e.g., those physicians with relatively fewer "alcoholic" patients must be substandard in their ability to recognize substance abuse). Hence a third reason for involving her colleagues: In the process of doing her research, Dr. Marshall may touch on sensitive issues. The questions she asks and the understanding she develops may have a powerful impact on her colleagues and on her relationship with them. She decides to talk with the colleague with whom she has the best rapport, Dr. Freund, and ask for his response to her ideas and concerns. In this hypothetical case he responds enthusiastically and reassuringly, encouraging her to bring her questions and ideas up at their next regularly scheduled group meeting. He suggests she phrase her presentation in a straightforward, nonjudgmental manner and predicts his partners will receive her without defensiveness.

Dr. Marshall has identified someone in the "culture" under study who can serve as a "key actor" (Fetterman, 1989; Jorgensen, 1989).

In effect she is given initial permission to observe, interact with, and learn from the group of people who interest her—a process sometimes called *gaining entrée* (Agar, 1986; Werner & Schoepfle, 1987b). This early interaction with gatekeepers, knowledgeable informants, or experts also yields feedback on one's research question or problem and provides information by which to identify other "key actors" or particularly important recorded data (Lincoln & Guba, 1985).

When she presents her questions and ideas to her colleagues and solicits their feedback in the setting of a meeting, Dr. Marshall is employing a strategy similar to a focus group interview (Morgan, 1988). This technique has the advantage of yielding responses to the same issue from multiple respondents in a shorter period of time than if each person were interviewed separately (Patton, 1990). One also can observe and note the interactions that occur between group members as they discuss the topic of interest. The researcher, however, needs to be aware of the potential constraints that groups can place on individuals' responses, and if resources permit she can obtain information in individual interviews with members for comparison with the data gained in the group setting.

In my hypothetical example Dr. Marshall intends to seek individual interviews with all five of her colleagues, thereby performing a *comprehensive sample* of the group that her initial question has bounded. The relatively small size of the group affords her this opportunity, as does the limited nature of her question. Were she interested in the practice patterns and beliefs of family physicians in her state, for example, she would have to choose certain individuals and practices (see below for a discussion of qualitative sampling strategies). Dr. Marshall must decide also what to sample. In this case the options might include the following:

> *Events*—the interaction between one of her partners and a patient in his practice already identified as a "problem drinker"; or the interaction with a patient not yet identified by problem list or encounter form, yet whose chart yields evidence that meet the diagnostic criteria for alcoholism
>
> *Places*—exam rooms; physician offices; (other practices?)
>
> *Persons*—her partners (all of them); their patients (which ones?)
>
> *Artifacts*—patient records; patient encounter forms (listing diagnoses for a given visit)
>
> *Activities*—face-to-face patient care; "telephone medicine"; dictating notes from patient visits

> *Time*—records of patient encounters before she joined the group; encounters from the past 6 months and those occurring during the next month; encounters occurring a year from now (how could she attribute meaning to apparent stasis or change over time?)

How to Sample

In addition to contemplating all the options before her of *what* to sample, Dr. Marshall also must decide *how* to sample. This contemplation includes considering whether to observe or to interview and, if interviewing, whether to speak to individuals, groups, or both; whether to record what she sees and/or hears (i.e., videotaping or audiotaping). It also includes deciding which of many purposive qualitative sampling strategies to employ (Patton, 1990). In my hypothetical case the initial presentation to the group surfaced some concerns from two of her partners about "interfering" with the flow of patient care. They worried about her presence in a patient encounter with one of her colleagues and about the limited time available to her to pursue these research questions. Given these responses, Dr. Marshall decides to limit her initial efforts to interviews with her colleagues and to analysis of their diagnostic data and selected medical records. This approach is approved by all in her group, and she makes a note to look for opportunities to further understand some of her colleagues' concerns during later individual interviews.

Dr. Marshall's comprehensive sampling of her group by means of interview and document analysis is one of several nonprobabilistic strategies one may use in qualitative inquiry (Goetz & LeCompte, 1984; Merriam, 1988; Patton, 1980). *Nonprobabilistic* underscores the distinction made earlier between the goals and resulting sampling strategies of qualitative versus quantitative inquiry. Patton (1990) has devised a typology of sampling that has 16 categories, shown in Table 2.1. Several of these categories deserve emphasis because they are typical of or critical for good qualitative inquiry in primary care.

Maximum variation sampling occurs when one seeks to obtain the broadest range of information and perspectives on the subject of study. Guba and Lincoln (1989) claim this is the preferred strategy for qualitative inquiry. By looking for this broad range of perspective, the investigator is challenging purposefully his or her own preconceived (and developing) understandings of the phenomenon

Table 2.1 Typology of Sampling Strategies in Qualitative Inquiry (After Patton [1990])

Type of Sampling	Purpose
Maximum variation	Documents diverse variations and identifies important common patterns
Homogenous	Focuses, reduces, simplifies; facilitates group interviewing
Critical case	Permits logical generalization and maximum application of information to other cases
Theroy-based	Finding examples of a theoretical construct and thereby elaborate and examine it
Confirming and disconfirming cases	Elaborating initial analysis, seeking execptions, looking for variation
Snowball or chain	Identifies cases of interest from people who know people who know what cases are information-rich
Extreme or diviant case	Learning from highly unusual manifestations of the phenomenon of interst
Typical case	Highlights what is normal or average
Intensity	Information-rich cases that manifest the phenomenon intensely, but not extremely
Politically Important cases	Attracts desired attention or avoids attracting undesired attention
Random purposeful	Adds credibility to sample when potential purposeful sample is too large
Stratified purposeful	Illustrates subgroups; facilitates comparisons
Criterion	All cases that meet some criterion; useful for quality assurance
Oppertunistic	Following new leads; taking advantage of the unexpected
Combination or mixed	Triangulation, flexibility, meets multiple intrests and needs
Convenience	Saves time, money and effort, but at expense of information and credibility

under study. This perspective also mitigates against the tendency to make the "messiness" of reality appear unduly "neat and tidy." Maximum variation sampling appeals particularly to the investigator who values critical inquiry (Fay, 1987), for the views of the powerful, as well as of the disenfranchised, are represented. If practical contraints preclude the use of this strategy, the investigator might defend the use of a more homogenous sample on the basis of seeking to understand a particular group of individuals particularly well, with some appreciation of the unarticulated diversity yet to be explored and some suggestions or plans for further study.

Patton (1990, p. 182) points out that maximum variation sampling "documents unique or diverse variations that have emerged in adapting to different conditions" and "identifies important common patterns that cut across variations." In practice, the investigator might ask a respondent, "Whom do you know who thinks very differently about this topic?" as a way of getting a wide range of opinion. Had Dr. Marshall been constrained to talk with only two of her colleagues, she might choose to talk with one of the two physicians with apparently more alcoholic patients and one of the three physicians with apparently fewer alcoholics in his or her practice.

In *critical case sampling* one looks for sources of data that are particularly information-rich or enlightening. An example in Dr. Marshall's study might be the colleague who has no alcoholic relatives (and so could not experience and learn from the disease in this way) and whose professional training on the topic was minimal, yet whose practice (as assessed by diagnostic distribution analysis) showed the highest proportion of alcoholic patients in the entire group. "If he can do it, anyone ought to be able to do it. Now, why can he do it?" This sampling strategy "permits logical generalization and maximum application of information to other cases because if it's true of this one case it's likely to be true of all other ['similar'] cases" (Patton, 1990, p. 182). In other words the researcher is looking for the particularly good story that illuminates the questions under study.

Theory-based sampling occurs when one samples for information in a focused manner, based on an a priori theory that is being evaluated and/or modeled. This sampling is different from the more commonly used *theoretical sampling* of Glaser and Strauss (1967). They state, "Theoretical sampling is the process of data collection for generating theory whereby the analyst jointly collects, codes, and analyzes his data and decides what data to collect next and where to find them, in order to develop his theory as it emerges. The process of data collection is controlled by the emerging theory" (p. 44). In my hypothetical case Dr. Marshall may wonder about the relationship between her colleagues' past experiences with alcoholic patients and their present practice patterns. She would therefore specifically gather interview data that might confirm or disconfirm the presence of such a relationship and characterize its form.

It is important to recognize the implication of theoretical and other purposeful sampling: The sample is selected serially and contingently (Guba & Lincoln, 1989). In other words the processes of framing and reframing the research question, sample selection, data gathering, data analysis, and theory construction occur concurrently in qualitative inquiry. This is the flexibility of theory that is fundamental to qualitative research. Merriam (1988) suggests that "purposive and criterion-based sampling occur before the data are gathered, whereas theoretical sampling is done in conjunction with data collection" (p. 51). Yet a priori, fixed sampling strategies seem antithetical to qualitative research. Good qualitative sampling, in my opinion, is always theory-based and theory-informing. Note that here and elsewhere in this chapter the terms *theory* and *understanding* are used as being essentially synonymous and are seen as shades of meaning around the same idea—a way of making sense of things.

Confirming and disconfirming cases are sampling strategies in which one looks for data that will support or challenge the investigator's understanding of the topic of study. Patton (1990) calls this a process of "elaborating and deepening initial analysis, seeking exceptions, testing variation" (p. 183). A related concept is that of "theoretical saturation" (Glaser & Strauss, 1967), or sampling to the point of redundancy (Lincoln & Guba, 1985). Not only does this technique provide more convincing evidence of the credibility of developed theory, but it also allows one to answer the question, When can I stop sampling?

This idea is illustrated in the commonly used technique of *snowball sampling* (Bogdan & Biklen, 1982; Patton, 1990).

> In this form of sampling one identifies, in whatever way one can, a few members of the phenomenal group one wishes to study. These members are used to identify others, and they in turn others. Unless the group is very large one soon comes to a point at which efforts to net additional members cannot be justified in terms of the additional outlay of energy and resources; this point may be thought of as a point of redundancy. (Lincoln & Guba, 1985, p. 233).

As sampling to the point of redundancy yields a more convincing explanation of events, so does searching for disconfirming evidence

—purposefully looking for negative cases (Lincoln & Guba, 1985). If some are found, the investigator must modify previous understanding to account for the new information. If none are found, both the investigator and the audience for the final report are still more convinced of the credibility and completeness of the theory contained therein.

The strategies of sampling to the point of redundancy or theoretical saturation, of searching for disconfirming evidence, and of maximum variation sampling have implications for sample size that should be considered in qualitative research design and implementation. Although the rules are not hard and fast, experience has shown that 6-8 data sources or sampling units will often suffice for a homogenous sample, while 12-20 commonly are needed when looking for disconfirming evidence or trying to achieve maximum variation (Lincoln & Guba, 1985; Marshall & Rossman, 1989; McCracken, 1988; Patton, 1990).

Sampling in qualitative inquiry generally has the following features, all of which underscore that responsiveness and development are essential characteristics of both qualitative inquiry in general and qualitative sampling strategies in particular:

1. The sample design, although preconceived (at least enough to answer the question, Where and with whom do I start?), is flexible and evolves as the study progresses.
2. Sample "units" are selected serially. Who and what comes next? depends on who and what came before.
3. The sample is adjusted continuously or "focused" by the concurrent development of theory.
4. Selection continues to a point of redundancy.
5. Sampling includes a search for negative cases in order to give developing theory greater breadth and strength (Lincoln & Guba, 1985; Kuzel et al., 1990).

To illustrate the notion of searching for negative cases, let us suppose that as Dr. Marshall gathers data and develops an understanding about the practice patterns of Drs. Able and Baker, she confirms a relatively high proportion of alcoholics and problem drinkers in their patient panels. Further, she creates a tentative explanation for this phenomenon. Dr. Baker, who happens to have considerable training in substance abuse, "attracts" alcoholic patients

Frequency of diagnosis:

Extent of previous training:	Rare	Not uncommon
Considerable	No examples from this physician group	One colleague with about 3% of their practice identified as alcoholic or problem drinkers; had required rotation in substance abuse in residency
Minimal	Two colleagues with minimal training in substance abuse and both with < 0.05% of patients identified as alcoholic or problem drinkers	One colleague with many undiagnosed alcoholics in his practice (via chart audit); one with no significant training in substance abuse and no affected relatives, yet has 2.5% prevalence of alcoholism among his patients - says he's "interested" in the problem

Figure 2.1. Previous Training in Alcoholism Versus Frequency of Diagnosis Among Patient Panel

because he is so effective in supporting their recovery. Dr. Able, however, shows behaviors with problem drinkers that actually enable them to persist in their dysfunctional state by substituting benzodiazepines for some of the alcohol they have been using. In this way he also "attracts" problem drinkers.

Searching for negative cases that would challenge this explanation, Dr. Marshall might look among her three remaining partners for one who has had appropriate training in substance abuse yet whose patient panel contains few identified alcoholics. If she could not find such a case among her partners, she might survey other family physicians in her community or her state and look for negative cases among those who have had extensive education in substance abuse. Conversely, Dr. Marshall could search for family physicians with relatively large numbers of alcoholics or problems drinkers in their patient panels (again, she must decide how to identify these patients) and interview those physicians about their attitudes and practice toward substance-abusing patients. This strategy might yield negative cases or variant cases, thereby challenging and expanding her developing theory. This theoretical sampling strategy may be represented graphically as a matrix (Figure 2.1). The investigator seeks to find data that pertain to each of the possible cells (Patton, 1980; Miles & Huberman, 1984). All of these approaches may produce interesting data and better theory, but the advantages must be weighed against the practical constraint of time available to Dr. Marshall.

In speaking with her colleagues about her research project, one of them suggests that she prepare a written report suitable for publication. Another colleague, however, has misgivings about the credibility of research based on such a small sample size and doubts that any such report has much chance of being published. Dr. Marshall has heard this concern before and is able to point out that good qualitative research is good because it investigates a question that is significant for the investigator, the respondents, and the audience for the report. A good qualitative report presents a convincing argument and allows for vicarious experience and learning. It is useful (Lincoln & Guba, 1985). As Patton (1990) suggests, one only has to consider the impact of the work of Piaget or Freud to realize that sample size is not the determinant of research significance. *The validity, meaningfulness, and insights generated from qualitative inquiry have more to do with the information-richness of the cases selected and the observational/analytical capabilities of the researcher than with sample size* (Patton, 1990, p. 185).

As she pursues her study, Dr. Marshall must work within the limitations of time and funding available for her efforts. In quantitative inquiry the researcher endeavors to make n only as big as it has to be for statistical significance. Similarly for the qualitative inquirer, one samples new sources up to but not beyond the point of redundancy. Furthermore, by using such pragmatic strategies as maximum variation or critical case sampling, the investigator focuses the majority of effort on information-rich cases and derives "more bang for the buck." Dr. Marshall may find that after the first three interviews, she is getting the same kind of information on a given topic, and she will choose, therefore, to devote relatively less time to that area in the fourth and fifth interviews in favor of exploring new, related topics or looking for information that will challenge the understanding she has thus far developed. For example, if the first three physicians she interviews all maintain that substance abuse is a critically important medical problem that family physicians need to identify among their patients, she may in subsequent interviews spend less time on whether the interviewee thinks it is important. She may instead focus on their self-assessment of their skills and on obstacles to effective diagnosis and therapy.

As a family physician Dr. Marshall enjoys some particular advantages as an aspiring qualitative researcher. Like most primary health care professionals, she has relatively easy access to individual respondents and groups of respondents, whether they are patients, colleagues, or trainees. Her professional position tends to reassure respondents that she can be trusted with intimate, meaning-filled knowledge—just the sort that qualitative investigation requires. Perhaps most important, she is suited for qualitative inquiry because she is comfortable with uncertainty, and "qualitative inquiry is rife with ambiguities. There are purposeful strategies instead of methodological rules. There are inquiry approaches instead of statistical formulas. Qualitative inquiry seems to work best for people with a high tolerance for ambiguity" (Patton, 1990, p. 185).

This tolerance is characteristic of both producers and consumers of qualitative inquiry but should not be taken to mean that "anything goes." The qualitative pursuit of knowledge has norms and customs, but they are less completely defined and fixed than those that guide quantitative inquiry. Qualitative inquiry, its strategies for sampling, and the theory it produces are more a reflection of the values and customs of the researcher, the respondents, and the audience for the results (Kuzel et al., 1990). In this way the doing and reporting of qualitative inquiry follow the "norms of social discourse" (Smith, 1990). It is incumbent on the investigator to make explicit the ethical, practical, and logical rationales for the sampling strategy employed, so the consumers of the work can make their own judgments of whether it is a good and useful story—well done and well told.

3 Participant Observation

STEPHEN P. BOGDEWIC

> If you are a successful participant observer you will know when to laugh at what your informants think is funny; and when informants laugh at what you say it will be because you meant it to be a joke.
>
> H. R. Bernard, 1988, p. 148

Introduction

Participant observation has been described as an oxymoron (Ellen, 1984). How is it possible to stand back and observe that of which you are also a part? While on initial reflection this may seem difficult, it is in fact a process that we use in everything we do. As a result, it can appear too simple to be considered a method. On the other hand, since this method is the province of a range of different social scientists, it also can be made to seem mystical, an art form that defies description. Somewhere between these two extremes lies a method that is of use to researchers in primary care settings. This chapter provides an introduction to the techniques, common practices, and procedures of this method, using examples from an investigation of the socialization of family medicine residents to illustrate major points.

Participant observation has its roots in social and cultural anthropology. The origin of this unique way of collecting data is attributed generally to Malinowski's (1961) fieldwork among the Trobriand Islanders. Malinowski is credited as being the first to use participant observation to generate specific anthropological knowledge (Ellen, 1984). The term *participant observation* can be traced to Lindemann (1924), who distinguished between *objective observers* who, primarily through the use of interviewing, approach a culture from the outside, and *participant observers*, who use observation to research a culture from within (Friedrichs & Ludtke, 1974).

Hammersley and Atkinson (1983) argue that regardless of the distinct purposes of social science, the methods it employs are simply refinements of processes we use in everyday life. It is no surprise then that participant observation has been defined in many, albeit similar, ways. Goetz and LeCompte (1984) see it as a means for eliciting from people the ways in which they construct their definitions of reality, and the manner in which they organize their world. Bogdan provides an operational definition that attempts to more completely encompass the method: ". . . research characterized by a prolonged period of intense social interaction between the researcher and the subjects, in the milieu of the latter, during which time data, in the form of field notes, are unobtrusively and systematically collected" (Bogdan, 1972, p. 3).

Jorgensen (1989) offers perhaps the most detailed definition. He defines the method in terms of seven distinct features: the insiders' viewpoint, the here and now of everyday life, the development of interpretive theories, an open-ended process of inquiry, an in-depth case study approach, the researcher's direct involvement in informants' lives, and direct observation as a primary data-gathering device. For Jorgensen the ultimate aim of participant observation is to "generate practical and theoretical truths about human life grounded in the realities of daily existence" (1989, p. 14). It is this definition of participant observation that guided the study reported in this chapter.

Why Participant Observation?

Most aspects of human existence can be studied using the method of participant observation. The fundamental reason to select participant observation over other research techniques relates to the significance of the cultural context in answering the research question. If the focus of interest is how the activities and interactions of a set-

ting give meaning to certain behaviors or beliefs, participant observation is the method of choice. The inhabitants of any organization
or group are influenced by assumptions that they take for granted.
These assumptions reflect the unique culture of a given organization. Rather than relying on the perceptions of inhabitants, participant observation affords the researcher direct access to these assumptions. Several advantages accrue to this method when it is used to
investigate cultural groups.

- As time in the field passes, the inhabitants are less likely to alter their
  behavior due to your presence; you are accommodated rather than
  reacted to. As a result your chances of witnessing the phenomenon
  as it actually occurs are greatly enhanced.
- Differences between real and verbal behavior are made apparent.
  Information obtained from interviews and questionnaires may not
  reflect actual behavior.
- Questions can be formed in the language of the inhabitants. Rather
  than constructing questions a priori, questions can be constructed
  using terms and colloquialisms characteristic of the people you are
  studying.
- The sequence and connectedness of events that contribute to the
  meaning of a phenomenon can be identified. Rather than attempting
  to piece an understanding together from various clues or repeated
  interviews, the context can be observed as it unfolds in everyday life.
- Many research interests cannot adequately be investigated by any
  other means. If, for example, your research question requires that
  you understand how trainees in one setting differ markedly in what
  they value from their counterparts in a similar setting, there may be
  no substitute for the method of participant observation.

It is apparent from the preceding list of advantages that participant observation would not be appropriate for all types of studies.
Jorgensen (1989) and Bernard (1988) suggest that it would, however,
be a likely choice when:

it would be considered an intrusion to have a complete stranger present
    to witness and record the situation of interest;
the situation of interest is obscured or completely hidden from the
    public; and
the inhabitants appear to have significantly different views than do
    outsiders.

Given these criteria, in several situations in primary care participant observation could prove useful. The various organizations in which the business of primary care takes place all have their own unique cultures. How many variations of primary care organizations exist? How will these organizations respond to such environmental factors as the economic strains on society, and the growing unmet health care needs of a large number of citizens? Likewise the various occupational groups that are involved in the delivery of primary care each function in accordance with particular norms, language, customs, and rituals. How do these occupations interpret and carry out what they each define as primary care? How do their definitions differ? To what values are the members of these occupations socialized during their training? In summary, any research question that requires an understanding of the processes, events, and relationships, the context of a social situation, is appropriate for the method of participant observation.

Costs are associated with using participant observation. It can be very time consuming. The fieldwork portion of a study can, and often does, take a year or even more to complete. It is possible, however, to conduct applied research in as short a time as 1-3 months (Bernard, 1988). The time required to conduct the study reported in this chapter was slightly less than 1 year. Whether participant observation is a suitable method depends entirely on the research question being asked and the overall design of the study.

A Primer on Participant Observation

In this section I describe the various steps in participant observation, using examples from a recent study of residency training in family medicine. Two interests prompted this investigation (Bogdewic, 1987). My primary interest was in knowing how residents in family medicine developed their professional identity. Through what stages did they pass en route to claiming the identity of family doctor? What factors or forces influenced how their identity was shaped? In addition I was interested in knowing how this identity formation process differed in the two major types of settings in which it occurred— university-based programs and community-based programs.

OVERVIEW OF THE PROJECT

The selection of methods for this investigation was guided by the question: What does it mean for family medicine residents to one day call themselves "family doctors"? I was less interested in residents' perceptions of their identity and more interested in those behaviors and other factors within the training setting that gave meaning to this unique professional identity. Since this meaning is culturally derived, I felt it was necessary to observe the residents in the context that formed their identity. Furthermore the resources required to conduct a time-intensive investigation were available. Two colleagues helped with data collection. Each of them observed at only one site, while I divided my time equally between the two sites. In addition to being participant observers, we each conducted key-informant interviews.

For three reasons, observations were limited to the outpatient care facility (Family Practice Center [FPC]) and those educational spaces that were located in or adjacent to it. First, the FPC is the social scene that most closely approximates the type of setting in which most residents will ultimately practice. Second, the FPC is the residents' home base. It is where they routinely interact, both formally and informally, with those who share a similar commitment to their discipline. The third factor was one of practical consideration: Family medicine residents rotate through numerous other teaching services, many of which are located at other hospitals; the logistics of arranging to be with the residents while they are on these other rotations was not feasible.

Interactions and activities that were observed included routine patient care activities (including interactions with support staff, preceptors, peers, and to a lesser extent, patients); educational conferences; one-on-one and small group teaching encounters; and informal interactions with staff, faculty, and fellow residents. Although observations occurred throughout an 11-month period, the bulk of the observations took place during the first 6 months of the study. Observation days were selected randomly, and observation periods occurred throughout each part of the day.

The majority of family medicine residency programs are located in community hospitals that have some university affiliation (American Academy of Family Physicians, 1991). The second largest category of programs is those based in university hospitals. This is one reason why both types of programs were included in this study. A second reason is that it has been my observation over the past 10 years that within academic family medicine is some general level of agreement that the two types of programs are significantly different. I have always been curious about these perceived differences and thought it would be fascinating to conduct my own comparison. Finally it was a manageable task to include both programs in this study since they are within 1 hour's driving time from each other.

GAINING ENTRY

Once a site has been selected that you believe provides access to the data in which you are interested, you need to gain permission to conduct the study. Several things bear keeping in mind. First, rehearse in advance the way you will answer the many questions you think you may be asked. Remember, no matter how well you frame your interest, no matter how credible you appear, you are asking permission to partake in private matters. Along those lines, take full advantage of anyone who can help you gain entry. Finally, the process of gaining entry is when data collection begins and data analysis starts.

In the resident socialization study, I had to gain entry into two settings. In the community setting this was accomplished by sending one letter to the residency director and then attending one faculty meeting. The primary concern expressed by the faculty in this meeting was a practical one—what is in it for us? How will we benefit from participating in this study? Once I adequately addressed this, I was given the go-ahead to conduct the study. When I asked about how I should present my proposal to the residents, I was informed that would not be necessary. I was told that the residents trusted that the faculty had their best interests in mind and that they (the residents) would support the faculty decision.

I sent the same letter to the residency director of the university program and was similarly invited to attend a faculty meeting to discuss my proposal. This is where the similarity ended. After considerable discussion, the faculty referred me to the group responsible for the management of the clinic where I would be spending the bulk of my time. The primary concern of this group was patient confidentiality. Once they were reassured this would not be a problem, the management group decided the residents needed to be involved in the decision-making process. Rather than letting me make initial contact with the residents, the chief resident first wrote the residents a memo briefly explaining what I wanted to do. I then wrote each resident, providing greater detail about the design and purpose of my study. Over the course of the next 3-4 weeks each resident responded back to the chief resident regarding his or her willingness to participate. They all agreed. All that was left was another meeting with the clinic management group and then the residency faculty, and I was in. This process took about 2 months.

In addition to gaining permission to conduct the study from each of the residency programs, I also had to contact the Human Subjects Committee in both institutions. Much to my surprise, formal approval was not required.

INITIAL CONTACT

Entry has been negotiated. Now what? How do you, a stranger, walk in the door without causing everyone's head to turn? The fact is, you cannot avoid it. People know you are not one of them and are curious to learn who you are and what you are doing there. Therefore what you need for your own comfort level, as well as that of the inhabitants, is a succinct way of introducing yourself and explaining why you are there. Even if they have been told by someone else the purpose of your study, they will want to hear it from you. The best rule to follow is **tell them the truth** (Bogdan, 1972). This does not mean you have to go into great detail; in fact, too much detail can alarm people. An honest, jargon-free, down-to-earth explanation will suffice. Among other things, such an explanation is much easier for someone to pass on to the other members of the organization.

One lesson I learned from my first few contacts in the field is the importance of being vague. My initial explanations to some of the staff about wanting to understand how the residency training program influenced identity formation were interpreted as my wanting to evaluate their organization. I quickly learned I was better off giving a much broader description of my purpose. Rather than putting any focus on their organization, I explained that I was primarily interested in what it meant to people to become family doctors. While this statement was essentially true, it was considered less threatening since it required no apparent judgments about the organization.

ESTABLISHING RAPPORT

Beyond initial introductions it is recommended the researcher approach the early days in the field with caution. At this point you do not know the routines and rituals of the situation. You cannot determine yet what is considered offensive or what roles are appropriate for you to play. Additionally you have not yet established trust with the natives. Behavior during this phase is guided as much by commonsense knowledge about considerate social interaction as it is by anything else (Bogdan, 1972). The goal at this stage is to develop trusting and cooperative relationships with the insiders in the field setting. Such relationships are necessary to gain access to important aspects of daily existence and to be trusted with dependable, pertinent information (Jorgensen, 1989).

Although the rules for establishing and maintaining rapport are not hard and fast, the following tips are worth considering:

Be Unobtrusive. At the outset you should be more observer than participant. This phase of participant observation has been referred to as "learning the ropes" (Geer et al., 1968; Shaffir, Stebbins, & Turowetz, 1980). Your behavior and attire should not draw attention to you. Your goal is to learn what it takes to fit in. No precise formula exists to follow; however, normal social cues such as body language and obvious shifts in feeling states or interactions are to be trusted.

Be Honest. People in the setting you are studying will have a limited understanding of why you are there. Questions about your interests and what you hope to find should be dealt with in an open and direct fashion. You may need at this time to assure people that their participation is voluntary, identities will remain anonymous, and all information will be treated confidentially (Jorgensen, 1989).

Be Unassuming. It is conceivable that you have some degree of technical or professional knowledge regarding the situation you are studying. Not only could this present a bias, it also runs the risk of threatening the subjects. If anything, play down your expertise. You already know what you know. That is not why you are in the field.

Be a Reflective Listener. This fundamental communication skill not only helps build rapport but is also an excellent way to learn the language of the inhabitants. The particular words used in a given social situation have a certain significance or meaning to the insiders. By reflecting back what you are hearing, you can better understand how the language in this setting differs from what you know, and simultaneously you can move the relationship to a deeper level.

Be Self-Revealing. Subjects have some degree of curiosity about you, particularly as time passes. A willingness to discuss common interests and life experiences can open the door to a more trusting relationship. You have to decide just how intimate your relations with subjects can become. Avoiding intimacy, however, and opting for a more aloof stance can limit your being accepted.

As rapport is developed, you are able to begin participating in the activities in the setting. These joint activities or shared experiences with the inside members mark the boundary between outsiders and insiders. Participating in them means that you have "joined," even if yours is a special type of membership.

THE MECHANICS OF OBSERVATION

Just what does "participation in the activities of the setting" mean? What do participant observers routinely do? One way to think about participant observation is to think of all the elements needed to tell a story—who, what, when, where, why, and how. To organize my fieldwork, I adapted the following framework from Goetz and LeCompte (1984):

Who is present? How would you characterize them? What role are they playing in the group? How did they enter the group? On what is their membership in this group based? Who did the organizing or directing of the group?

What is happening? What are people doing and saying, and how are they behaving? How did this activity/interaction begin? What things appear to be routine? To what extent are the various participants involved? What is the tone of their communication? What body language is being used?

When does this activity occur? What is its relationship to other activities or events? How long does it last? What makes it the right time (wrong time) for this to occur?

Where is this happening? What part do the physical surroundings contribute to what is happening? Can and does this happen elsewhere?

Do participants use or relate to the space or physical objects differently?

Why is this happening? What precipitated this event/interaction? Are different perspectives on what is occurring evident? What contributes to things happening in this manner?

How is this activity organized? How are the elements of what is happening related? What rules or norms are evident? How does this activity or group relate to other aspects of the setting?

Obviously not all of these categories will be recorded in a single observation. They provide one way of thinking about the range of possible ways to begin the adventure of learning about a social situation. Most of the above questions are ones that we unconsciously process as we encounter social scenes on a routine basis. Of course we also unconsciously apply our own biases and interpretations to these scenes, often without giving them any additional thought. The difference for the participant observer is that consciously recording the specific details of what we might normally take for granted begins to show how meanings are constructed in this particular organization or setting. To the novice fieldworker it may at first seem like busy work to pay attention to such details as how people are physically located within a room. These details can, however, open doors to realizations that can contribute in ways previously unimagined to the story that is unfolding.

In the study of family medicine residents, one routine location for my observations was the preceptor room. This is the place in the outpatient clinic where individual faculty members and community practitioners (preceptors) are available to provide consultation and supervision to the residents. Residents usually come to this room with some question they would like answered or to ask the preceptor to see the patient with them. For the first few weeks my observations were not guided by any framework. I was simply "learning the ropes." Soon afterward I began applying some structure to my observations. One of the first things I noticed, that I had not noted previously, was the difference between residents' presentation styles in the two settings. In the community program, when residents presented a patient to the preceptor, they almost always remained standing; residents in the university program, more often than not, sat down. This one difference colored the ensuing interaction with the preceptor. It also led to the development of a new category that served as a filter for screening other observations. One final comment about the above framework: It only specifies the various elements of an observation; it does not indicate the possible "types" of observations. Spradley (1980) distinguishes three types or levels of observation: descriptive, focused, and selective. *Descriptive observations* occur early in the study and are the least systematic. They are guided by the general question, What's going on here? Werner and Schoepfle (1987a) have described this level of observation as the "shotgun approach." Every attempt is made to observe as much as possible. *Focused observations,* which are more selective than descriptive observations, represent choices the researcher has made based on both areas of interest and on what has been learned from being in the setting. The product of such observations may be categories or taxonomies that begin to provide initial structure to one's understanding. *Selective observations* are highly focused and enable the researcher to compare the attributes of various categories or activities. Spradley (1980) suggests the three levels of observation be thought of as a funnel. Each level has a narrower focus.

Before beginning your fieldwork, or during your first few days in the field, *map the territory.* This means literally diagramming the physical spaces in which you are spending time. This map provides one context for the interactions you observe. It enables you to consider differences, such as the difference between group space and personal space, from a more global perspective than may be available in any other manner. It helps you see where you are spending your time and where you are not. Last, the exploration required to draw the map is one way of becoming familiar with the setting.

THE PARTICIPATION CONTINUUM

Observation is the more passive dimension of the participant observer role. By definition, participation connotes some form of active involvement. Before considering the factors that influence the extent to which one can participate, it is useful to consider ways of conceptualizing the participant observer role.

Jaeger (1988) distinguishes between three different stances participant observers can take: the active participant, the privileged observer, and the limited observer. Jaeger's characterization depicts participation as an all-or-none situation. By contrast, Junker (1960) poses four theoretical social roles for conducting fieldwork: complete participant, participant as observer, observer as participant, and complete observer. This characterization depicts participation as a function of degree.

The identity of the "complete participant" is completely concealed. This person joins a group ostensibly as a regular member but with the sole purpose of conducting research. A variation of this role is seen in the work of Konner (1987). Having achieved considerable success as an anthropologist, Konner decided, in his mid-30s, to attend medical school. His training in anthropology provided an excellent foundation for providing a thorough account of his journey through medical school.

At the other end of the continuum is the "complete observer." Hammersley and Atkinson (1983) point out that complete observation has advantages and disadvantages similar to complete participation. In both situations the researcher does not interact as a researcher with those being studied. This minimizes the problem of reactivity. Both of these roles, however, make it difficult, if not impossible, to question and interview subjects. Likewise both of these roles may limit just what can be observed. Most fieldwork lies somewhere between these two extremes.

The distinction between participant as observer and observer as participant is blurred. Junker (1960) characterizes the former as marked by "subjectivity and sympathy" and the latter as a somewhat more detached role characterized by "objectivity and sympathy." Obviously the overlap is significant between these two roles. Distinguishing them as separate is one way of encouraging the researcher to move about the continuum and to adopt the posture best suited to the situation.

The extent to which the researcher both chooses to participate and is allowed to participate depends on several factors. The purpose of the study and the particular nature of the setting are the foremost factors. My primary interest in the resident socialization study was to see the training program through the eyes of the residents. Because the setting was not highly structured, I was able to participate in a range of resident activities. I attended lectures with them, ate meals with them, sat in on their small group and one-on-one teaching encounters, and served as a sounding board to them just as their peers often did.

It is important to keep in mind that the goal of participation is not to see how many different ways the researcher can become involved in the activities of the organization. You are concerned primarily with collecting data. Participation is a way of establishing rapport. It is also how you find ways to fit in the organization that do not disturb the setting or interfere with your function as an observer (Bogdan, 1972).

INFORMANTS

Researchers who attempt to learn the insiders' view of a particular social and cultural scene do not do so alone. They are aided by knowledgeable individuals from within the culture—informants. Informants are defined as "native speakers," engaged by the participant observer to "speak in their own language" (Spradley, 1979). Informants teach the researcher through modeling and interpreting and by supplying information. Together with the researcher, informants help edit the story as it is being discovered.

Every member of a cultural group is a potential informant. Each has commonsense knowledge of his or her social world and can teach you something. Because it is usually impossible to cultivate relationships with every member, however, researchers select informants and vice versa. Selection is based on several factors. In general you want someone who has been in the culture long enough so that they no longer think about it. Informants who fit this description are more inclined to provide an insider's account or analysis. By contrast, anyone who steps beyond the insider role and offers an analysis based on specific frameworks, such as those of social science, should be avoided (Spradley, 1979). Informants might also be selected because they represent a particular category of actor. In studying the developmental process of identity formation among residents, for example, it was essential to locate informants within each of the three year groups.

Informants who have special knowledge, status, or access to observations denied the researcher are referred to as "key informants" (Goetz & LeCompte, 1984). Perhaps the best advice for selecting key informants comes from Bernard (1988). He suggests that you seek informants who are observant, reflective, articulate, and also who know how to tell good stories. These are the people with whom to develop and maintain relationships throughout your time in the field. A more thorough consideration of the use of informants is provided in Chapter 4.

Field Notes: A Dialogue With Self

Once a level of comfort and trust is established, the adventure of being in the field blossoms. What may amount to routine activities for the inhabitants become pieces of an intricate puzzle to the participant observer. The temptation to continue observing and participating rather than stopping to record the experience is strong. **Field notes cannot, however, be trusted to memory.** The richness and detail of an experience will be lost as a new and unexpected phenomenon occurs. The habit of regularly recording experiences as soon as possible after they occur is essential.

Field notes represent an attempt to provide a literal account of what happened in the field setting—the social processes and their contexts. Obviously it is not possible to record everything that transpires. What eventually gets recorded depends on the style and preference of the researcher, the research questions being asked, the particulars of the setting, and the methods used to record data. Three fundamental questions are to be considered with regard to field notes (Hammersley & Atkinson, 1983): what to record, how to record it, and when to record it.

WHAT: THE CONTENT OF FIELD NOTES

The general rule of thumb for what to record, especially during the early stages of fieldwork, is **"If in doubt, write it down."** Even with a particular research question in mind, one cannot be certain of what will contribute eventually to an understanding of the phenomenon of interest. Descriptions must include enough of the context surrounding the activity so that meaningful comparisons and contrasts can be made during analysis. Until the habits and skills of accurately recording observations are fully developed, it is very helpful to use a framework or checklist for constructing the context. Spradley (1980) proposes one such framework:

1. Space: the physical place or places
2. Actor: the people involved
3. Activity: a set of related acts people do
4. Object: the physical things that are present
5. Act: single actions that people do

6. Event: a set of related activities that people carry out
7. Time: the sequencing that takes place over time
8. Goal: the things people are trying to accomplish
9. Feeling: the emotions felt and expressed (p. 78)

A framework such as this encourages thick description, and "rich field notes" are those endowed with quality descriptions (Bogdan & Biklen, 1982). Beyond the descriptive part of field notes, however, is a reflective part. Because the researcher is the primary research tool in a participant observation study, it is essential that the researcher's personal journey be included in the field notes. Before even entering the field, it is important to record your feelings, hunches, known biases, assumptions, and even expected outcomes. Doing so provides a baseline against which you can compare what actually emerges as the study develops. Once the study is underway, the reflective dimension of field notes falls into several categories (Bogdan & Biklen, 1982):

1. Reflections on Analysis. Throughout the investigation themes will emerge, new hunches or possibilities will surface, patterns will develop, connections will be made, and you will experience confusion over what you are seeing. Reflecting on these dimensions of the fieldwork experience is the beginning of the dialogue you have with yourself throughout the study, and from which your analysis takes form.

2. Reflections on Method. As a participant observation study develops, the strategies and processes used to explore various aspects of the setting change. This happens as a result of learning more about the environment and also being afforded new opportunities for observation and/or participation. In addition, not everything you attempt will work. Reflecting on how and why you select new strategies or on how you deal with difficult situations provides, in the end, an accurate record of what the study actually entailed.

3. Reflections on Ethical Dilemmas and Conflicts. By its very nature, fieldwork places the researcher in intimate contact with the lives of the observed. Decisions such as what to record, how to handle privileged information, what types of relationships are appropriate, and how to handle value conflicts are common occurrences. Reflecting on these issues is both an important part of the "story" and a way of working out concerns.

4. Points of Clarification. Not all reflections require in-depth thought. Without having to go into any detail, it is useful to include sentences in your notes that point out errors or that clarify something about which you were previously confused.

5. Reflections on the Observer's Frame of Mind. While every attempt should be made to explore one's preconceptions prior to entering the field, it is inevitable that field experiences will challenge many of the researcher's assumptions. Patients, for instance, actually play more of an educational role with residents than I imagined. By reflecting on this process of discovery, the researcher not only moves from the imagined world to the empirical world but also documents important analytic constructs.

A critical aspect of the observer's frame of mind involves feelings. When our thoughts, assumptions, values, and reflections are challenged, we respond emotionally, as well as intellectually. The experiences we have in the field are not merely observed and recorded, they are also felt. **Reflecting on feelings is essential.** Only through such reflection can the researcher determine how he or she is influencing the field experience.

At one point in working with residents who were feeling significant stress from their training experience, I realized that I enjoyed the fact that they seemed to feel good when they were interacting with me. On reflection I realized I enjoyed it so much that I sometimes shied away from discussing certain things with them that might shift the feeling state. I learned from this that I was less secure than I thought about being in this particular setting. Once I realized this, I chose to change my behavior. I did not want to deny myself and the residents an opportunity to learn from all of their feeling states, including those of frustration, sadness, and anger. I did two things differently. First I made a conscious effort not to send cues that would shift the feeling state, cues such as tone of voice, eye contact, and only permitting brief pauses between comments. Then I asked a few key informants who were seniors what I might do to make it easier for the other residents to explore the total range of their feelings. These informants not only suggested certain questions I might ask based on their understanding of some of the stresses and challenges of residency training, but they also launched into a more serious level of discussion regarding some of their own concerns. In essence they were modeling for me what they thought might work.

HOW: THE FORM OF FIELD NOTES

Most field notes are not written in the field. The "field notes" that are most often referred to represent an expanded account of a variety of information obtained in the field during a given observation session and then later assembled. Various technologies can be used to obtain this information. These will be discussed later in this section. For now, the focus will be on the various types of "notes" that are generated during a participant observation study. Although the term *field notes* is often used interchangeably for these various notes, each serves distinct purposes.

Jottings. The participant observer must be sensitive to what is considered normal and appropriate behavior while in the field if he or she is to be granted access to the range of possible observations. For this reason it is unlikely that the researcher will have the opportunity to write any extensive notes during observation sessions, since this behavior is likely to be conspicuous. Such situations as lectures, where note taking is normal, are an exception. For the most part the initial notes the researcher takes can best be described as jottings.

The word *jottings* is an accurate description of what the researcher is usually able to do in the field—jot down phrases, or even just a key word, that capture some aspect of the observation. Later, when the expanded account of the observation session is being developed, jottings serve as memory triggers. A small notebook, one that might even fit into a pocket, is used commonly for recording these abbreviated notes. No particular format is suggested, since the primary objective is to capture some key phrase, or descriptor, without drawing attention to the process of doing so. What actually gets written is a matter of style or preference. Discovering the best way to write brief notes, or a condensed account, in a particular setting usually requires some experimentation. The ploy of "frequent trips to the bathroom" is one method that has been the brunt of much humor among experienced fieldworkers.

Log or Field Diary. It is valuable in doing fieldwork to have a record of how you spend your time. Such a log has many benefits. It can be used for planning future sessions; for recording the amount of time spent in the field, as well as for any associated expenses; for easy reference in reviewing who has been interviewed and where the most frequent observations have occurred; and as an appointments calendar. By providing a historical record of the entire fieldwork experience, analysis of the log can generate additional insights to the study.

Field Notes. The term field notes is used here to describe the expanded account, or permanent notes, that are the core of a participant observation study and the foundation for eventual analysis. It is therefore essential that they are as complete and accurate as possible. Field notes are written as soon as possible after an observation period. (This is covered in greater detail in the following section.) In no time at all, the number of actual pages can swell to unimagined proportions. Therefore, to manage the data, it is important that field notes be well constructed. This requirement entails several issues.

First, each page must be properly labeled. For example, a space could be reserved in the upper right-hand corner of the page for noting name of the observer, date, location, time of the observation period, and page number. The cover page on a set of notes for a given observation session could also include a title that might prove useful in recalling that particular session (e.g., "The Stormy Seminar on Liability," "The New Preceptor").

In addition, each page should have a wide margin down one side. This margin enables you and others to make comments on the notes, comments that can then be used to reflect on feeling states, possible meanings, or even theoretical hunches about what may be happening. This margin is also useful in coding the notes. Coding is a fundamental analytic process—it is more fully described in Chapter 5. Basically, coding addresses the issue that facts do not speak for themselves (Jorgensen, 1989). Therefore, as field notes are written and reviewed, it is important to make side notes that identify and label issues that seem relevant to what is being studied. These issues might include themes, relationships, key words or questions, patterns, sequences, and so forth (e.g., ways of being esteemed; how to look responsible, etc.).

Another consideration in writing field notes is how to record dialogue accurately. The actual words that participants use are important. Each culture has its own language, which means the language has a particular meaning for the inhabitants of the culture. The word(s) that the researcher might select for describing a phenomenon could easily have a completely different meaning from what was intended by the subject. It is essential then that dialogue be recorded accurately.

Unless dialogue is recorded mechanically, which is not always possible or desirable, the researcher must depend on jottings and memory to reconstruct dialogue. A consistent method for distinguishing the accuracy of dialogue is essential. The following is one suggested method:

Verbatims: If you are certain you have the actual words used in a sentence or phrase, or a key word that was expressed, place it in double quotes (" . . . ").

Paraphrase: Citations in which you have a lesser degree of certainty but are reasonably sure of what was said can be placed in single quotes (' . . . ').

Observer's Comment: Words themselves can be misleading. Someone can say "yes" when in fact it is clear he or she meant "no." Often the context of an exchange is better understood by inserting an explanatory comment or description. This interjection can be separated from the rest of the text by the use of brackets ([. . .]).

Finally, be liberal in starting new paragraphs. Any event or circumstance that is new to the scene being observed merits a new paragraph. If someone new enters the room or if the mood or topic changes, start a new paragraph. By doing so, your notes are much easier to both read and code. Another way of indicating a shift or break in the observation, or a subset of observations, is simply to insert a break line in the text (see Figure 3.1).

Journals, Memos, or Notes on Notes. The "field notes" that have just been described represent the descriptive part of the written record. While it might be possible to include the reflective part of the fieldwork experience in these field notes, the preferred way to proceed is to keep a separate or parallel set of notes for this purpose. Reflective notes are literally the notes you write to yourself about the descriptive accounts that you have developed—notes on notes. Included in them are your thoughts, confusions, and understandings of personal, methodological, and analytic aspects of the fieldwork

Location: Preceptor Room   Observer: SPB
                                                      Date: 2/2/87
                                                      Time: 1:30-5:30
                                                      Page: 3

follow up →

Upon returning from the noon conference I made my usual pass through the staff lounge, only to find no coffee or people. I then headed for the clinic. As I approached the nursing station en route to the preceptor room I was asked by one of the nurses if 'I could be helped'. I briefly explained my presence. She had no questions, thanked me and went about her business. She did not indicate in any fashion that she knew about my study and appeared too busy to talk at the moment. ....[I am surprised. I thought I had become a pretty common fixture in this setting by now. Maybe she knew about the study by simply did not connect it to me personally. I need to follow-up on this]....

Key informant problem??

I entered the preceptor room and found it vacant. From the stack of charts sitting on the lone table it is apparent that a preceptor is close by. ....[The preceptors often try to catch up on completing their patient charts while they are precepting.].... Before I even sit down Dr. H. enters. He shakes my hand and says, "How's the study going? I don't mean here (this setting), just in general." I make a few vague general comments about what a challenging experience this has turned out to be. [I am reluctant to discuss "the study". I would rather discuss what is happening around us. Dr. H. has been a key informant for me. I am concerned that what this may mean to him is that we (he and I) will usually be engaged in editorial/analytical comments about the study, rather than the activities that are occurring in the setting. I need to give some thought to how this happened and what I can do to change it.]

We are interrupted by a call that Dr. H. receives from a patient. As he chatted, in an animated fashion with the patient, he turned to me with a big smile on his face and whispered, "this is a great couple". Several times during the conversation he called the patient "sir". Two more times he covered the receiver and commented on 'what a great couple they were'. He closed the conversation by saying that he would have 'my nurse call you back to let you know if the hospital could do a chest x-ray on Saturday'. I was curious to see what Dr. H. would have to say about this "great couple", but just as he finished the call a resident came into the room and asked Dr. H. to see a patient with him. JR (second-year resident): "I've got a kid with a rash that won't go away, could you take a look at it?". Without asking any questions, Dr. H. stood up and said "sure, let's go", and departed the preceptor room with the resident.

resolution:
my way

While they were gone one of the senior residents (BL) came in, sat down, and we exchanged greetings. I had spent quite a bit of time with this resident a few days ago, during which we were talking about her father who was a surgeon. Within moments we were interrupted by another senior student (WD) who came into the preceptor room ostensibly to ask the other senior what type of medication she preferred for a particular condition. They discussed the options and then disagreed about the medication despite what the literature had to say. When WD left I asked the remaining resident if she was comfortable with the disagreement. She replied, "Sure, there really isn't a right answer." ....

Figure 3.1. Sample Page of Field Notes—Expanded Account

experience. Such notes enable the researcher to gain analytical distance from the data (Strauss & Corbin, 1990). They are the *sine qua non* of a participant observation study. Throughout the time in the field—the data collection stage—numerous themes, hypotheses, insights, and theoretical ideas emerge. These are recorded at the time they occur. The understandings that surface from them provide the direction for the next steps in the study. In this sense the final analysis that eventually is achieved reflects a cumulative learning experience. The journal or "notes on notes" track the intellectual and emotional journey of the researcher. They explain how the learning and discovery process evolved.

WHEN: THE PROCESS OF WRITING FIELD NOTES

Participant observation studies can continue for extended periods of time. During that time both the researcher's focus of interest for the study and the understanding of what the data mean take several turns before the investigation is complete. It is therefore essential that the researcher develop and utilize effective habits for writing field notes. Otherwise, invaluable data that is left to memory is lost. What follows are hints for writing field notes that can help the researcher develop these habits:

1. *Record your notes as soon as possible after the observation.* Nothing can substitute for a fresh impression. The longer you wait before writing notes, the greater the risk of losing data. You may forget details or might uncouple what you observed from what you felt. If enough time passes, you may even fail to record anything. This failure means you must schedule your activities in the field so that you have ample time to write your notes immediately following observation sessions. *The discipline of daily writing is a must in a participant observation study.*

2. *Do not discuss your observation with anyone until you have it recorded.* It can be tempting to talk with others about what you have observed. Events in the field can be exciting, particularly when you begin to see connections that you believe are significant. Doing so, however, easily alters what you eventually record. You will have plenty of time later to share your thoughts and excitement.

3. *Find a private place that has the equipment you need to do your work.* Ideally, being able to use the same location each day can contribute to your sense of purpose and minimize distractions. In any event, find a convenient, quiet location where you can work undisturbed for several hours.

4. *Plan sufficient time for recording.* Estimating the time required to record properly a given observation session takes some amount of practice. Until you have gained this type of experience, it is best to give yourself more time than you think it will take. One hour of observation easily takes 3-6 hours to record. With this in mind, it is a good idea to limit initial observations to 1 hour and plan recording time accordingly. Gathering large amounts of data without sufficient time for recording usually produces poor notes.

5. *Do not edit as you write.* It is possible to record notes according to topics or themes; however, the natural, chronological flow of the session usually provides the best organizing framework. Therefore wait until you have completed your notes before you go back over them and edit or add as necessary. Along those same lines, if days later you recall something from an observation that you failed to record, go back and add it to your notes. This rule of thumb has one exception: If a particular observation session was lengthy, or the course of events complex, or a given conversation involved, consider making a brief outline of the major topics before starting to write; doing so can reduce the tendency to reread notes as they are being written.

Recording notes is a laborious task. Observation sessions can leave you feeling drained or can leave you feeling exhilarated. In either case the last thing you feel like doing at the end of a session is sitting down and concentrating on writing a detailed account of what transpired. This is something you must discipline yourself to overcome. Otherwise, when you are in the advanced stages of analysis and realize your data are thin, you will be able to do nothing, except perhaps gather additional data. Rich data cannot be generated retrospectively. Writing expanded accounts of your notes in a timely fashion is therefore the most essential habit and skill you will need to develop in order to conduct a participant observation study.

Technologies for Recording and Managing Field Notes

Paper and Pencil. The mental image that first comes to mind when thinking about doing field notes is usually the indispensable paper and pencil. While limited in their use, paper-and-pencil notes are often the only alternative. Tape recorders and portable computers would be conspicuous in many settings where paper and pencil seem natural. For instance, in both educational and clinical settings, a fair amount of writing activity usually is going on. In such settings a researcher who is jotting brief notes that will later serve as cues would hardly be noticed. Beyond "jottings," paper-and-pencil notes are of questionable value. Given the technology that currently exists, it makes little sense to handwrite expanded accounts.

Audio Recording. Tape recorders are an excellent tool for making notes. They can be used to record both jottings and more expanded accounts. In the resident socialization study, my assistants and I used a minicassette recorder to record brief reminders, cues we later used in writing more complete notes. This recorder was the same type that many of the physicians were using to dictate notes for patients' charts. Its presence was seen as "normal." This same recorder was used then to develop one version of an expanded account. My home was approximately 1 hour away from the study location and, because of both the privacy it offered and the availability of a computer, was an excellent location for writing field notes. On the drive home I dictated an account of the observation session. "Talking through" the day's activities was excellent preparation for sitting down at the word processor and letting the day's events flow onto paper. Once the typed version of the notes was completed, the recording that was made on the drive home was listened to for any additional data.

Tape recorders are also the optimal way to record both dialogue and interviews. In some instances, such as lectures or certain meetings, tape recorders are not uncommon and usually go unnoticed. Likewise, many people, once an interview gets underway, forget that a recorder is in use.

Like written notes, tape recordings must be transformed before they can be subjected to complex analysis. Transcribing tapes is both time consuming and expensive—factors that must be weighed in deciding how much recording will be feasible.

Computers. Personal computers have many advantages for recording and managing field notes. With nothing more than a basic word processing program, it is possible to record, file, and perform various analyses of your recorded data. With the advent of portable computers, all of these functions can be performed in the field. The knowledge required to use a computer for writing field notes is learned in a very short time. The advantages and possibilities of using computers in conducting qualitative research are covered in depth in Chapter 7.

Photography and Videotaping. Both photography and videotaping provide unique visual records of observations. Still photographs capture details, as well as more global perspectives of a setting. Videotaping has the advantage of showing how scenes develop and how the movements and actions of the actors are related. Both of these technologies are, in most situations, obtrusive. The opportunity to use them depends on the unique characteristics of the setting. For instance, family medicine residents are videotaped routinely during their patient encounters. Without having to impose any equipment in the setting, I was able to watch residents perform the core act for which they had been training.

It is important to remember that permission to use audio and visual recording devices must be obtained for each instance in which they are to be used. Under no circumstances should you take for granted that permission to conduct the investigation also includes permission to take still or motion pictures or to tape-record conversations.

Summary

In a participant observation study the researcher is the primary instrument for both data collection and analysis. Much of what we are routinely aware of is guided by what we have come to expect, the norms to which we are accustomed. Therefore the details of a scene, as well as the difference between the figure and the ground, often do not capture our conscious attention. In a participant observation study, until our focus becomes very refined, one cannot tell which details matter. It is therefore essential that the researcher be capable of "seeing" what is before him or her, rather than what he or she is accustomed to seeing. This does not require genius; *it requires practice.* It is a skill that can be developed. For example, one way of developing the skill of observation is to practice writing descriptions of events that have become an ordinary part of your life from as many perspectives as you can imagine. Regularly scheduled meetings that you attend might be an excellent place to start. This skill is further developed by inviting a colleague to write descriptions of the same event and then comparing them. Of course it could be argued that the best way to develop the skills of the participant observer is in the field. Certainly it is true that to become adept at these skills nothing can substitute for the actual experience of participant observation. Each of the needed skills, however, can be developed and strengthened before ever entering the field.

The method of participant observation is not for everyone. It is a method that asks a great deal of the researcher and offers no promise in return. Such research can consume a great deal of time and energy.

And in the end, all the data in the world will not necessarily lead to a useful interpretation. The best way to ensure that the data are rich and have captured some essence of the scene being studied is to be armed with the necessary skills, to be open to possibilities you have not yet imagined, and to be willing to look at yourself as intensely as you look at the events you are studying. In participant observation, who you are and what you see cannot be separated, only understood.

4 Key Informant Interviews

VALERIE J. GILCHRIST

Introduction

The purpose of this chapter is to familiarize the reader with a research approach commonly used by ethnographers, which is useful in primary care research. This represents what Arthur Kleinman has called, "the translation of concepts from other fields into new ways of conceptualizing and analyzing health care problems" (Kleinman, 1983, p. 540). This method of qualitative data collection is another form of "research listening" as described by Miller and Crabtree (in press). This chapter developed from a literature review, my own research experience, and taped telephone interviews with experts in the field.

"Social science is a terminological jungle where many labels compete" (Lofland & Lofland, 1984, p. 3); therefore I will define terms as I use them (Field & Morse [1985], Kirk & Miller [1986], and Patton [1990] were helpful in clarifying terms). This chapter is titled "Key Informant Interviewing"; all three of those terms require clarification.

Informant is viewed by some social science researchers as both pejorative and inadequate to capture the relationship between the researcher and the individual providing information. Michael Agar, in a telephone interview, described the term in the following manner:

AUTHOR'S NOTE: I would like to thank Ben Crabtree and William Miller, the editors of this volume, for their constant encouragement. I am grateful for the review and helpful comments of Melinda Graham, M.Ed., Margaret Wilkinson, Ph.D., and William Scott, Ph.D. A thank you to all my co-workers at the Aultman Family Practice Residency program, and especially Laura Licklider, for their support. Finally, I am indebted to those "key informants" who made this chapter possible.

I called the independent truckers I worked with in the last ethnography I wrote, "teachers." I decided that was really the proper term. It showed the kind of respect I feel for their knowledge. It showed the kind of role that they were really in, with reference to me, in terms of teaching me about independent trucking. But there's a lot of choices available.

Other terms that have been used are *consultant, friend, respondent, actor, participant, interviewee,* and *source.* I will use the term *informant* to mean "the individual who provides information," simply because it still seems to be the most commonly used term in the literature.

An *interview* usually means some sort of formal discourse. In the present context, it describes the relationship between the ethnographic researcher and the key informant from which is negotiated an understanding of the culture. A key informant provides information through formal interviews and informal verbal interchanges or conversations. The informant may also provide the researcher with references—for example, a genogram, a picture, a map. The informant provides the researcher with introductions and interpretations. Finally, informants communicate with the researcher in a myriad of nonverbal ways—how they dress, when and how they speak, and the influence of context on their actions.

Key informants differ from other informants by the nature of their position in a culture and by their relationship to the researcher, which is generally one of longer duration, occurs in varied settings, and is more intimate.

After I was asked by Drs. Miller and Crabtree to prepare this chapter, the initial literature review left me with lots of material but only my own sense of what would be most useful for primary care clinician-researchers. I felt it would be more helpful also to gather perspectives of ethnographic experts and other qualitative researchers in primary care. These interviews allowed me to sharpen the focus of the chapter. These "key informants" on key informants also allowed me to experience what I was writing about. They probably shaped this chapter in ways that at this time I do not yet appreciate.

Each interview began with the same six to eight general questions concerning the following: the individual's understanding of this method, how they personally had used key informants, the advantages and disadvantages of working with key informants, how it complemented other types of research, and any advice they might have

for beginning primary care researchers. Each interviewee, at the conclusion, was asked for any texts or papers he or she might recommend and also for the names of other individuals whom I might
wish to interview. As the interviews proceeded, they became more
focused. The interviews took 20-45 minutes. All interviews were
transcribed and transcriptions forwarded to the interviewees for
review. I made the decision to seek no more interviews when no new
information or references came to light during the interviews. Direct
references to the interviews are cited by the informants' initials in
the text.

I had met Drs. Helman, O'Toole, Bauer, and Lewis previously and
already knew of their expertise. Dr. Cecil Helman (CH), a British
anthropologist at University College and Middlesex School of Medicine, has written several books and papers in medical anthropology
and in family medicine. Dr. Peter O'Toole (PO), a sociologist at Kent
State University, had taught me a graduate course in qualitative methods. He has written extensively in medical sociology. Dr. Larry
Bauer (LB), a social worker by training, now directs faculty development at Ohio State University. Dr. Barbara Lewis (BL) is a qualitative researcher in the Department of Family Medicine at the University of Colorado. I also asked Drs. Crabtree and Miller for their
recommendations concerning experts in the field. They recommended CH and BL and also Drs. Bodgewic, Agar, Morse, and Weller.
Dr. Michael Agar (MA) is a professor of anthropology at the University of Maryland. He is probably the most well known of those I
interviewed. His writings in ethnography are extensive and innovative. Dr. Janice Morse (JM), from the University of Alberta, has been
a leader in qualitative health research. She not only writes extensively in the field but edits the journal *Qualitative Health Research*.
Dr. Susan Weller (SW) is a medical anthropologist in the Department
of Preventive Medicine and Community Health at the University of
Texas Medical Branch, Galveston. She has written a methodology textbook and several articles pertinent to primary care. SW recommended
Dr. Jeffrey Johnson (JJ). Dr. Johnson also had come to mind because
of his book *Selecting Ethnographic Informants* (Johnson, 1990). He is an
anthropologist at the University of East Carolina. Dr. Steve Bodgewic,
the author of the previous chapter on participant observation, when
approached for an interview, replied, "You don't want to talk to me.
You want to talk to George. Why, he comes up with things I've never
even thought of!" Dr. George Noblit (GN) is a professor of education

at the University of North Carolina, Chapel Hill. He also has written extensively and has done several ethnographic studies in the school system.

The examples I use throughout this chapter come from the published articles in the family medicine literature, my interview experiences preparing this chapter, and two other examples that I hope are imagined easily by the clinician-researchers to whom this book is directed. The first example concerns one of my patients. Early in 1991 I was approached by the mother of a 15-year-old female in my practice who, according to this mother, had withdrawn from the family. "Susan" simply said these were "bad times" for her. Intrigued by Cecil Helman's (1991a) description of a "family's culture," I set out over the next few weeks and months to explore with Susan what she meant by "bad times." Armed with the ethnographers' approach of listening and learning from Susan, I tried to see her world from her perspective and later developed some translations with her as we discussed these "bad times." Another example of a study is a brief one that grew out of my department's need to develop plans for the future of one of our family practice centers. This center is 14 miles away from the hospital and the offices of our program. It serves both a small town and the surrounding rural area with a large Mennonite population. One of the receptionists in our office is Mennonite, and she became my key informant as I explored that culture in general but also more specifically with regard to how this Mennonite community used health care services.

Ethnography and "Key Informants"

Ethnography is what those of us who are not anthropologists think anthropologists do. The popular image is captured by the vision of Margaret Mead in her tent, taking notes from the natives. Although ethnography traditionally has entailed studying cultures to which the researcher is a stranger, this has changed (Patton, 1990). Agar (1980) describes ethnography as representing both content (usually a book) and process. It is the aspect of process with which this chapter is concerned. "Such work requires an intensive personal involvement, an abandonment of traditional scientific control, an improvisational style to meet situations not of the researcher's making, and an ability to learn from a long series of mistakes" (Agar, 1986, p. 12). Ethnography, according to Agar, is also crucially dependent on the researcher as an essential component of the research process. "Ethnography is neither subjective nor objective. It is interpretive, mediating two worlds through a third" (Agar, 1986, p. 19).

Ethnographers do not start with a hypothesis to test, but rather they attempt to discover a group's culture, or shared sense of reality. "Rather than studying people, ethnography means learning from people" (Spradley, 1979, p. 3). An essential element of the ethnographer's approach is that he or she takes the attitude of a student or child in relationship to the group being studied and attempts to find patterns, the implicit framework, within the culture. The ethnographer learns about the culture in basically three ways: (a) observation—what people actually do, as well as examination of artifacts of any sort, (b) discussion—what people say they think, believe, or do, and why, and (c) reflection—what the ethnographer infers or interprets (Helman, 1991b). Participant observation is described in chapter 3 by Steve Bodgewic. A large part of this chapter will deal with the "discussion" means of learning about a culture, recognizing that the separation of observation and interviews is artificial. For example, "the manner in which an informant discusses an issue, thus revealing patterns of personal choosing, is, for the ethnographer, just as important as the revelation of social patterns themselves" (Dobbert, 1982, p. 114). In the field the researcher or research team will learn by simultaneously observing multiple aspects of people and settings while talking to individuals and making interpretations. Ethnography is the context for key informant interviewing.

Who Is a Key Informant?

"Although almost anyone can become an informant, not everyone makes a good informant" (Spradley, 1979, p. 45). Historically the key informant was often the anthropological researcher's link to the tribe. He or she might have been the translator. It was often the individual with whom the researcher developed a special friendship. Rather than thinking of key informants as distinctly different from any other individual or informant, I think it is more helpful to view key informants as individuals who are able to teach the researcher. The teacher may vary according to the topic and the relationship between the individuals. There are often many teachers, or there could be one special teacher or mentor. As GN stated, ". . . a key informant for me may not be a key informant for you."

Key informants are individuals who possess special knowledge, status, or communication skills, who are willing to share their knowledge and skills with the researcher and who have access to perspectives or observations denied the researcher (Goetz & LeCompte, 1984). For example, in my study of our local Mennonite culture, my key informant was our receptionist. She possessed the special knowledge and the access to the culture which I did not have. Another example is when I requested interviews with ethnographers in preparing this chapter. All but one openly shared their information and perspectives. One, however, felt that I really should not conduct research in this manner and directed me to the library. This reaction acutely exemplified the fact that the researcher's relationship to the key informant has to be such that the informant is willing to share his or her knowledge and skills. During the investigation of the adolescent's family, she, my patient, was my key informant. Her mother was also a key informant. Clinicians will realize immediately the different perspectives key informants demonstrate, as well as the interpretation and subsequent negotiation that involves the clinician. Schein (1987) writes about the need for the clinician's approach in ethnographic research. I would echo Stein's (1990) call for an ethnographic perspective within clinical work.

The ideal key informant is described as "articulate and culturally sensitive" (Fetterman, 1989, p. 58). This cultural sensitivity may or may not be analytic. "Some informants use their language to describe events and actions with almost no analysis of their meaning or significance. Other informants offer insightful analysis and interpretation of events from the perspective of the native or folk theory. Both can make excellent informants" (Spradley, 1979, p. 52). The informant, however, needs to be thoroughly enculturated and currently active within his or her own culture in order to represent accurately that culture to the researcher. Ethnographic texts often include warnings about the translator or the first person to approach the researcher. These individuals, by their very ability and willingness to straddle two cultures, often do not represent the native culture (Lofland & Lofland, 1984; Patton, 1990; Pelto & Pelto, 1978; Spradley, 1979). *Articulateness* often refers to the ability to be a good storyteller or an everyday life philosopher. GN described one of his key informants in this manner.

So he could take, kind of stand outside a little bit and look at it. He was also a real good storyteller and, so I could do things like say, "Tell me about someone who would say this." And then he would be able to render perspectives for me of different groups in the organiza- tion . . . but [he was] someone who is heavily vested, with some experience and a known role and connections with other people.

The Researcher/Informant Relationship

As stated previously, the key informant teaches the researcher. The researcher attempts to see reality as the informant sees it.

I want to understand the world from your point of view, I want to know what you know in the way you know it. I want to understand the meaning of your experience, to walk in your shoes, to feel things as you feel them, to explain things as you explain them. Will you become my teacher and help me understand? (Spradley, 1979, p. 34)

This is what the researcher asks of the key informant.

The researcher also represents a crucial component of the research process. Agar (1980) describes the understanding that evolves out of the relationship between the informant and researcher as a "joint construction of reality." Each person contributes a perspective. It is not that the informant simply describes what happens in his or her culture, but that the ethnographer's very questions, as well as subse- quent interpretations, are within the context of his or her own cultural assumptions or traditions. "Having been socialized into culture means that the sensory clues we perceive from the external world and from within ourselves are filtered, selected, and interpreted according to meaningful patterns we have learned" (Burkett, 1991, p. 110).

This may present specific difficulties to those researchers who choose to investigate cultures with which they are at least somewhat familiar. Rather than questioning some aspect of a culture, an as- sumption is made that may not be correct. For example, I often have assumed that families act in a loving manner toward their members only to be reminded that it is not true in all cases. The kinds of ethnographic questions I will later describe are helpful in counter- ing those assumptions. As BL said, ". . . good informants can actually be difficult to locate, but there's two sides to the equation. You have to not only have a good informant, but you also have to have a good interview." The point is that the researcher fashions the ethnographic account as much as the informant.

This relationship between the researcher and informant is not static. Like any relationship, it develops over time, founded on mutual trust. The informant may start as a respondent, answering questions; then may become an interpreter, explaining observations and expanding on questions; later may become more of a teacher asking questions; and finally may become a collaborator. Ethnographic accounts frequently are shared with key informants, "which serves both an ethical and a methodological function" (MA). PO described to me writing his account of a vocational rehabilitation program with his key informant, one of the rehabilitation counselors.

Why Use Key Informants?

One might appropriately ask, Why use key informants? Why not just interview everyone you possibly can and get all the different perspectives you possibly can without relying on the interpretations of just a few select individuals?

The simplest answer is the *pragmatic limits* that constrain the researcher. One generally cannot interview everyone or observe everyone. One cannot be in all places at all times. If one is going to use only a few key individuals, it is better to understand the limits of their information based on who they are and to develop a relationship with them to ensure the richness of that information. Efficiency also plays a role in the choice of key informants, especially in the face of limited resources. Gregor and Galazka's (1990) article in *Family Medicine* nicely describes how they used key informants to investigate the need for geriatric services in their community. Key informants provided them the information they needed in a cost-effective manner.

Key informants also can provide the researcher both *access* and *sponsorship*. This access may mean access to information that is unavailable except from the key informant—for example, a description by a senior faculty member of what the Family Practice Center (FPC) was like when it first started. Access also may be afforded individuals, based on the key informant's status within the community. I would be treated very differently if I simply walked into a Mennonite community meeting or Bible study rather than being introduced by my key informant. Likewise some aspects of the "adolescent culture," which my patient Susan described, are denied me because of my personal characteristics—in this case my age. Other common limiting personal characteristics include gender and race. An example of sponsorship in a medical setting is described by Bosk (1979) in his study of medical mistakes. When Bosk approached a senior surgeon, asking for his cooperation, the surgeon said his sponsorship would be "the kiss of death" and that Bosk had best obtain entrée through the house staff. He gave him the telephone number of the chief resident.

As discussed earlier, the key informant may become a *research collaborator*. This is another reason to use and treasure key informants. The key informant first answers questions and provides the explanations—what, when, who, why, and how (Schatzman & Strauss, 1973). As the researcher begins to formulate interpretations, it is the key informant who will expand, modify, and clarify these interpretations. The key informant will be able to help transform the researcher's translations of the native culture into something with meaning in the researcher's own culture. A key informant is a *translator* both literally and figuratively.

How Do You Select Key Informants?

In the past, little was written about how the researcher went about finding key informants, although anthropology is full of stories about how this relationship went awry (Wax, 1971). Good luck or personal contacts somehow magically lead to the perfect key informant who is "trustworthy, observant, reflective, articulate and a good storyteller" (Johnson, 1990, p. 30). Thankfully, more recent accounts describe who the key informants are, how they are selected, and how the relationship with the researcher evolves. What follows is largely abstracted from Johnson's book *Selecting Ethnographic Informants* (1990).

Key informants are not selected randomly. Random sampling, as one type of probability sampling, assumes that the characteristic under study is represented equally in a study group. The knowledge or perspective the researcher is seeking, as well as the inclination and ability to share that with the researcher, is not equally distributed within a study group. Also the members of a culture are often not easily identified or defined as members of a study group. The selection of key informants represents nonprobability or information-rich sampling

Figure 4.1. Selection Criteria for Finding Key Informants (Adapted from Johnson, 1990)

(see Chapter 2). The selection attempts to yield a small number of informants who provide representative pictures of aspects of information or knowledge distributed within the study population. This nonprobability sampling is also referred to as purposeful, strategic, or judgment sampling. "It is not opportunistic, but rather guided by the ethnographer's theoretical or experimentally informed judgments" (Johnson, 1990, p. 27).

Johnson describes two sets of selection criteria to be used sequentially in finding key informants (see Figure 4.1). The first set of selection criteria differ based on one's approach. One of these, referred to as "theory driven," results from "the use of prior theoretical knowledge in constructing a framework" (Johnson, 1990, p. 24). For example, an investigation of the FPC might include interviews with representative members of functional groups such as those in education or patient care, or professional groups such as physicians, nurses, secretaries, residents, or groups based on other characteristics such as length of employment in the FPC. One could assume reasonably that their perspectives of what life in the FPC is like would differ.

Johnson calls the second set of criteria "data driven" or exploratory, which results from "the emergent nature of the within-group and between-group comparisons, eventually leading to the discovery of categories that can help in developing grounded theory" (p. 24). For example, an investigation of the FPC might start with a survey of the various roles within the FPC. A factor analysis might then separate those who had different roles—education, patient care, research, administration—and the individuals who scored strongly in each of those directions could be interviewed.

Gregor and Galazka (1990) used a snowball method for identifying key informants from the researchers' initial contact with an individual known to staff members (emergent or data driven) and later specifically sought representation of the black community (theory driven). Johnson also gives examples representing compromises within these frameworks.

This first set of selection criteria, driven by theory and/or data, results in a pool of potential key informants. Within that pool the researcher seeks out those who are willing and able to work with the researcher—selection criteria II. Sometimes good key informants are acquired serendipitously, and thus only selection II criteria are considered. For example, I might have struck up a friendship with the Mennonite woman at the flea market with whom my children were playing, and she might have become an excellent key informant. I would have to discover, however, her position in her community and to document how she became a key informant.

Interviews

Clinicians are generally good interviewers. Some of us even teach the subject! The ethnographic interview differs from the medical interview, however, in its openness.

> Because the researcher's aim in using informants is to uncover patterns and not to get questions answered, the researcher cannot, like the interviewer, direct the conversation. Indeed, by directing the conversation, the researcher can only uncover patterns predicted in advance. . . . [W]ith an informant, the basic aim is to determine what patterns the informant sees and considers important enough to bring up. (Dobbert, 1982, p. 114)

The emphasis is on listening. "The question is not, how do you talk to an informant? But, how do you listen to an informant?" (Dobbert, 1982, p. 118). The astute clinician will recognize that these two features —following the direction of the informant and astute listening— characterize a good interview in primary care too. The doctor-directed, focused interview, concentrated on diagnosis, may characterize the interview of some areas of medicine, but the parallel between the descriptions of ethnographic interviews and "patient-centered interviews" in primary care is striking (McWhinney, 1989).

Just as in medicine we ask certain types of questions (Can you describe the pain? Where does it hurt? What makes it better? What makes it worse?) to better understand and develop a picture of a patient's pain, so does the ethnographer ask certain types of questions to help develop an understanding of that person's culture. Spradley (1979) identifies three different types of questions and principles that guide their use. Although the clinician-researcher may find the names unfamiliar that Spradley uses to categorize these questions, the types of questions will be recognized readily. I will use my own investigation of our local Mennonite community and of the life of my adolescent patient for examples.

DESCRIPTIVE QUESTIONS

Descriptive questions, Spradley's first category of questions, are often introductory. The clinician-researcher would recognize them as very *broadly open-ended questions*. A *grand tour question*, a type of descriptive question, attempts to elicit a rich story that is completely directed by the informant. One may ask about a typical situation, such as, What's a typical day like for you? or be more specific, What happened yesterday? What happens on Mondays? The researcher may ask the informant to focus on an activity or task. When I was inquiring about the Mennonite community in our area, I asked my informant to locate the members of her community on a map. When I was trying to understand what were important activities in the life of my adolescent patient Susan, I asked her to describe her weekly school schedule.

Spradley describes *mini-tour questions*, which focus on a smaller unit of experience, for example, after-school work. As questions become more focused the researcher may ask for examples: Can you give me an example of something about which one might consult a community healer? Can you describe some situation that might result in an argument at home? The researcher also might ask the informant for any experience he or she may have had in a particular setting: Tell me about the last time you talked to a community healer; Tell me about the last argument you had at home. It is essential to be aware that you the researcher may not be using the same language or terms as your informant. What Susan described to me as "bad times" she described to her girlfriends as "bummers," "downers," "fights," "one of those times," as well as "bad times," depending on the situation.

STRUCTURAL QUESTIONS

The ethnographer generally chooses to investigate some areas of a culture in more depth than others. Spradley's second category of questions, structural questions, function to focus further the researcher's inquiry. I think of these questions as *questions of inclusion*, expanding and enhancing the description of the particular area of research interest. In reference to the two examples that I am using, I asked questions in an attempt to develop an understanding of the structure of that aspect of the culture referred to in the Mennonite community as "health care" and of the times in Susan's life that she referred to as "bad times."

Spradley's *verification questions*, a type of structural question, seek to prove or disprove the researcher's understanding of what aspects are included within the area of interest. A domain verification question I posed to our receptionist was "Are there different kinds of health care within your community?" Other verification questions are used to discover whether specific terms that the researcher has heard are within the area of research interest. For example, a question I asked our receptionist was "Is 'manipulation' considered a kind of health care?"

One not only needs to know the terms within the area of interest but also their relationships. An example of this type of question is, Is a chiropractor a type of health care? or Do you go to a chiropractor for health care? Other structural questions described by Spradley include those that ask for examples of what is included within the area of study—both in general, What are the different kinds of health care in your community? and more specifically, What elements would your community elders think necessary to provide for optimal health care in your community?

In order to enhance the richness of the description of the area of interest, one may use what Spradley calls substitution frame questions, or one might use card sorting questions. *Substitution frame questions* remove one term and the informant is asked to replace it with another. For example, "When I feel ill I go to bed" is replaced with "When I feel ill I ____." *Card sorting questions* are a type of pile-sorting exercise. The researcher lists terms, each on separate cards, and asks the informant to separate them according to a category. For example, Which of these are health care providers—the health food store owner, family members, chiropractor, MD, public school nurse, urgent care center staff, midwives, community elders, neighbors? Writing terms on cards helps elicit, verify, and discuss various aspects of a particular area of interest. (For further discussion of pile sorts, see Weller & Romney, 1988.)

Other examples of structural questions that I used when I was trying to understand Susan's "bad times" are as follows: Are there different kinds of bad times? What kinds of bad times do you have? If it's a bad time when your folks are fighting, can you fill in the blank with some other examples such as, "It's a bad time when _____." Would you say that when you're quiet, that's a "bad time"? When you're angry? Sad? Is a "bummer" a kind of bad time?

In this example it was obvious that I had to verify constantly that the term I used for a situation was appropriate. One can confirm this by asking directly. For example, Is this how you would talk about "bad times" to your girlfriend? In other settings the limits of the language may not be as obvious but just as important.

CONTRAST QUESTIONS

Contrast questions further clarify the area of research interest. I think of these questions as those dealing with *criteria of exclusion*, rather than inclusion, or the multiple types of relationships within a given area. For example, the area of health care includes various treatments, practitioners, different patient ages, problems, and issues of decision making, to mention only a few. Susan's "bad times" varied by the precipitant, her effect at the time, and who was involved.

Once the researcher has a sense of the differences between various terms, he or she can present this to the informant for verification. I asked, "Am I correct in understanding that there's a difference between how a fever would be treated by your grandmother, the health food store owner, and a physician?" Contrast questions also require some knowledge on the part of the researcher. These questions begin with a known characteristic and ask about contrasts within that category. For example, I knew that within health care there were various practitioners—chiropractors, physicians, the health food store owner, knowledgeable community members, midwives. I could ask then, "You said you'd go to a chiropractor for a backache—can you go through other types of illness and tell me when you would and wouldn't go to a chiropractor?"

Comparisons and contrasts may be made using terms the researcher has verified as part of the area of study, the researcher asking the informant to identify differences between terms. For example, "What's the difference between a chiropractor and a physician?" Another example is the triadic contrast question, in which three terms are presented to the informant and she or he is asked, "Which are alike and which are different?" I asked Susan, "You have used different terms at times and I want to see if I understand. Are 'bummer' and 'bummed out' the same while 'burnt out' means something else?"

Another variation on pile sorts, called *contrast set sorting questions* by Spradley, differs from card sorting questions in that the terms are ones the researcher already has grouped in some manner. Terms relating to various treatments such as vitamins, antibiotics, salves, various herbs, and poultices can be resorted by your informant according to whatever parameters the informant thinks are important. My informant in this example chose cost, the practitioner's recommendation, and the age of the person likely to use it.

Finally it is helpful to use rating questions. These questions seek to discover the values placed by the informant within any categorization that the researcher is developing. Examples I used were "What is the best type of health care?" and "What is the worst time with your parents?"

PRINCIPLES OF ETHNOGRAPHIC QUESTIONING

Clinicians will be able to imagine an abundance of questions to use in their research. The function of these ethnographic questions is to expand and then enrich the researcher's understanding of what the informant is describing. This requires, above all, *constant vigilance.* One cannot assume, without verification from the informant, that your understandings and assumptions are the same as the informant's. This is especially important for most clinician-researchers who will work within their own culture or one very similar. This brings to mind an example with which many physicians are familiar. Your 30-year-old obese patient says she's taking "the pill." The physician assumes this is the birth control pill, but the patient actually means her diabetes pill!

Spradley also outlines some principles surrounding the asking of ethnographic questions. All the different types of questions—descriptive, structural, and contrast—should be asked concurrently and repetitively. Ask the same questions at different times to elicit all the possible examples, similarities, and differences surrounding any event or construct. Explain why you are asking the question, and put it in context. Most researchers feel it is unethical to hide the primary focus of the research, although specific themes may be shared differently with different people. For example, to one individual in the Mennonite community I might say, "I'm interested in your community," while to another, "I'm interested in how you define health and keep healthy," and yet to another, "We're looking at how your community uses health care resources to see if we should increase our services here." It is also helpful to put the questions in a cultural, as well as personal, framework. For example, "You described using Union Salve for cuts and rashes. Are there any other times when you might use it? Would most people in your community use this for rashes?"

Language

A discussion of how the researcher tries to understand a culture by means of a verbal interchange with another individual is not complete without at least a brief discussion of language. "Language is a way of organizing the world" (Patton, 1990, p. 227). Spradley goes on to say that language functions "not only as a means of communication, it also functions to create and express cultural reality" (Spradley, 1979, p. 20). Consequently the researcher's questions will frame the respondent's answer. "[I]nterviewing assumes that questions and answers are separate elements in human thinking. . . . Ethnographic interviewing . . . begins with the assumption that the question-answer sequence is a single element in human thinking. Questions always imply answers" (Spradley, 1979, p. 83). The researcher should attempt to phrase questions as they might be asked in the native culture.

"Every ethnographic description is a translation" (Spradley, 1979, p. 22). This quote not only reflects the fact that the researcher must translate from the native culture to the researcher's culture, but that the information also must be filtered by both the informant and the researcher. What each one of us sees and remembers from any setting depends very much on who we are. "As an exclusive or dominant method of ethnographic inquiry, the dialogic mode boxes the informant into an ethnographic present defined by Western, middle class discourse and alienates her or him from the historical, interpenetrating settings that informant and ethnographer may come to share" (Sanjek, 1990, p. 405).

Validity/Trustworthiness

What is a valid or truthful ethnographic account? Because qualitative ethnographic research is so much a reflection of the researcher as the research instrument, validity has been difficult to define. GN defines a valid ethnographic account as one in which "the second person finds the same story. My belief is that if I'm good enough, other people would find a story that resonates with mine. Not that it would necessarily be the same, but we would be able to understand the other person's story from our own. And that is as close as you get."

How does a researcher develop a trustworthy description of a setting or culture? How does a reader know when to believe what is written? Four criteria modified from Kuzel and Like (1991) provide a framework for evaluation. (See also Borman, LeCompte, & Goetz, 1986; Howe & Eisenhart, 1990; Kirk & Miller, 1986; Lather, 1986b; Sanjek, 1990).

Member Checks. This refers to the recycling of analysis back to key informants. This recycling should be documented in the study account, preferably with mention of the informant's comments. The research relationship may also change the key informant. Rather than not acknowledging this possibility, Lather describes including an assessment of what has changed, called *catalytic validity.* "My argument is premised not only on a recognition of the reality-altering impact of the research process itself, but also on the need to consciously channel this impact so that respondents gain self-understanding and, ideally, self-determination through the research participation" (Lather, 1986a, p. 67).

Searching for Disconfirming Evidence. "The job of validation is not to support an interpretation, but to find out what might be wrong with it. A proposition deserves some degree of trust only when it has survived serious attempts to falsify it." (Cronbach as quoted in Lather, 1986a, p. 67). Searching for disconfirming evidence involves both purposive sampling and prolonged engagement. Documentation of the selection process leading to key informants allows the researcher to seek accounts from other informants who may differ from the key informant in critical ways. This purposeful sampling of individuals and the inclusion of conflicting, as well as complementary, accounts strengthens an ethnographic description. The sampling and inclusion also allow consideration of potential biases due to informants' stakes in specific outcomes or due to their position in the organization. Prolonged engagement also allows the researcher to confront the conflicts any informant may exhibit. Do they do what they say they do? Informants will report more accurately on events that are usual, frequent, or patterned and less accurately on things that are not readily observed or are inferential (Johnson, 1990). Prolonged engagement allows the less readily observable aspects of the setting to become visible.

Triangulation. This is an essential check for the researcher. Triangulation refers to both the use of multiple data sources, for example multiple informants, and of multiple methods, such as participant observation and informant interviewing, as well as the use of various records. One informant may give highly reliable but invalid information. I would go beyond what one usually thinks of in terms of triangulation to include multiple theoretical perspectives. "Valid-rich ethnography must make explicit as many . . . theoretical decision(s) . . . as possible by reporting when and why judgments of significance are made" (Sanjek, 1990, p. 396). This quote implies, of course, a rejection of any one objective reality. "The attempt to produce value-neutral social science is increasingly being abandoned as at best unrealizable, and at worst self deceptive, and is being replaced by social sciences based on explicit ideologies" (Hess as quoted in Lather, 1986a, p. 67).

Thick Description. This is "a thorough description of the context or setting within which the inquiry took place and with which the inquiry was concerned . . . [and] a thorough description of the transactions or processes observed in that context that are relevant to the problem, evaluand, or policy option" (Guba & Lincoln as quoted in Kuzel & Like, 1991, p. 153). This description should use "native language" and describe not only the final analysis of the study but also how that analysis was obtained. Also needed is "an accounting of the relationship between field notes and the ethnography based upon them. . . . " (Sanjek, 1990, p. 401). This accounting starts with recognizing one's initial suppositions and assumptions. Lather calls for a "systematized reflexivity which gives some indication of how a priori theory has been changed by the logic of the data" (Lather, 1986a, p. 67).

Applications in Primary Care

Key informants have been used to plan for health services delivery in many different settings (Penayo, Jacobson, Caldera, & Burmann, 1988). It is also easy to see how an investigation of other issues within a more circumscribed culture, such as a hospital, might benefit from key informant interviewing. In our hospital we have a high turnover of ICU nurses. I suggest that, rather than distribute questionnaires, interviews with key informants are a more informative approach. Many of the problems we confront professionally have been illuminated by such ethnographic studies as Bosk's (1979) study of mistakes and Smith and Kleinman's (1989) study of management of one's emotions in medical training. What I find personally most exciting is the application of some of the methods of anthropology and the ethnographic approach to our everyday contact with patients. CH's view is that "every patient is an informant" and that the clinician's access to the culture of a particular family is through our patient or "key informant." Howard Stein (1990) characterizes an ethnographic approach to patient care as "quintessentially contextual and open-ended."

In conclusion, here are what I consider to be the critical features that ethnography and a discussion of key informants offer us for our research and for our patient care:

1. An abiding respect for context as influencing the clinician-researcher, the patient-informant, and their constructed reality.
2. A consideration of the clinician-researcher as part of that context. "Doing ethnography differs from many other kinds of research in that the ethnographer becomes a major research instrument" (Spradley, 1979, p. 76).
3. An awareness of the constraints imposed by language. This awareness includes an acknowledgement of the extent to which questions frame

responses and the róle of translation in constructing a joint reality. "For a consultation to be a success there must be consensus" (Helman, 1990, p. 118).

4. An understanding that a truthful account is obtained not by trying to eliminate bias but by comprehending it. "The ethnographic method is as much concerned with how and why we observe as with what we observe, for the former heavily influences the latter" (Stein, 1990, p. 206). (See also Crabtree & Miller, 1992; Kuzel & Like, 1991.)

Readers of this chapter are not likely to become ethnographers. The long term relationships with our patients, however, can be thought of as relationships with key informants. Techniques from ethnography can enrich our research and our practice. "Naturalistic research is first and foremost emergent. Today's solutions may be tomorrow's problems" (Lofland & Lofland, 1984, p. 19). I urge the researcher to reject the "tyranny of methodology" and use whatever method best answers the question at hand and honestly report what is done.

PART III

Interpretation:
Strategies of Analysis

5 A Template Approach to Text Analysis: Developing and Using Codebooks

BENJAMIN F. CRABTREE
WILLIAM L. MILLER

Introduction

Qualitative research often results in large volumes of verbal text that must be interpreted and summarized using one of a number of text-based analysis techniques. Text data include transcripts from focus group interviews (Chapter 12) or depth interviews (McCracken, 1988; Miller & Crabtree, 1992), participant observation field notes (Chapter 3), key informant interviews (Chapter 4), or historical documents and transcripts (Chapter 9). Data from these sources can be analyzed, using a number of different approaches, as overviewed in Chapter 1. In this chapter an approach to text analysis is presented in which a template in the form of "codes" from a "codebook" is applied as a means of organizing text for subsequent interpretation. This approach is illustrated using participant observation field notes from research on health-seeking behaviors of community-dwelling elderly persons.

Deciding on a particular analytic approach depends on the goals of the analysis and the stage of the research. Field notes and participant observation data already have been "filtered" through an observer and may not require the open interpretive process needed for most interview transcript data. Researchers wishing to confirm an already well-defined hypothesis may also be better advised to use a structured approach, such as that provided by a priori codebooks or content analysis. These approaches are often more time efficient than more unstructured styles, such as the editing approaches described by Crabtree and Miller (1991) and Addison (Chapter 6), albeit with a trade-off with respect to the potential for discovery of new interpretations.

The style of analysis described in this chapter differs from an editing style (cf. Crabtree & Miller, 1991) in two critical ways—when "codes" are defined, and how interpretations are made. Researchers using an editing style generally make observations in the margins of the text during a systematic reading of the text and then organize these observations into categories or "codes" that are then reread for further interpretation, as illustrated by Addison in Chapter 6 (also see Glaser & Strauss, 1967; McCracken, 1988; Strauss & Corbin, 1990). This process is presented schematically on the lower left in Figure 1.4 of Chapter 1 (p. 18). When using a template, on the other hand, the researcher defines a template or codes before an in-depth analysis of the data (either a priori or based on preliminary scanning of the text)— the process being represented on the upper right in Figure 1.4 of Chapter 1. While these representations are somewhat simplistic and overly linear, they serve to illustrate that the same basic processes are occurring, only in a different fashion. In the editing style, the researcher makes interpretations (observations) of segments of text, and these interpretations then are used to make further abstractions, while the researcher using a codebook identifies segments of original text that are sorted and used to make further abstractions (note where the recursive arrows occur in each). Both approaches allow the text to alter the "codes," unlike a more structured approach such as basic content analysis (Weber, 1985).

Coding and sorting textual materials based on codebooks is one of several qualitative analysis approaches using structured or semi-structured templates. Another commonly used form is basic content analysis, a quasi-statistical approach that looks for regularities in terms of words, themes, or concepts, using a classification procedure (Weber, 1985). A less apparent template is the sociolinguistic approach described by Spradley (1979) in which the analyst applies certain semantic criteria to the interviews in the search for domains and relationships (see Chapter 1, p. 27).

Several approaches may be taken to creating the codebooks that serve as the template. The approach used reveals the paradigmatic assumptions of the researcher. The most structured and closed approaches rely on a priori codes, based on either the research question or theoretical considerations. This structured approach is recommended by Miles and Huberman (1984), who acknowledge, "We think of ourselves as logical positivists . . . soft-nosed logical positivism, maybe" (p. 19). At the other extreme, researchers read over large amounts of the text and then formulate the codebook, a style well described by Willms and colleagues (Willms et al., 1990). We take the middle ground, beginning with a basic set of codes based on a priori theoretical understandings and expanding on these by readings of the text. Miles and Huberman (1984) have suggested test-coding a number of pages of text and modifying the codebook accordingly, making it possible for many codes to originate from interpretive observations.

Once a codebook has been prepared, different approaches may be taken for using the codebook, in particular: (a) using codes as a data management tool in which segments of similar text are printed for subsequent reading and analysis, and (b) coding the text and then counting the frequency of different code occurrences as a means of identifying key areas for further investigation. In this chapter, the former approach is illustrated.

To illustrate the use of codebooks for the analysis of text, we use a field study designed to discover how elderly persons living in a rural community make decisions about dealing with musculoskeletal pain. This study uses a combination of participant observations collected over a year at a community senior center and a series of life history interviews of community-dwelling elderly persons utilizing the senior center. The participant observation field notes are used to illustrate the process of coding and interpreting textual materials, since these type of data more readily lend themselves to this style of analysis than do interview transcripts.

Health-Seeking Behaviors of Community-Dwelling Elderly

Musculoskeletal problems are a frequent concern of the elderly (Kelsey et al., 1979). While it has been observed that there is often considerable variation in functional status or in health care utilization among elderly with similar degrees of physiologic impairment, the literature presently offers little understanding about these observations (Levkoff, Cleary, Wetle, & Besdine, 1988; Rosner, Namazi, & Wykle, 1988). This anomaly generated the research question, "Why is there a discrepancy among musculoskeletal physiology, functional status, and illness behavior?" This research question asks for description, meaning, and an answer to the generic questions, Who are these people, and what are they doing? For this reason we selected qualitative methods based within a constructivist paradigm (see Chapter 1) for the research project. The long-term goal of the study is to identify patterns that can be used by family physicians to facilitate the health care of this population.

Initial fieldwork, using participant observation as the primary method of data collection, focused on defining the investigator's role in the community under investigation, establishing informal ties, and charting a basic map of the community. The research site was a small geopolitically bounded community in rural, central Connecticut near a large university. The fieldwork activities were centered around a senior center and an associated housing development. For over a year an anthropology doctoral student spent several days each week actively participating in the activities at the senior center. This participation included playing bridge, reading newspapers in a low-vision group, attending exercise classes, helping in the organization of special activities, and participating in the numerous social events occurring at the senior center. The participation observation field notes were typed directly onto a computer file by the fieldworker.

Participation observation field notes recorded over a 1-year period form the basis of the analysis in this chapter. It should be remembered that, in qualitative research, data analysis proceeds simultaneously with data collection. The initial data analysis reported here illustrates the process of coding the participation observation field notes. Coding immerses the researcher into the often massive and confusing jungle of text and has three primary purposes: (a) to identify "chunks" of text to facilitate future data retrieval and analysis, (b) to identify key data areas, and (c) to generate initial cultural hypotheses.

Developing and Applying a Codebook

The goal of this analysis strategy is to code a large volume of text so that segments about an identified topic (the codes) can be assembled in one place for interpretation. Once these segments are assembled, several strategies may be used for making further interpretation, just as a number of strategies may be used for constructing the codebook.

Assuming the use of a computer, text analysis consists of a series of steps:

1. Entering and printing field notes (or transcribing interviews) and creating an ASCII version (see below) of the field notes or transcripts if not already in ASCII format (for variation see Chapter 7)
2. Creating a codebook
3. Hand-coding the printed text in the margins, while making memos on 5 x 7 index cards
4. Computer-coding of the text into a software program and sorting and printing segments with the software program to get all similar text in one place
5. Reading these segments and making interpretations

While this process seems linear, the analyst must recall that constructivist inquiry is an iterative process, requiring continual interaction between collection and analysis of data (cf. Addison in Chapter 6).

ENTERING AND PRINTING TEXT

It is possible to perform the analysis described in this chapter using a number of different computer software programs or doing the entire analysis by hand. The amount of time saved by using computer text-analysis software packages to sort and print the data makes it well worth the time becoming familiar with the computer processes. For this particular study, we used Qualpro (Blackman, 1987; Tesch, 1990) as the program for coding, sorting, and printing segments of text. Another alternative is that described by Reid (Chapter 7), in which codes are embedded into the text itself and the search facilities of a word processor are used to retrieve text.

In the senior center analysis, a general purpose text editor, Kedit (Mansfield Software Group, 1987) was used for entering the field note data. For those not wedded to a particular word processor, the use of a "plain vanilla" text editor such as Kedit may be a useful addition, since they generally save files in an ASCII format (American Standard Code for Information Interchange), a generic way in which computers can store data (also see Chapter 7). Researchers using word processing programs such as WordPerfect or Word Star need to convert their text to ASCII format before analysis, since text-analysis programs require data to be in an ASCII format. This requirement is due to the word processor's embedding special characters in the text (e.g., for bolding, paging, etc.) that are meaningful only to them. Fortunately most word processors are able to save the text in an ASCII format.

During the participant observation fieldwork on the elderly health-seeking behaviors project, the field-worker made "jottings" (see Chapter 3, p. 61) during the day but had easy access to a computer for entering data each evening. Each day's field notes were typed into a continuous file that was identified by date, time, and place. After several months this file became too large to handle easily, growing to an excess of 2,000 lines. A new file was then begun, and so forth. In transcribing the life-history interviews, each interview was saved as an individual file. Most text-analysis software programs are able to code and search multiple files.

A useful strategy is to have hard copy of the text printed on wide-margin computer paper, to allow ample room for coding the text, and then bound into the type of binders used by computer programmers. It is also very helpful if the computer image text (text seen on the computer screen) has a line-by-line, page-by-page correspondence to the text found in the bound volumes. This identicalness can save a lot of paper (and trees), because most analysis programs require a numbered, printed version of the document (or at least you will need to know the line numbers—also available on the screen with most text editors). Thus editing and corrections to text should be complete before coding begins. It is very discouraging to find that all your line numbers have changed after you have begun coding!

DEVELOPING A CODEBOOK

The first step in coding is the development of a codebook or template. Before beginning, the researcher must decide on the level of detail to be coded, a decision generally related to the type of data (e.g., field notes vs. interviews) and the level of previous understanding. In constructing the codebook, the researcher is always walking a fine line between premature closure and creating codes so encompassing that every line of text requires coding. At one extreme the analysis resembles content analysis, while at the other extreme the researcher is inclined to read the text and to decide that everything is important. The codebook is a data management tool: It is used to organize segments of similar or related text for ease in interpretation and to search for confirming/disconfirming evidence of these interpretations. How detailed the codebook becomes is a function of where the researcher is in the research process. For example, preliminary studies may require a much broader net to catch alternative explanations than a study designed to enlighten several specific hypotheses emerging from earlier research.

In the analysis of the senior center field notes, the goal was to capture broad categories of information around several initial concerns found in the literature. These include health seeking/illness behaviors, senior center activities, and diet and health beliefs, as shown at the upper portion of Table 5.1. The advantage of using these broad categories is that large amounts of text can be coded rapidly and that coded segments are longer with broader context preserved, allowing the researchers to access more text for interpretation with a given search. The disadvantages are almost the same: Many coded segments of peripheral use would not have been captured with more specific codes; some coded segments are very long, making reading tedious; and a given segment may contain multiple ideas, which makes later sorting more difficult. To illustrate, compare Table 5.1 with the codebook used by Willms, Johnson, and White (Figure 11.4 p. 200 this volume) for their study in which an extensive coding system was developed to capture greater detail.

A preliminary codebook often is based on an initial conceptual model and/or a literature review. Miles and Huberman (1984) offer some useful suggestions for the development of a codebook, including having individual members of the research team independently coding a number of pages of text to test for both intercoder reliability

Table 5.1 Preliminary Code Manual for Senior Center Field Notes. The Boldface Codes Were Identified After Coding Process Had Begun

HEALTH SEEKING/ILLNESS BEHAVIOR	HSB
SENIOR CENTER ACTIVITIES	SC-ACT
DIET & HEALTH HABITS	DIET
TALKING ABOUT DEATH	**DEATH**
DONATIONS (e.g. Time, Things, Money)	**DONATIONS**
LACK OF COMPETITION (e.g. in games)	**LACK OF COMP**
RISK-TAKING BEHAVIOR (e.g. driving)	**RISK-TAKING**
PEER GROUP IDENTIFICATION	**PEER GROUP ID**
CONFLICT/CONFLICT AVOIDANCE	**CONFLICTS**
THRIFT	**THRIFT**
RESEARCHER ROLE	**ROLE**

and the utility and appropriateness of the codes. The codebook can then be modified to correct for deficiencies.

Another strategy for revising a codebook, which proved useful in our study, is to first code the text with the broad preliminary codes, retrieve and read these, and then develop refined subcodes based on these larger segments of text. For example, Table 5.2 is a rather large segment of text that was coded as "health seeking/illness behavior." Clearly many different ideas fall within this segment, including descriptions of the doctor-patient relationship, medication strategies, and the health decision-making process. After reading many such large segments, all about health behaviors, additional subcodes become evident. In fact this process led to the revised codebook that is partially displayed in Table 5.3.

The codebook not only contains the original a priori codes and the more detailed subcodes, but also incorporates additional codes that emerged while perusing the text (see bold portion of Table 5.1). These latter codes note some key features/patterns that provide a better understanding of the social and interpersonal context of this group of elderly and provide deeper insights into the health-seeking processes of interest. These include "talking about death," "conflict/

Table 5.2 Sample of Participant Observation Field Notes to Be Coded with Line Numbers Added (Not Corrected for Typographical Errors and Names Changed for Confidentiality)

Beverly is back and waiting in the library with Jane	2804
for group to begin. When I come in she is busy rubbing	2505
her knees and shins. These have been bothering her for	2806
several weeks. Beverly tells me that she is not sure	2807
what is the matter with her, but it is either her	2808
bones, her veins, or her muscles. Jane suggests to her	2809
that she strained her knees bending them in order to	2810
avoid bending from the waist while she was recovering	2811
from her cataract surgery. Beverly has been putting a	2812
heating pad on her knees. She puts a wet piece of	2813
sponge inside her heating pad so that the heat will be	2814
moist. Her doctor suggested to her that she try the	2815
heat. He offered to give her some pain medication but	2816
she refused since she wantd to see if she could control	2817
it with just the heat. She feels that she is already	2818
taking a lot of medicine for her high blood pressure	2819
and doesn't want to add to it. She told me "I'd rather	2820
take a pill than lose a pound." Last fall (??) she	2821
said that she had been having some side effects from	2822
her high blood pressure medication. I aske her what	2823
exactly bothered her and she said that the medication	2824
caused her to have pains and unpleasant feelings in her	2825
breasts, "her sex organs." She had told the doctor	2826
about this "He didn't do anything," so she decided to	2827
stop taking the medication. She had some other	2828
medication left from an earlier time and she took this	2829
plus I think she was also taking something else that	2830
had been prescribed for her for her high blood	2831
pressure. She did this for about three months until	2832
she began to feel that "my system was really upset."	2833
She returned to her doctor who took changed her	2834
medication. (I'll try to get this in an interview with	2835
her, I've forgotten the names of the meds and some of	2836
the details of this story). Beverly thinks that her	2837
present problems with her knees might be related to a	2838
fall that she took last fall. She tripped going out	2839
the door.	2840
Beverly, like Jane, reads a lot about the	2841
medications she is taking. She likes to discus her	2842
ideas with the doctor and she likes to feel that she is	2843
in control of her own treatment. Jane and Beverly	2844
talked about drug interactions, Jane thinks that the	2845
doctors can't possibly keep all the information about	2846
the different drugs in their heads. She thinks that it	2847
it sthe patient's responsibility to be aware of what	2848
drugs they are on and possible side effects and	2849
interactions. She recently read about a computer	2850
program for doctors that will help them with this	2851
problem (keeping all the info about drugs straight).	2852

Table 5.3   Modified Code Manual for Senior Center Field Notes Illustrating
the More Detailed Codes Used for "Health Seeking/Illness
Behaviors"

HEALTH SEEKING/ILLNESS BEHAVIOR	HSB
Health Beliefs	HSB-BELIEFS
Illness Experience	HSB-ILLNESS
Hospital Experience	HSB-HOSP
Doctor/Patient Relationship	HSB-DOC/PAT
Medications	HSB-MEDS
Pain	HSB-PAIN
Illness Impact	HSB-IMPACT
Role of Family/Peers	HSB-FAM/PEER
Personal Decision-making	HSB-DECIDE
Coping	HSB-COPING
Money/Access	HSB-MONEY

conflict avoidance," "risk-taking behavior," "lack of competition,"
"thrift," "donations," and "peer group identification." Additionally,
codes pertinent to the role and participation of the researcher are
defined as a means of capturing possible influence of researcher
context and the topics of conversation/observation. Given the iterative nature of constructivist inquiry, further revisions of the codebook may be necessary as a better understanding of the data unfolds.

To accommodate text-analysis software programs, it is best to
limit the maximum number of characters in any code. For example,
Qualpro (Blackman, 1987) has a maximum code length of 15 characters, while THE ETHNOGRAPH (Bee & Crabtree, 1992; Seidel,
Kjolseth, & Seymour, 1988) has a 10-character limit. This limit is not an
issue when using a word processor as described by Reid in Chapter 7.

HAND-CODING TEXT

Computer-coding of text entails telling the software program where
each segment begins and ends; however, it is advisable to hand-code
a hard copy (printed version) initially with a pencil (Bee & Crabtree,
1992; Miles & Huberman, 1984; Seidel, Kjolseth, & Seymour, 1988;
Tesch, 1990). To do so, the analyst generally needs a printed copy of
the text that also has the line numbers printed on it. This requirement is not as simple as it might seem because the analysis software
is coding and sorting the version that is in the computer, which may
or may not be identical to that on the hard copy. Note that this is not

a problem if using the style described by Reid in Chapter 7, since paragraphs are being coded within the software program. Fortunately the analysis software programs are able to print numbered versions of the field notes for this process—which unfortunately results in the creation of a duplicate copy of all the field notes! We have found it is possible to bypass the printing of the numbered copy by using a split screen editor (using Kedit) with the file being coded on the top screen and the file used by the analysis software program to identify the segments (refer ahead to Table 5.4) on the bottom. Since the editor has line numbers on the screen, it is possible to hand-code on the printed field notes and follow the computer version for line numbers. Codebook in hand, segments then are marked in the margins.

Whenever coding is taking place, the researcher should be making "memos" in text margins or on file cards of interpretive insights that come about from being closely involved with the data. The researcher should be open also to the potential for codebook modifications that might emerge as these "memos" take on more focused meaning.

COMPUTER CODING AND RETRIEVING TEXT

It is not the intent of this chapter to advocate the use of any particular computer software package or to describe in detail the use of any specific software program. Different software programs have advantages and disadvantages, making them more or less useful for a particular study or style of analysis (see Reid in Chapter 7; Tesch, 1990). For example, THE ETHNOGRAPH provides superb searching and retrieval facilities but is discouraging by limiting line length to a maximum of 40 characters, thus considerably expanding the total number of pages (see Bee & Crabtree, 1992). Qualpro is used here to illustrate the template style of analysis because it is very simple to use and is extremely easy to code. Yet its simplicity can be a major drawback by limiting the types of searches it can perform. **One should certainly not develop an analytic strategy based on software, but rather select the software according to analysis needs.**

The goal of computer coding is to match text data with the organizational strategy of the codebook. Most text analysis programs have both an interactive mode accessed through a menu, as well as another "batch" mode in which a separate computer file identifies the text segments. The simplicity of this latter approach in Qualpro was a

Table 5.4   Code File (.COD) That is Used to Match Codes with Line
Numbers of Text in Qualpro

> **HSB-ILLNESS, 2804 , 2840**
> **HSB-PAIN, 2805 , 2818**
> **HSB-FAM/PEER, 2809 , 2812**
> **HSB-DECIDE, 2812 , 2818**
> **HSB-MEDS, 2815 , 2837**
> **HSB-BELIEFS, 2815 , 2821**
> **HSB-DOC/PAT, 2815 , 2835**
> **HSB-PAIN, 2823 , 2828**
> **ROLE, 2835 , 2837**
> **HSB-BELIEFS, 2837 , 2840**
> **HSB-DOC/PAT, 2841 , 2852**
> **HSB-MEDS, 2841 , 2852**
> **DOCTORS, 2815 , 2852**
> **HSB, 2804 , 2852**
> **MEDS, 2815 , 2852**

major factor for using the program for this particular analysis. An
individual file is created for each of the field note files to be coded,
with the stipulation that this file is required to have the same file
name as the text file and .COD as its three-letter extension. The code
file contains the code name from the codebook, the starting line, and
the ending line for each segment, as shown in Table 5.4, and then is
processed by the program. The analyst can request frequency counts
of occurrences of each code or the printing of text segments in which
all instances of a particular code are found within the text.

In our senior center example, we first coded all the data with the
preliminary codebook (Table 5.1); however, note that one does not
necessarily need to use all the codes if some are clearly outside the
immediate question of interest. One of the preliminary codes, "health
seeking/illness behavior," was noted with a code of HSB and yielded
153 segments from the nearly 200 pages of single-spaced participant
observation field notes. Because this code category is very broad,
some segments were extremely long, occasionally exceeding one page
of single-spaced print. These large text segments were printed and
hand-sorted, marginal notes were written on each, and a hierarchi-
cal system of subcodes, similar to that used by Willms, Johnson, and

Table 5.5 Sample Segment of Text About Doctor/Patient Relationship
(Code HSB-DOC/PAT) Retrieved by Qualpro

****

File NOTES3   Code HSB-DOC/PAT found in lines 2815 to 2835

2815 moist. Her doctor suggested to her that she try the	2815
2816 heat. He offered to give her some pain medication but	2816
2817 she refused since she wantd to see if she could control	2817
2818 it with just the heat. She feels that she is already	2818
2819 taking a lot of medicine for her high blood pressure	2819
2820 and doesn't want to add to it. She told me "I'd rather	2820
2821 take a pill than lose a pound." Last fall (??) she	2821
2822 said that she had been having some side effects from	2822
2823 her high blood pressure medication. I aske her what	2823
2824 exactly bothered her and she said that the medication	2824
2825 caused her to have pains and unpleasant feelings in her	2825
2826 breasts, "her sex organs." She had told the doctor	2826
2827 about this "He didn't do anything," so she decided to	2827
2828 stop taking the medication. She had some other	2828
2829 medication left from an earlier time and she took this	2829
2830 plus I think she was also taking something else that	2830
2831 had been prescribed for her for her high blood	2831
2832 pressure. She did this for about three months until	2832
2833 she began to feel that "my system was really upset."	2833
2834 She returned to her doctor who took changed her	2834
2835 medication. (I'll try to get this in an interview with	2835

All the codes in lines 2815 - 2835 are:
HSB-ILLNESS HSB-PAIN HSB-DECIDE HSB-MEDS HSB-BELIEFS
HSB-DOC/PAT HSB-PAIN ROLE DOCTORS HSB MEDS

****

White in Chapter 11, was created. The .COD file then was updated to include these new codes, and the smaller, more specific text segments were printed for interpretation.

The passage in Table 5.2 is a single segment retrieved by the original code of HSB; however, the revised codebook refined the specificity of the original code considerably. This revision is seen easily by comparing the coding of this same passage into numerous overlapping segments as illustrated in Table 5.4. For example, the subcode for "doctor/patient relationship" (HSB-DOC/PAT) was coded to include lines 2815 through 2835. The Qualpro output for this particular segment is shown in Table 5.5. Note that the program provides information on which file was searched, as well as a summary of other codes that overlapped the segment. A search of all three field note files yielded 63 segments that contained information regarding doctor-patient relationship. These were printed for further interpretation.

MAKING INTERPRETATIONS

Once segments have been organized and printed, the goal is to summarize the data. As with other steps described in this chapter, the researcher has different options about the best way to proceed. One option is to cut the printed output into individual segments and to sort them in the manner described by Addison in Chapter 6. Another option is to read through all the segments about a particular topic and to determine tentatively which themes seem to be recurrent. These themes then can be color-coded with different highlighter pens and read repeatedly for a better understanding. Once themes become salient, the researchers must create strategies for finding disproving cases, often requiring going back and collecting additional data. (See Miles & Huberman [1984] for some strategies for evaluating completeness of data.)

A number of themes emerged from the doctor/patient relationship segments which seemed important to this group of elderly persons. One of these was a theme of "not wishing to consult with physicians because they don't listen and take time." A few examples of segments addressing this issue, retrieved by the HSB-DOC/PAT subcode, are presented in Table 5.6. These and many other segments create a picture of dissatisfaction among these elderly persons due to prolonged exposure to health professionals who fail to communicate adequately (from the elderly person's perspective). Over time they become reluctant to consult physicians and develop expectations that physicians will not show concern about their individual problems and just classify them as "old." This theme also finds credence when reading segments retrieved by the HSB-MEDS subcode, in which patterns of sharing prescription medications and deciding to stop taking their own prescription drugs is common (this latter interpreted by their physicians as noncompliance). As segments from other "health seeking/illness behavior" subcodes are interpreted, other connections are found until a coherent description is possible and hypotheses are formulated.

The credibility, dependability, and confirmability of these and all future hypotheses are verified using triangulation, reflexivity, member checking, and independent audit (Kuzel & Like, 1991; Lincoln & Guba, 1985). The long-range goal remains to link these and future hypotheses into explanatory cultural models that explicate the

Table 5.6   Sample Segments From Field Notes From a Search of Doctor/
Patient Relationship (Code HSB-DOC/PAT) that Support a Theme
of Physicians Not Taking Time or Listening to Patients (Names
Changed to Protect Confidentiality)

Bea did go to the doctor (Johnson) to have her blood pressure checked. She said that he yelled at her for not having it checked in three years. He did a bunch of tests, including some blood work, and what sounded like an electrocardiogram. . . . Bea didn't seem to know what any of the tests were really for. I asked her what the doctor had said about her sweats, and she said "He didn't say nothing much, I don't think he thinks much of me." She said that he said something about cancer and she has to go back and have some more tests. Again she complained that she would be happy if he would just treat her blood pressure and not do all these tests. One thing she was upset about was that the doctor does all these tests and then you never hear anything more about them. I asked if we could get together again sometime right after her next appointment (Sept 9) to talk about it and she said that would be fine, adding "Maybe you can tell me more than my doctor."

He mentioned another doctor that he likes. I asked why he liked this doctor and he said that he treated you like a person and was willing to sit and talk to you. He feels free to make suggestions regarding his own treatment and health to this doctor, feels that the doctor respects his opinion, and takes his suggestions into account. Bob feels that you have to aggressively seek treatment because many doctors are too busy to provide you with the correct services, and that you have to push to get what you need.

Janet complained that when you go to the doctor's you are given an appointment, but then you must sit and wait. . . then you wait again in the examining room. Finally you see the doctor, but only for a few minutes and he never seems to have the time to answer any of your questions. Beverly said that she used to bring a list of questions with her whe she went to see Dr. Joseph but he never seemed to want to really take the time to answer them. At first he said that he would go over them, but later just looked at them and put them in her file. She said that if something was really important he would answer it. Finally he suggested that she switch to Dr. Howard. She likes him better and feels that he is more willing to answer questions. she said that at Joseph's she usually wsa not kept waiting and that apparently his priority was getting his patients in and out as fast as possible.

Edward is very bitter about the treatment he received for Masters. Janet said that doctors never take time to really look for what's wrong with you that they have full waiting rooms and the spend too much time looking at their watches and thinking about their pocketbooks and not enough time really taking time to take care of their patients and find out what is really wrong with them. Mary added that she thinks doctors are too quick to categorize people. She said that if you are old and fo to the doctor that right away the doctors assume that your have arthritis or diabetes, or have some other older persons disease. She thinks that doctors assume if you are in pain or have some problem that is because you are old, and that this is why they don't take time to find out what is really wrong. Carloe agreed with this.

context-dependent, decision-making processes elderly persons in this community use to manage their musculoskeletal problems. The transferability of these models to the family physician's office then will be evaluated.

Discussion

The template analysis style has advantages and disadvantages when compared with other analysis methods. Making the codebook and coding the text is relatively quick, reproducible, and easy to grasp for those skeptical of qualitative research. On the downside is a potential for missing information, especially if the codebook is produced in a completely a priori manner and the analyst runs the danger of not looking beyond the codes.

Clear descriptions of exactly how to develop and apply codebooks to text data are scarce. Tesch (1990) provides some insights and overviews several software options, while the workbook originating from educational research published by Miles and Huberman (1984) is probably the most complete description. The examples and educational context of the latter do not readily transfer to primary care research. The manual for THE ETHNOGRAPH software program (Seidel, Kjolseth, & Seymour, 1988) provides a description from the anthropology and sociology traditions for coding and retrieving data that is very similar to those we apply here (also see Bee & Crabtree, 1992). The analysis strategy in this chapter initially began as a test of the approach described by Miles and Huberman (1984) but gradually evolved to be more like the approach briefly summarized by Altheide (1987) as "Ethnographic Content Analysis."

The coding of text need not lead directly to computer applications, as well described by Addison in Chapter 6. Once the text is coded, it is possible to cut and paste (sort) the segments without ever using the computer. This process requires multiple copies of field notes, since codes are not mutually exclusive and the same segments of text need to be sorted into different places. Some logistical difficulties also arise if the codes are modified over time.

Another simplified approach, one using colored highlighter pens, was demonstrated to us by Terrie Wetle, a sociologist at the Institute of Living in Hartford, Connecticut. In her analysis of depth interviews of case managers, she developed a simple codebook in which pink indicated ethical concerns, green meant a client type, orange represented a communication among provider issue, and blue marked a case manager management strategy. After marking a transcript, she had her secretary copy the computer version of the transcript to a new file and delete everything except the colored text. Thus, for each transcript, she had four files, each with only those segments pertaining to a particular code.

Alfred Reid in Chapter 7 illustrates yet another simplified approach (also see Pfaffenberger, 1988), in which coding is done directly on the field notes within a word processor. In using this approach, the codebook strategies described in this chapter also apply. One potential drawback to the word processor approach arises when multiple files need to be searched. This situation is not uncommon when extensive participant observation field notes are involved. This is less of a problem when analyzing interview data, since each interview is usually coded and interpreted separately.

The analysis of a mountain of information-rich, purposefully sampled, qualitative text data can easily appear insurmountable and quixotic, especially to researchers proficient in quantitative methods. There is reason enough to pause and briefly tremble. The template approach to text analysis described in this chapter, however, is one specific way for quantitatively trained primary care researchers to take the first step into qualitative analysis.

6 Grounded Hermeneutic Research

RICHARD B. ADDISON

Introduction

Hermeneutics is an awkward word with a long tradition. It simply stands for the business of interpretation. The word is thought to derive from Hermes, the Greek messenger god and trickster, who carried messages from the gods to the people. His role was to interpret these messages from the gods and to make them understandable to humans.

The central task of hermeneutic analysis is "the process of bringing a thing or situation from unintelligibility to understanding" (Palmer, 1969, p. 13). Trying to understand, take meaning from, or make intelligible that which is not yet understood is not only the central task of hermeneutics, it is an essential aspect of our being in the world (Gadamer, 1976; Heidegger, 1927/1962).

As an approach to understanding written texts, hermeneutics has long been applied to fields as diverse as biblical exegesis, legal interpretation, and linguistic and literary analysis. It was not until the end of the 19th century that a hermeneutic approach for studying the human sciences began to gain prominence (Bleicher, 1980; Palmer, 1969).

In this chapter I will provide a brief summary of a grounded hermeneutic approach to research, give examples of such research, list the central aspects of grounded hermeneutic research, describe the

AUTHOR'S NOTE: I wish to thank Margo Addison, Bruce Denner, Martin Packer, Don Ransom, Tony Stigliano, Todd Straus, and Richard Zimmer for their critical comments on earlier drafts of this chapter.

step-by-step research practices I employed in a grounded hermeneutic investigation of individuals becoming family physicians, outline the account I generated, and offer some helpful standards for evaluating qualitative research.

AN APPROACH TO RESEARCH

A grounded hermeneutic approach is not a method in the sense of a prescribed set of techniques that can be applied to any research project. A hermeneutic approach cuts below specific methods or techniques. For the research described in this chapter, I adapted a grounded theory method (Glaser, 1978; Glaser & Strauss, 1967; Strauss, 1987) and applied techniques developed in participant observation-related research (Agar, 1980; Erickson, 1977; Garfinkel, 1967; Geertz, 1973, 1983; Mehan & Wood, 1975; Schatzman & Strauss, 1973; Schwartz & Schwartz, 1955) on a hermeneutic framework (Bernstein, 1976, 1983; Bleicher, 1980, 1982; Caputo, 1987; Dreyfus, 1986, 1991; Habermas, 1968, 1977; Heidegger, 1927/1962; Lather, 1986a; McCarthy, 1978; Packer & Addison, 1989; Rabinow & Sullivan, 1979; Ricoeur, 1981).

I call the hermeneutic approach described in this chapter *grounded* for two reasons: first, it seeks to illuminate social, cultural, historical, economic, linguistic, and other background aspects that frame and make comprehensible human practices and events; second, it is grounded in the everyday practices of individuals in ongoing human affairs (see Kuzel, 1986, on naturalistic or constructivist research).

ASSUMPTIONS OF A GROUNDED HERMENEUTIC APPROACH

A grounded hermeneutic approach embodies certain assumptions or understandings about the world, the people in it, research activity, and the relationships among these. Briefly these assumptions and their implications for conducting research are as follows:

1. Participants of research are meaning-giving beings; that is, they give meaning to their actions, and these meanings are important in understanding human behavior.
2. Meaning is not only that which is verbalized; meaning is expressed in action and practices. To understand human behavior, it is important to look at everyday practices, not just beliefs about those practices.

3. The meaning-giving process is not entirely free; meanings are made possible by background conditions such as immediate context, social structures, personal histories, shared practices, and language. When something is noticed as missing, wrong, or problematic, illuminating these background conditions can allow change to occur.

4. The meaning and significance of human action is rarely fixed, clear, and unambiguous. Meanings are not limited to preestablished categories. Meaning is being negotiated constantly in ongoing interactions. Meaning changes over time, in different contexts and for different individuals.

5. Interpretation is necessary to understand human action. Truth is not determined by how closely beliefs correspond to some fixed reality. It is never possible to achieve an objective, value-free position from which to evaluate the truth of the matter. Facts are always value-laden, and researchers have values that are reflected in their research projects.

EXAMPLES OF HERMENEUTIC RESEARCH QUESTIONS

Certain classes of problems and concerns in primary care research are particularly well suited to a grounded hermeneutic approach. These include questions aimed at (a) understanding the meaning and significance of complex human interactions and events in the context of their everyday settings, and (b) understanding the relationship between behaviors, practices, or events and the sociocultural, historical, political, and economic background against which they take place. At this time, several promising investigations in process are employing hermeneutically informed approaches. These studies ask such questions as how physicians deal with medical mistakes (Newman, 1991), how the social and cultural context affects the doctor-patient relationship for patients with Type II diabetes (Bartz, in preparation), how patients think about their hip fractures (Borkan, Quirk, & Sullivan, in preparation), how women decide how to feed their infants (Marchand, 1991), what happens when elderly patients are discharged from the hospital to home (McWilliam, 1991), how to understand barriers to providing primary care to HIV patients (Epstein, in preparation), and how family practice resident-physicians deal with dying patients and their families (Dozor & Addison, in preparation). Other primary care research studies have used aspects of an interpretive or hermeneutic approach (e.g., Benner, 1984, 1985; Brody, 1990b; Crabtree & Miller, 1991; Frankel & Beckman, 1982;

Kleinman, 1988; Mishler, 1984; Mizrahi, 1986; Stein & Apprey, 1985; Willms et al., 1990).

CENTRAL PRACTICES OF GROUNDED HERMENEUTIC RESEARCH

Even though a grounded hermeneutic approach is not a method in the sense of a set of techniques, it is possible to list the following seven practices that are central to grounded hermeneutic researchers:

1. Immersing oneself in the participants' world in order to understand and interpret the participants' everyday practices
2. Looking beyond individual actions, events, and behaviors to a larger background context and its relationship to the individual events
3. Entering into an active dialogue with the research participants, research colleagues, research critics, the account itself, and his or her own values, assumptions, interpretations, and understandings
4. Maintaining a constantly questioning attitude in looking for misunderstandings, incomplete understandings, deeper understandings, alternative explanations, and changes with time and context
5. Analyzing in a circular progression between parts and whole, foreground and background, understanding and interpretation, and researcher and narrative account
6. Offering a narrative account of the participants' everyday practices that opens up new possibilities for self-reflection and changed practices
7. Addressing the practical concerns of the researcher and the research participants against a larger social, cultural, historical, political, and economic background

Accordingly, grounded hermeneutic researchers approach a particular problem from a concerned, involved standpoint; immerse themselves in the participants' world; analyze human actions as situated within a cultural and historical context; offer a narrative account of how a problem developed and is maintained; and offer directions for positive change. These practices will be illustrated in the following step-by-step discussion of my research practices.

Becoming a Family Physician

For many years I had been interested in the long and arduous education and training involved in becoming a physician. I saw this intense, stressful process as a problem for the trainees, their families, and their patients. I wanted to better understand what becoming a physician was like for the individuals involved, how the practices of resident-physicians became problematic, and whether positive alternatives were possible.

CHOOSING AN APPROACH TO THE PROBLEM

The method of inquiry must fit the problem and goals of the research question. To address the questions detailed immediately above, I knew that questionnaires or self-report surveys would be inadequate for capturing the complexity and richness of the everyday practices of individuals as they became physicians. I wanted to understand what they actually did as they began their residency, not just what they thought they were doing, believed they were doing, intended to do, or said they did. This is the kind of question that can be addressed effectively by a grounded hermeneutic investigation.

NARROWING THE FOCUS

After talking to many people in the field of medical education, I informally visited different training programs. I observed different primary care specialties (pediatrics, family practice, internal medicine, as well as some observations in emergency medicine residencies), in different settings (county, private, HMO), in different locations (urban, semiurban), and with different affiliations (university based, university affiliated, community). After 9 months I chose one university-affiliated family practice residency program in a semiurban county setting.

CLARIFYING INITIAL UNDERSTANDINGS

I tried to clarify my initial understandings about the problematic aspects of family medicine and residency training. These understandings centered around two issues. First, increasing technological expertise was demanded of physicians who had chosen family medicine; this would create a contradiction for them in their training if they envisioned themselves as healers rather than technicians. Second, stress and impairment in physicians, as evidenced by poor patient care, burnout, dropout, marital problems, substance abuse, depression, and suicide, seemed to be far more problematic than ever before.

I decided to focus on the first year of residency, long recognized as most stressful in terms of its encompassing demands and most significant in terms of inculcating attitudes, beliefs, values, and practices (Bloom, 1963; Mumford, 1970). Habits and patterns of behaving and interacting that are forged at this time often extend beyond internship and residency into personal and professional lives.

IMMERSING MYSELF

The program I chose to look at had accepted nine new residents. I narrowed my focus to observing these nine residents in one residency setting at the beginning of their residency training in order to gain as thick and comprehensive an understanding of their everyday existence as possible.

I presented myself as a psychologist and researcher who was studying how individuals become physicians. I followed the nine first-year residents solidly for a year and intermittently for the next two, observing them in almost every aspect of their lives. I followed some more closely than others, as I found some residents more welcoming of my presence, some more verbal, and some more critically reflective. I openly recorded observations about what I saw, what I felt, how I was doing research, what I understood and did not understand, and what I thought was important. I interviewed the residents, their spouses, and others associated with their education and training, asking questions about what I observed. I read the enormous volume of memos, schedules, and documentation that was churned out by the hospital, the residency, and the residents themselves.

Immersing myself in the everyday activities and practices of the residents was important for me to develop an understanding of what these activities meant to them. For example, when I accompanied them to their first surgery conference, the surgery coordinator made them stand up and recite differential diagnoses. He called on one of the first-year residents who was very uncomfortable talking in front of groups. She sounded unsure of herself, hesitated, and the coordinator quickly moved on to someone else. I felt her embarrassment; it reminded me of how my seventh-grade teacher ridiculed me in front of the class because I spoke my answer too softly. When I later interviewed the resident, I told her that I knew how she had felt at the moment. She went on to talk about a wealth of similar experiences in medical training when she had felt embarrassed, chagrined, abused, and demeaned. As a resident she sometimes did not attend conferences held by certain physicians. I saw these dynamics repeated with other residents in other interactions. Out of this I came to an interpretation about the importance of such interactions in constituting residents' practices.

This type of analysis is essentially and necessarily a hermeneutically circular process: I moved from immersing myself in the residents' everyday existence wherein I developed an experiential understanding of their practices. I then made this understanding explicit in the form of an interpretation of the meaning of their practices. I then incorporated this fuller interpretation into my further observations and immersion to understand more or different aspects of their existence.

CONCURRENTLY COLLECTING, FIXING, AND ANALYZING

Hermeneutic analysis is a necessarily circular procedure. Even now as I attempt to describe this process by writing words, sentences, and paragraphs that follow one another in linear fashion, I am aware of the difficulty of communicating the circular feel of my research procedure. While I was still immersed in observing resident practices, taking notes, and recording interviews, I began analyzing the notes and interviews. I moved back and forth between collecting, analyzing, reflecting, and writing in a way that cannot be laid out or predicted in advance.

All of the collecting, coding, and analyzing was done in light of my practical research question: the problematic aspects of becoming a family physician. Although I analyzed far more data than I eventually used, my selection of data was determined by this question.

I had my notes and interviews transcribed onto only the left half of the page, saving the right half for text analysis. I treated the social action I observed as a type of text (Ricoeur, 1979). I "fixed" events, behaviors, interactions, dialogues, and practices in the form of a text so that I could interpret and analyze them. Although texts are usually thought of as written material, audiotaped and videotaped material (see Chapter 8) also have been used as hermeneutic texts, usually along with a transcript of the tapes. Thus the typed transcripts of my audiotaped interviews, my handwritten notes, and my reflections on both of these became the text for analysis.

I used two different types of analysis for developing my account. The first type, often referred to as "in vivo" coding (Strauss, 1987), consisted of selecting from transcripts residents' words or phrases that stood out to me as potentially significant for understanding how the residents were becoming family physicians. For example, I coded such words as *punting, pimping, dumping,* and *surviving.* These were terms residents used that later became categories in the developed account. I used as much in vivo coding as possible.

I also used a second and more global type of analysis. This type of analysis was like the reflective process notes I take after seeing psychotherapy clients. In this latter type, I recorded comments and notes on what the residents' words or practices reminded me of, on what I felt to be significant, on what I thought their practices meant and were connected to, on what I did not understand, on how I thought my presence influenced their practices, and on the implications of their practices for their professional socialization. For example, one of these notes read:

> I went up to see (a 21-year old patient who was dying): the guilt of not spending enough time with him, and the discrepancy I noticed between the people around him who know he's going to die, and his not talking about death, or not having anyone to talk to about dying . . . . I feel guilty at not spending enough time with him, and I'm sure the residents do too.

This note developed into an analysis of residents' difficulties in dealing with dying patients.

Again, collecting, coding, and analyzing data occurred concurrently. Interpretation and analysis began as soon as I started observing residents and collecting data. For example, one of my early notes read: "I sit at the nurses' station . . . trying to hide out and write my notes. I am feeling absolutely overwhelmed with the amount of input." Another note read: "I feel tired, not at my best, even though I got five hours sleep, considered a good night on call (white cloud). The residents must get used to this." These notes and others around this issue helped me understand how "totalizing" their lives as residents were.

I started to put all of these codes and notes on index cards. I cut up relevant sections of my transcribed notes and interviews that were too long to fit on index cards. I began to sort the hundreds of cards and longer selections into piles that seemed to have a common thread. I looked for patterns and relationships between cards and piles of cards. I looked for themes that organized piles of cards. Every horizontal surface above floor level was filled with cards and cut-up transcripts. I began to see progressions and flows. I started making lists of groups of practices, people, reactions, and events, and connecting these lists on big sheets of white paper. Since no horizontal surfaces were left, I removed pictures and prints and tacked these lists and categories onto walls.

Suddenly, 3 or 4 months after beginning, out of this wealth of seeming chaos, I had a flash of clarity: The central organizing theme for the residents as they began the residency was "surviving." It seemed to both describe and unify their practices in a way that made sense. On finding such a unifying theme, I set out to learn how they survived and how they did not survive that first year of residency.

DEVELOPING THE ACCOUNT

I therefore began to reanalyze my transcripts, interviews, notes, and index cards with reference to surviving. I began seeing a different, more cohesive organization that seemed to incorporate previously scattered experiences and practices. I constructed a diagram that encompassed most of the lists and categories from my wall charts. This beginning diagram or attempted pictorial whole of what happened to these individuals as they began their residency looked something like a child's drawing of an extraterrestrial's digestive system. It was the first of many such attempts to make diagrammatic sense out of their existence.

SPIRALING AROUND
THE HERMENEUTIC CIRCLE

The above progression illustrates the circular movement of hermeneutic research from understanding to interpretation to deeper understanding to more comprehensive interpretation. After immersing myself in the residents' lives (understanding), I began to analyze my notes and interviews (interpretation) to make sense out of them. My flash of (deeper understanding of) how surviving played such a central role for them led me to reanalyze my transcripts, diagrams, and models in light of the centrality of surviving (more comprehensive interpretation). Following this, I returned to observe and interview the residents (aiming for greater understanding and even further development of the interpretive account). Thus, as I moved around the hermeneutic circle, my understanding continued to deepen and my account became more coherent, cohesive, and comprehensive.

QUESTIONING THE ACCOUNT

I tried always to keep my critical voice active, questioning my notes, looking for contradictions, inconsistencies, gaps, omissions, and ambiguities in the developing account. For example, I knew that two strategies the residents employed for surviving—"helping" and "isolating"—were only part of a larger story. It was not until I questioned the conditions under which residents survived by isolating themselves and the conditions under which they survived by helping that I was able to push the account further. It was then that I came up with the more comprehensively explanatory modes of "Covering-Over" and "Over-Reflecting."

This is only one example of how questioning an account serves as a key element of hermeneutic research. It is essential for developing and refining any account of human practices.

ENTERING INTO A CRITICAL DIALOGUE
WITH OTHER RESEARCHERS

Since I worked alone and was not part of a research team, I joined a weekly analytic seminar of other health care student researchers led by a sociologist and health care researcher (see Strauss, 1987, pp. 167-168). At various stages, I also presented the developing account to other colleagues and teachers. One mentor (an educational sociologist) cautioned me about identifying too strongly with the residents' plight and encouraged me to expand my interpretations. Bonding or identifying too closely with the research participants is a frequent occurrence in participant-observation research. Although my bonding with them helped me understand their everyday practices, I also needed to stand back, reflect on, and question my understanding. Another mentor (a psychologist and behavioral scientist) filled in valuable pieces of local history. Another primary care physician and researcher pointed out logical inconsistencies in my account.

SHOWING THE ACCOUNT
TO RESEARCH PARTICIPANTS

When I felt ready, I tried to explain the working diagram to the residents. I received many helpful comments and questions about various aspects of the diagram. I was also greatly surprised at the initial reaction I received: No first-year resident could sit through my brief presentation of the account without either crying or becoming extremely anxious. One first-year resident told me of his reaction:

> I had an incredible amount of anger about everything that was on that sheet. I mean, everything that was bothering me was on there in some way . . . and all the arrows went exactly the way the arrows in my brain were going . . . but I was unaware of a lot of them at the time. . . . And I looked at them all and . . . within fifteen seconds my eyes were just welling up with tears. . . . It just made me feel so uncomfortable. (Addison, 1989, p. 49)

I took this reaction to the diagram as a sign that the account was a powerful one; it had some significance for the residents. I also interpreted this type of reaction to mean that they had no broader understanding of what was happening to them as they carried out their everyday tasks and responsibilities. This understanding of their limited range of reflective vision became a central element of the developed account. Additionally their reaction told me that I needed to be sensitive and careful about whom I presented the account to, when I presented it, and how I presented it. I needed to think through the implications of showing the account to individuals already experiencing a great deal of stress.

REFLECTING ON INITIAL UNDERSTANDINGS

One of the essential elements of hermeneutic research is the inclusion of the researcher in the hermeneutic circle. Since no privileged position exists from which to observe human behavior, researchers' beginning understandings inevitably influence how researchers carry out their observations, what questions get asked, what data get selected, how data get interpreted, and what findings get reported.

An example of how these early, sometimes taken-for-granted understandings can affect the course of inquiry (and how understandings can change during the course of inquiry) involved the residents' choice of specialty. As noted above, when I began my study, I was very interested in the split between why I thought individuals chose family medicine: because they wanted to be healers; and what they would be doing as they learned family medicine: learning the technology of medicine. I thought this split would be the central contradiction in their everyday existence. I came to understand that although this contradiction was important to the residents, it was not nearly as central as I thought. I learned that individuals chose family medicine for a variety of reasons: because they thought it would be challenging, because they would meet interesting people, because they thought it would allow them to perform a great variety of procedures and give them enormous breadth of knowledge, because they thought they would not be accepted in other specialties, and because they saw themselves as altruistic healers. I only came to this fuller interpretation after I reflected on my professional choices: I became a psychologist instead of a family physician and a psychotherapist who eschews technical or cookbook approaches to psychotherapy. Once I saw how my professional choices affected my developing understanding of the residents, I began to see some of the other reasons why the residents had chosen family medicine. At the same time, the split I had identified as central (technician-healer) became far less central. By moving in a circular fashion between reflecting on my evolving account and my developing understandings, these understandings changed as my interpretation of their everyday practices evolved.

CONTINUED OBSERVATIONS

At the same time, I continued observing and interviewing to flesh out underdeveloped portions of the account and to correct aspects that were not yet coherent or cohesive. For example, the residents were troubled by their outpatient clinics, the kind of setting in which they would be spending most of their time after residency. One of their complaints about their clinics was that they had too many patients to see; they always felt rushed and harried. When I questioned the faculty as to the rationale for the number of patients residents were required to see, they replied that residents needed to learn how to see patients quickly and efficiently now in order for them to earn a decent living after residency. After continued questioning of other medical educators, I identified another and perhaps more important reason for the number of patients in the residents' clinics: The outpatient facility needed the income from these visits.

In addition to showing the value of continued questioning, the above example illustrates how it is impossible to interpret sufficiently the significance of a singular event without reference to the larger context within or upon which the event took place. I moved back and forth between foreground (the residents' dissatisfaction) and background (the economics of the clinic and hospital). Again this circular, back and forth movement is central to a hermeneutic approach to analyzing research data.

REVISITING THE PROBLEM

From my immersion and analysis, I constantly returned to the problem at hand: how individuals became family physicians. I wanted to make sure the account addressed this question directly and did not wander off on interesting and important points that were not quite relevant to my specific question.

REFINING THE ACCOUNT
BY WRITING IT UP

As I began to fill in the gaps, inconsistencies, and mistaken understandings of the developing account, my diagrams changed, looking less indigestive and otherworldly, more digested and cohesive. I grew more confident of the account and began to write it up as a narrative whole. Even at this stage, I saw other aspects of the account that did not quite hang together. I had to go back and reinterview and reobserve to fill in missing connections or sections that were unworkable.

THE ACCOUNT ITSELF:
SURVIVING THE RESIDENCY

Since the focus of this chapter is the process of analysis, I will provide only a brief summary of the account. A more detailed narrative can be found elsewhere (Addison, 1984, 1989).

In summary, I found "surviving" to be the unifying theme of the residents' everyday practices. As they began the residency, they were confronted by certain immediate issues (work and information overload, time pressures, sleep deprivation, inexperience, responsibility, control, and dying patients). They encountered different groups of people (other residents, nurses, receptionists, faculty, attending physicians, and significant others) whom the residents sometimes found helpful, and sometimes found to be sources of abuse. In response, residents adopted certain strategies for dealing with these stressful issues and interactions. Strategies ranged on a continuum from helping to isolating and included learning the ropes, forming teams, covering, punting, dumping, and pimping. These encounters took place against a background of conflicts and contradictions in the fabric of the residency.

These contradictions occurred in two arenas. I called the first arena *spheres of existence*. It consisted of three spheres: work, education, and life outside of residency. As residency progressed, the purpose and balance of the spheres changed radically. Work became all-encompassing, education became defined as doing procedures, and life outside became negligible.

I labeled the other arena of conflict and contradiction *models of medicine*. Although residents entered the residency hoping to learn family medicine, they soon found themselves torn among the medicine practiced and taught by specialists and subspecialists, the medicine practiced and taught by general practitioners, and the medicine taught by behavioral scientists. Their ideals and their everyday practices were in conflict. They found no family medicine role models, especially in the hospital where they spent most of their time.

At times they found themselves "Covering-Over" these conflicts and contradictions; at times they found themselves "Over-Reflecting." When they became buried in the Covering-Over mode, they barreled through their work, forgot their ideals, and lost sight of their own place in the process of becoming a family physician. When they became paralyzed in the Over-Reflecting mode, they became overwhelmed, had difficulty becoming involved in learning family medicine, and thought of quitting. Residents bounced back and forth between these two extremes in a jarring fashion without seeing what was happening to them. They defined the whole of their existence by the mode they found themselves in. What was missing was the opportunity to perceive the larger picture of this movement, to reflect on the disparity and contradiction between their ideals and their everyday practices, to learn to move more flexibly between Covering-Over and Over-Reflecting, and eventually to begin to integrate these two disparate modes into one workable mode of being a family physician.

THE HERMENEUTIC AND NARRATIVE
CHARACTER OF THE ACCOUNT

The product of my inquiry was a comprehensive hermeneutic and narrative account grounded in the everyday practices of the residents. I do not believe that the account corresponds with, represents, or reconstructs "reality." Rather, I generated an interpretive account that looks at a crucial period in the process of becoming a physician; provides an interpretation of how distress developed and was maintained; describes the conditions, context, and problematic atmosphere of the process; discusses the costs and significance of the process for residents, their families, and health care; and suggests directions for improving physician training. The account can be modified as time, social conditions, and individuals change.

Conclusion

Grounded hermeneutic research is an extremely well-developed and powerful approach to meaningful, difficult, and complex human research questions. It addresses practical concerns of the researcher and research participants. It aims to describe and uncover significant background conditions, understandings, and practices that contribute to the problem at hand. It takes into account the values, attitudes, beliefs, and practices of the researcher. It can produce a cohesive, interpretive account of research participants' everyday practices. Such an account can open up new possibilities of self-reflection and action for the participants. It is my hope that this chapter will encourage researchers to recognize its value for addressing primary care research questions.

7 Computer Management Strategies for Text Data

ALFRED O. REID, JR.

Introduction

Newcomers to qualitative research, as well as those more experienced, often find themselves daunted by the sheer volume of data involved and the necessarily labor-intensive process of analyzing it. In addition to careful thought, imagination, and insight, qualitative data analysis can require long hours of coding, sorting, and summarizing. Computers cannot perform *analysis* of qualitative data, but they can perform many of the labor-intensive tasks of data *management* quickly and accurately, freeing the researcher's time and energy for the more interesting and rewarding work of analysis.

Personal computers and word processing software are rapidly becoming commonplace as administrative and clerical tools. The primary purpose of this chapter is to show how these commonly available tools can facilitate the management and manipulation of qualitative text data. When turned to this purpose, word processor functions fall into three broad categories. As with most qualitative categories, these are neither linear nor mutually exclusive in their relation to each other. The first of these, *data preparation,* involves the initial entry and "cleaning" of text data. Data entry includes typing field notes, recording jottings or analytic memos, or transcribing interviews. Cleaning data may include checking for spelling errors and inconsistencies, minor editing for clarification, numbering lines, and perhaps formatting and printing. The purpose of *data identification,* the second category, is to divide text data into analytically meaningful and easily locatable segments. This process can be as simple as dividing text into paragraphs at each shift in topic. It may also include attaching notes, memos, or even formal codes to text segments. The final category, *data manipulation,* includes searching for particular data elements (words, phrases, or data segments) and sorting or retrieving them.

The extent to which word processing functions are beneficial depends substantially on the analysis style (see Chapter 1) most appropriate for the project. Using a word processor for initial data preparation is worthwhile regardless of the type of analysis. Data identification and manipulation can be done using a growing variety of specialized software. Crabtree and Miller (Chapter 5) illustrate the use of one such program, Qualpro. Such software can be expensive, however, both in financial terms and in the amount of time required to learn how to use it. Moreover, for novices at either qualitative research, computers, or both, it may not be immediately evident which specialized program is most suited to the task. Mastery of a small number of word processor functions can emulate many of the features of the more specialized programs and give researchers a sounder basis on which to choose other software, should it be required. The bulk of this chapter is devoted to step-by-step explanations of word processor-based data management strategies. Before turning to that topic, however, it is useful to point out some of the unique aspects of computer-based qualitative data management, and also to highlight the small subset of word processor capabilities needed to put such strategies into action.

Beginning Assumptions

Computers have become nearly universal analytic tools for numerical data. This fact, along with the ubiquity of the quantitative approach, strongly influences the image most of us have of computers as research tools. In quantitative analysis, computer programs can compute statistics that allow us to say, with more or less confidence, that the data support or do not support our hypotheses. No such programs exist for text data. Computers can manipulate data in ways that greatly facilitate the analytic decisions we make, but computers cannot guide us in judging the soundness of those decisions. *Computers do not analyze qualitative data. They help manage it.*

In using a computer, we must also reconsider some of the ways we typically interact with information. Most of the text that most of us see is on paper, and we employ a variety of methods to manage and process it, including highlighters, colored pens, sticky notes, scissors, paper trays, and file folders. Word processors can emulate, and even improve on, many of these tools, but they can also influence the way we look at text, often literally. For example, the visual frame for text is most often the 8-by-11 inch page (several, if we have a sufficiently large tabletop to work on). On most PC word processors the video monitor provides a "window" through which we can view only about 24 lines of text at a time. Scrolling through a document 24 lines at a time can be cumbersome, and so it is still often desirable to work with a printed copy of text data.

Another point to bear in mind concerns the variety of word processing software. Each word processor is, in effect, its own language that tells a computer (on your behalf) how to format, display, store, and print text. Documents created by one word processor generally cannot usefully be read by any other program. This situation can become problematic if documents must be shared among colleagues who may not have access to a common word processor or if different software (a specialized text management program, for example) may be used at some later point in the analysis. Special programs are available that convert documents from one word processor's format to another or to a very basic common format (such as ASCII), and some text management programs are capable of "importing" documents created in some of the more common word processors. Such "translations" are rarely perfect, however, and the more advanced features of a word processor one uses (footnotes, nonprinting comments, columns, different type styles), the more difficult it becomes to translate documents accurately into any other program.

For the reasons stated above, the data management strategies presented here rely largely on functions that are easily portable between programs and, within limits, between different computer systems. This approach makes good use of the fundamental power of word processors to manage text but maintains the flexibility to move data from one program to another and to share data among researchers conveniently.

Three points of clarification are in order before I turn to the practical business of managing data. First, most of the examples of word processor functions contain general directions for their use. These directions have been tested on word processing programs for both the Macintosh and IBM-PC-compatible computers. For consistency, however, accompanying figures reflect the format of the WordPerfect word processing program for IBM-PC-compatible computers. Regardless of which word processing program you use, you should consult the user's manual for specific information on how each function works. Second, the uses for word processing functions explained in this chapter are meant to be suggestive rather than exhaustive, a list of ingredients rather than a recipe. Use the examples as a way of learning how the processes work, but also use your imagination in adapting them to your own projects. Third, I offer a word of caution. Computers excel at doing complex or highly repetitive tasks quickly and consistently. These two characteristics place enormous power at the disposal of qualitative researchers, and like most powerful tools, they can be destructive as well as useful. A single keystroke can make changes in a document that would take many hours to accomplish manually, but *the changes may not be what you wanted.* Most experienced computer users have learned that computers do what you *tell* them to do, not necessarily what you *want* them to do. For this reason, it is wise to practice new or unfamiliar functions on a spare copy of a data document, applying it to the "real" data only after you are sure the function works as you intend it to.

Useful Features of Word Processors

Word processors have become powerful, versatile, and varied in their ability to manage text and in the approach they take to the task. As a result, users' manuals have become large, intimidating documents in which it is not always easy to find what is needed. Happily the functions most useful for managing qualitative text data are relatively few and are accessible in all commonly available word processing programs. Below is a description of the word processing functions that should be mastered in order to manage qualitative data effectively.

File Management. If you will be working with documents directly on a computer, it is important that you understand the basic commands or menu choices your computer and word processor use to manipulate files. They include:

Copy a file from one disk to another
Retrieve a file from disk storage into the word processor
Save a file, updating the disk copy but keeping the file on-screen
Store a file on disk and clear it from the word processor's screen
Store a file in ASCII format

If it is at all likely that you will want to share data with other researchers who use different word processors or different computer systems, it is valuable to learn how to save documents in ASCII format. ASCII (American Standard Code for Information Interchange—pronounced "askee") defines a set of alphabetic characters, numbers, and symbols that most computers can understand. When a word processor saves a file in ASCII format, it removes all of its own codes or special characters, leaving only the plain text. The conventions described later in this chapter use only characters and symbols that are part of the ASCII character set.

Most word processor manuals address the topics of file management and format in sufficient detail and clarity to provide all the information the novice analyst needs to understand file management and format. They have the additional advantage of being oriented to the particular computer system and word processor that you are using. For those who find their software manuals unsatisfying or who simply want to know more on this subject, a wide variety of books has been written. Remember that change occurs rapidly in the computer world; the information in books on computer-related topics has a short shelf life. For this reason, such books tend to be relatively expensive if they are up to date, and relatively cheap if they are not. Discounted older editions are rarely a bargain.

Document Editing and Navigation. Reading, annotating, and manipulating text all depend on the fundamental ability to move easily from one point in a document to another. On paper, we tend to take document "navigation" for granted, visually scanning pages and turning them back and forth, highlighting text and jotting notes. In using a PC, however, you must explicitly tell your word processor which part of a document you want to look at next and what you want to do when you get there. Here are the functions you will need to master.

Cursor movement from one place to another. The following units determine how far the cursor will go.

- Character: one space forward or back
- Word: to the next space or tab, forward or back
- Line: up or down a line, staying in the same column
- Beginning/End of Line: to the first or last character of the current line
- Beginning/End of Document: to the first or last character of the document
- Blocking Text: indicates to the word processor where a particular unit of text begins and ends. This process involves moving the cursor to the first character of the text unit, activating the blocking function, and then moving the cursor to the last character of the text unit.
- Copying and Moving: Once a unit of text is blocked, it can be moved to a new location (and deleted from its current one) or copied to a new location, leaving the original location intact.
- Auto Date: reads the PC's internal clock and inserts the current date and time into an on-screen document. This feature provides a convenient date/time stamp for field note entries, analytic memos, and so on.

Word Search. This feature is an extension of the ability to move around in a document, the computer equivalent of visually scanning pages for a particular word or phrase. It allows your computer to find any and all occurrences of a specified character string. A character string for our purposes will most often be a word or phrase but can be any set of contiguous characters and spaces, including numbers, symbols, and even such attributes as boldface or underlining. The literal nature of computer software makes this feature particularly powerful, though sometimes counterintuitive. For example, in most word processors a search for the string "drug" would find, in addition to the word itself, *drugs, druggist, drug-induced,* virtually any word that included "drug" in its makeup. With a little thought, this facility can be made exclusive to search for very specific words or inclusive to search for several variations of the same word. A search for " prescription drug " (note the beginning and ending spaces) would find only the specific phrase "prescription drug." On the other hand, a search for "tox" would find *toxin, toxic, detoxification, antitoxin,* and any other word containing the string "tox."

Search and Replace. This variation on the word search feature systematically replaces one character string with another throughout a file. Most word processors have two variations on the function—one that stops and asks for confirmation before each replacement, and one that makes all the substitutions at once.

Spelling Checker. Spelling checkers work by comparing each word in a document to a list of acceptable spellings. If a word is not found on the list, the program stops and either asks the user to correct a misspelling or, in many programs, offers the opportunity to add a word to the list. Spelling checkers improve the reliability of text data by ensuring that words are spelled consistently; if they are not, the value of having the word processor search for words is diminished. Consistency of spelling is particularly important if codes are added to the text.

A spelling checker can also be useful analytically. For practical reasons the list of acceptable spellings is fairly limited; names of people, technical terms, and a variety of "unusual" words are not included, and even correctly spelled words of these types will be identified as misspelled. Repeated references to the same name or use of the same unusual term throughout an interview, for example, may provide a first glimpse at an important concept or analytic category. Spelling checkers are integral parts of most word processors. If your word processor does not have one, separate speller programs are available, but you may want to consider switching to a word processor that has one built-in.

Macros. A macro is a simple key combination or command that initiates (i.e., is a "macrocommand" for) a whole series of keystrokes or command sequences. As a simple illustration, consider recording a field note outline format in a macro. Such an outline might look like the one in Figure 7.1, giving the date and time of observation, observer's initials, and a set of topic headings for notes. Gillespie (1986) describes a more sophisticated set of macros for field note management, as well as a number of other examples of word processor macros for qualitative data.

In most word processors, macros are created by placing the word processor in "keystroke recording mode." Thereafter the word processor records anything typed at the keyboard (or clicked on with

```
April 10, 1991        5:15 pm      [AOR]

Space:

Actor:

Activity:

Object:

Act:

Event:

Time:

Goal:

Feeling:



D:\DOC\CAREERS\NOTE01.TXT                  Doc 1 Ln 1" Pos 1"
```

Figure 7.1. Field Note Template

the mouse) until the recording mode is turned off. Keystrokes and commands recorded in this way can be assigned to a shortcut key or to a command and then "played back" as many times as needed. The steps to create the field note outline macro in Figure 7.1 are shown in Figure 7.2.

To begin a field note entry, press the macro's shortcut key to bring the outline to the screen and begin typing. The note headings provide convenient reminders of areas that should be covered, but any that are not needed can be deleted.

Guidelines for Managing Text Data

The word processor functions described above provide the basic tools needed to manage qualitative text data. We turn now to a series of concrete examples illustrating how to use these tools to create data documents (field notes, interview transcripts), to insert new information into existing documents (analytic notes, codes), to search documents for both general and specific pieces of information, and

Function	WordPerfect Prompt	You enter:
Initiate Macro Define		Ctrl-F10
Name macro. **NOTE:** You can use either a shortcut key (e.g. Alt-s) or a character string to name the macro. Use the shortcut key Alt-f for this example	Macro:	Alt-f
Describe macro	Description:	Optional--type in a brief description
Use autodate to enter the current date		Shift-F5 1
Type in your initials, fieldnote headings, and any other material you wish to include in the template		
Terminate macro define		Ctrl-F10

Figure 7.2. A WordPerfect Macro to Automatically Generate a Field Note Template (The macro assumes you are beginning with a blank screen.)

to sort and retrieve data. The figures used for illustration show information as it would be displayed by WordPerfect 5.1 on an IBM-compatible PC; however, the guidelines that accompany them apply equally well to any computer system that provides the word processing functions described above.

DATA PREPARATION

Regardless of the analysis style used, the first step in data preparation is to record the data in word processor files. In initially entering data, the flexibility of word processing software makes it possible to devote most of one's concentration to capturing all of the data without being too concerned about careful typing and accurate spelling. With the aid of a spelling checker and the ease with which documents can be edited, data can be "cleaned up" quickly and conveniently. Using consistent abbreviations for frequently occurring words or phrases, particularly those that are difficult to type, can substantially speed up initial data entry. Abbreviations can be "expanded" all at once, using the word processor's search-and-replace function or one at a time during spelling checking. Alternatively, words or phrases can be assigned to macro shortcut keys. Figures 7.3 and 7.4 show a section of interview transcript before and after cleanup. In Figure 7.3 text appears just as it was initially transcribed from an audio recording, with "misspelled" words (i.e.,

```
I. Let's talk for a few minutes about professional clbtion.  I
notice from your vitae you have clbted with a number of different
people.  Who initiated the clbtion?

I've thought about that a little bit recently because, on balance
now, I think most of my work is clbtive.  In the early stages, in
work with Jim Fischer and Ed Lowrey in this department, I was
distinctly junior and they were distinctly senior and I was
invited to participate.  I would say I did most of the work on
those things and I had most of the ideas.  I mean it wasn't me
implemting their ideas.  I had most of the ideas and defined the
projects and did most of the work.  The thing with Colin Ramsey
was something that was more like the subsequent clbtions--things
that couldn't have been done otherwise because they merged very
different kinds of skills.  He was a 20th century expert with
knowledge about some stuff in that period--I had some ideas about
what it all meant and how to make an argument out of it, and that
was a genuine clbtion in which different skills were brought in.
Since then, all my clbtions have been with people in other
disciplines.  And so they ... I like that idea;  I like the
interdisciplary thing.  I think it's really exciting and I learn a
lot from it and do some things I couldn't do by myself.  It also
got me a fellowship and in a much broader sense was good for me.
I did get to the point of resenting some of the ... at first I
D:\DOC\CAREERS\INT10.TXT                    Doc 1 Ln 1" Pos 1"
```

Figure 7.3. Raw Interview Transcript with Spelling "Errors" Highlighted

```
I. Let's talk for a few minutes about professional collaboration.
I notice from your vitae you have collaborated with a number of
different people.  Who initiated the collaboration?

I've thought about that a little bit recently because, on balance
now, I think most of my work is collaborative.  In the early
stages, in work with JF and EL in this department, I was
distinctly junior and they were distinctly senior and I was
invited to participate.  I would say I did most of the work on
those things and I had most of the ideas.  I mean it wasn't me
implementing their ideas.  I had most of the ideas and defined the
projects and did most of the work.

The thing with CR was something that was more like the subsequent
collaborations--things that couldn't have been done otherwise
because they merged very different kinds of skills.  He was a 20th
century expert with knowledge about some stuff in that period--I
had some ideas about what it all meant and how to make an argument
out of it, and that was a genuine collaboration in which different
skills were brought in.  Since then, all my collaborations have
been with people in other disciplines.  And so they ... I like
that idea;  I like the interdisciplinary thing.  I think it's
really exciting and I learn a lot from it and do some things I
couldn't do by myself.  It also got me a fellowship and in a much
D:\DOC\CAREERS\INT10.TXT                    Doc 1 Ln 1" Pos 1"
```

Figure 7.4. Interview Transcript After Cleanup

Function	WordPerfect Prompt	You enter:
Initiate Macro Define		Ctrl-F10
Name Macro. For this example, use the abbreviation to be replaced as a macro name.	Macro:	clbt
Describe macro	Description:	Optional
Move to the top of the document		Home Home Up
Initiate search & replace without confirm		Alt-F2
	w/ confirm? No (Yes)	Enter
Type in the abbreviation	-> Srch:	clbt F2
Type in the complete word	Replace with:	collaborat
Terminate macro define		Ctrl-F10

Figure 7.5. A WordPerfect Macro to Replace an Abbreviation Used in Transcription or Note Taking With the Complete Word

those not recognized by the spelling checker) and typing abbreviations highlighted. Figure 7.4 shows the same section of text with "corrected" misspellings and expanded abbreviations in bold type. Abbreviations were expanded, using the search-and-replace feature of the word processor. Here are the steps involved:

1. Move the cursor to the beginning of the file.
2. Invoke search and replace without confirmation.
3. Search for "abbr," and replace with "abbreviation."

Figure 7.5 shows how to create a WordPerfect macro to expand the abbreviation "cblt" that appears in Figure 7.3. Choose abbreviations carefully—they should not occur naturally as part of another word. For example, "ob" would be a poor choice to abbreviate *obstetric* since it might result in words like *obstetrictain* or *obstetricject* or *jobstetric*.

The cleanup process in this document also provides the opportunity to protect the anonymity of specific individuals named in the interview. Among the words the spelling checker did not recognize were the names of particular individuals referred to by the respondent. The analyst replaced the names with generic references to preserve anonymity. If the identity of individuals named in this way is analytically important, confidentiality can still be maintained by using systematic codes or pseudonyms for each named individual in place of actual names. Use of the spelling checker, search-and-replace function, and macros as outlined above can be done very quickly, even for a relatively large number of data files. Once these automatic preparations are complete, an initial careful reading of the text should be done to ensure the integrity of the data. At this point it may be desirable to print the data and indicate changes on the printed copy for later entry into the word processor file.

Here too is the point at which the type of analysis and the choice of analysis style affects what you do next with the data. For an immersion/crystallization-style analysis, a clean printed copy of the text may be all that is needed. Leaving a wide margin on the printed copy will provide room for annotations. Addison's editing style (Chapter 6) and Crabtree and Miller's template-style analysis (Chapter 5) could also begin with word processing. Beyond initial data preparation, a quasi-statistical analysis would require more specialized software to produce frequency distributions of words or phrases or key-word-in-context (KWIC) lists. Most such software provides only rudimentary data entry capabilities or assumes that data already exist in ASCII format. In this case as well, using a word processor for data entry and cleanup is an effective first step.

Word processing software can be directly useful beyond the process of data preparation, however. The next two sections of this chapter describe an adaptation of elements of the editing and template-analysis styles that takes advantage of the functions available in most word processors.

CODING DATA

The document in Figure 7.4 has been coded in a rudimentary way, though it may not seem so at first glance. The transcriptionist indicated material spoken by the interviewer with "I:". During the initial reading of the transcript, the analyst used blank lines to separate the text into analytically distinct parts. The breaks in text are easy to see and also easy to relocate if later analysis requires the text be reorganized. Conventions like these, though simple, provide the foundation for effective use of the power of computer software in managing text data.

```
@10-105 @M @PROF @COLLAB @FACULTY
I've thought about that a little bit recently because, on balance
now, I think most of my work is collaborative.  In the early
stages, in work with JF and EL in this department, I was
distinctly junior and they were distinctly senior and I was
invited to participate.  I would say I did most of the work on
those things and I had most of the ideas.  I mean it wasn't me
implementing their ideas.  I had most of the ideas and defined the
projects and did most of the work.

@10-106 @M @PROF @COLLAB @FACULTY
The thing with CR was something that was more like the subsequent
collaborations--things that couldn't have been done otherwise
because they merged very different kinds of skills.  He was a 20th
century expert with knowledge about some stuff in that period--I
had some ideas about what it all meant and how to make an argument
out of it, and that was a genuine collaboration in which different
skills were brought in.  <<"Genuine" collaboration involves
different skills--something neither of the collaborators could do
alone.>>  Since then, all my collaborations have been with people
in other disciplines.  And so they ... I like that idea; I like
the interdisciplinary thing.  I think it's really exciting and I
learn a lot from it and do some things I couldn't do by myself.
It also got me a fellowship and in a much broader sense was good
D:\DOC\CAREERS\INT10.TXT                        Doc 1 Ln 1" Pos 1"
```

Figure 7.6. Interview Transcript With Codes and Analytic Notes Inserted

Figure 7.6 shows part of the same transcript to which codes and analytic comments have been added. Codes appear on a separate line at the beginning of each paragraph. This convention makes it easy to scan codes visually. The inclusion of "@" as part of each code distinguishes codes from otherwise identical character strings that may occur naturally in the data. It is not necessary to use this specific character to distinguish codes; any character will do, provided it appears nowhere else in the data. In the second paragraph in Figure 7.6, an analytic comment on the nature of "genuine" collaboration is set off by "« »". Again, the particular character(s) used for this purpose do not matter, provided they are used only for this purpose. In addition, characters used to set off comments should be easy to identify visually. As the use of "« »" to identify analytic comments implies, codes need not necessarily be put all in the same place, and they need not follow the form "@CODE". Any consistent and identifiable convention can serve as a code. Consider for example the following phrase:

I did get to the point of resenting some of the . . . at first I liked the balance of work on that because I liked being in control, which I really was.

The respondent begins to talk about his resentment of a situation but stops in midsentence to point out what he liked. If such a rhetorical occurrence is analytically important and if the ellipsis (or some other convention) is used consistently to indicate it, then the ellipsis becomes a code.

The explicit codes in Figure 7.6 fall into three categories: (a) The number codes indicate the document and the location within the document of each coded entry. Thus "@10-105" denotes document 10, paragraph 105. This information is crucial if data are to be reorganized according to analytic concepts; the location code provides a quick, simple means of finding the original context of any coded passage. (b) The next two codes stand for characteristics of the respondent, in this case a male (@M) with the academic rank of professor (@PROF). (c) The remaining codes refer to concepts expressed in the text of the paragraph. The sample data in the figures contain relatively few codes; however, many more could be included if necessary. In field notes, for example, additional codes could indicate the setting, the role of the researcher (whether observer, participant/observer, interviewer), the number of people observed, and background information on some or all of the participants.

The process of entering codes is greatly facilitated by word processor macros. In the interviews used in this example, location and respondent characteristic codes are constant throughout an entire document (except for paragraph numbers). The analyst took advantage of this consistency and assigned "@10- @M @PROF" to a single macro key; each concept code was also assigned to a macro key. To code each paragraph, the analyst first entered the location/characteristic codes and then whatever concept codes were called for. After coding the entire document in this way, the analyst returned to the beginning, searched for each occurrence of "@10-", and entered sequential paragraph numbers all at once. Figure 7.7 shows part of a document that lists each code, along with the macro key that enters it and a brief definition. This list can be updated easily as the coding system evolves, and a printed copy serves as a memory aid during coding.

Coding qualitative data, especially early on, is still a highly fluid process. New analytic concepts emerge, old ones are combined or rethought, and, as a result data must be recoded and reorganized. This process will, of course, affect the number of paragraphs but will not require renumbering since numbers only have to be unique, not

```
CODE            MACRO        DEFINITION
@ADVICE         Alt-A        getting or giving advice
@BESTWORK       Alt-B        ease in working
@CAREER         Alt-C        general comments about career
@CHILDREN       Alt-D        relating to children
@COLLAB         Alt-E        collaboration
@DIFWORK        Alt-F        difficulty in working
@FACULTY        Alt-G        relations with faculty
@FAMRESP        Alt-H        family/home responsibilities
@FRIENDS        Alt-I        relations with friends
@GRADSCHL       Alt-J        graduate school
@IDEAL          Alt-K        ideal situation
@LOUSY          Alt-L        opposite of ideal
@MENTOR         Alt-M        relations with mentor
@RSCHPROJ       Alt-N        typical research project
@SPOUSE         Alt-O        relations with spouse
@SPOUSWRK       Alt-P        spouse's job/career
@STUDENTS       Alt-Q        relations with students
@TEACHING       Alt-R        teaching/classroom activities
@TENURE         Alt-S        comments related to tenure
@TYPDAY         Alt-T        typical day
@WHEREWRK       Alt-U        where respondent works
@WHYACAD        Alt-V        decision re:academic career
@WORK           Alt-W        work/professional responsibilities
D:\DOC\CAREERS\INT10.TXT                  Doc 1 Ln 1" Pos 1"
```

Figure 7.7. Analytic Codes With Definitions and Associated Macro Keys

sequential, to serve their function. Two (or more) paragraphs can be combined simply by removing the blank line separating them and deleting any codes they have in common. To divide a single paragraph into several, insert blank lines and code lines at the appropriate points. Decimal points may be used to avoid duplicate paragraph numbers. For example, if paragraph @10-106 in Figure 7.6 were later divided into three, the first would remain @10-106, the second would be @10-106.1, and the third @10-106.2.

A word of caution is in order regarding numbering paragraphs to identify their original location. Many word processors provide an automatic numbering function that seems to solve the problem caused by merging or splitting paragraphs. This function works by placing a code where the number should be. This code tells the word processing software to display a number that is always one greater than the number displayed by the previous code. Thus, if two paragraphs are merged (and a number deleted) or if a single paragraph is split (and numbers added), the word processing software will readjust the numbers automatically to keep them sequential. Ironically this function serves our purpose only as long as paragraphs remain in their original context. If, for example, all the paragraphs relating to a specific concept are copied into a separate document for analysis, the word processing software will renumber each paragraph to reflect its relative position in the new document, and information needed to find a paragraph's original context will be lost.

REORGANIZING DATA

Up to this point the emphasis has been on preparing and coding data for analysis. Of course, dividing text into analytic units, assigning codes to them, and recording notes and observations all require analytic decisions, and once documents have been coded, it is possible to use the word processor to search for each text segment assigned to a specific code. In many cases these functions alone are sufficient for the analytic task at hand. Often, however, it is useful to reorganize text into separate documents for each content code. In the sample data shown in the figures, for example, a separate document could be created for each of the content codes listed in Figure 7.7. Word processing programs can greatly facilitate this process.

Although the specific commands or menu choices needed to reorganize data vary considerably among different word processors, the logic of the process varies very little. The list below outlines each logical step as it would need to be conveyed to the word processor so that the entire process can be recorded in a macro. This process assumes that the cursor is at the very beginning of the document and that paragraphs are separated by blank lines. Before actually recording the macro and applying it to real data, it would be wise to "rehearse" the process on a test document to ensure that you are using the appropriate functions in your word processor and that they produce the results you expect.

1. Search for @CODE.
2. Search backward for a blank line. (What the word processor actually searches for may be referred to as a "hard" carriage return or paragraph marker.)
3. Activate "block" or "define" mode. This instructs the word processor to begin copying text into a temporary holding area.
4. Search forward for a blank line.
5. Turn off the block mode.
6. Copy the blocked text, and append it to a separate document.

Function	WordPerfect Prompt	You type:
Move to top of document (N.B. Do this **before** you start the macro)		Home Home Up

Function	WordPerfect Prompt	You type:
Initiate Macro Define		Ctrl-F10
Name macro. For this example, use the character string to be searched for (**@char**) as the macro name	Macro:	@char
Describe macro	Description:	Optional--type in a brief description of the macro
Search for character string (use **@char** in this example)		F2
	-> Srch:	@char F2
Search backward for a blank line (i.e. for two hard returns together)		Shift-F2
(Note: WordPerfect automatically inserts the last string searched for when you initiate another search)	<- Srch:@char	Enter Enter F2
Initiate blocking		Alt-F4
Search forward for a blank line (i.e. for two hard returns together)		F2
	-> Srch:[HRt][HRt]	F2
Append blocked text to a file. Using the search string in the file name will make it easy to locate secondary data files. Use **@char.fil** in this example)		Ctrl-F4 1 4
	Append to:	@char.fil
Invoke the macro you just created. When the macro is run, this step will cause it to run repeatedly until the search for **@char** fails.		Alt-F10
	Macro:	@char
Terminate macro define		Ctrl-F10

Figure 7.8. A WordPerfect Macro to Find Blocks of Text Containing a Specified Charater String and Copy Them Into a Separate File (The macro assumes that blocks of text in the original file are separated by blank lines, i.e., two hard returns.)

Once recorded, the macro can be repeated as many times as necessary to copy each paragraph containing a specific code. In most word processors, invoking the macro just created as a last step will cause the macro to repeat itself until it finds no more occurrences of @CODE. The macro listings in Figure 7.8 demonstrate how to do this is WordPerfect. Macros of the same form can be created for each code and can then be used to begin building secondary data docuents that comprise only the paragraphs containing a specific code.

Macros like the one described above can save considerable time, particularly when large amounts of data are involved. By the same token, they also can do considerable damage if they contain errors. As macros become more sophisticated and powerful, it becomes more important to test them thoroughly before using them on real data.

The secondary documents created in the process outlined above can then be examined to answer a variety of analytic questions. Do like-coded paragraphs express a common theme or concept? Do additional themes emerge? Should new codes be developed? Do some existing codes seem related to the same theme or concept? Should they be combined? This process can, and should, begin well before all the data are coded so that emerging analytic insights can be incorporated into the coding process. Since the original context of each coded paragraph can be located quickly and easily, already-coded documents can be updated with little difficulty.

The general procedure for locating a particular text string and for putting all the paragraphs containing it in a common place, or any part of it, can be adapted to virtually anything that appears consistently in data documents. Such items might include particular words or phrases (other than codes) of analytic interest, analytic comments, or other identifiable notes. Within a secondary document for a particular code, for example, it may be useful to examine all paragraphs containing analytic comments. This can be done simply by substituting "<" (or whatever character is used to set off comments) for "@CODE" in the search process or macro.

When working with secondary data documents especially, it may be useful to sort paragraphs within the document by categories. A slight variation on the macro steps above can do this.

1. Search for the desired character/string.
2. Search backward for a blank line.
3. Activate the block or mode.
4. Search forward for a blank line.

Function	WordPerfect Prompt	You type:
Move to top of document (N.B. Do this **before** you start the macro)		Home Home Up

Function	WordPerfect Prompt	You type:
Initiate Macro Define		Ctrl-F10
Name macro. For this example, use the character string to be searched for (**@char**) as the macro name	Macro:	@char
Describe macro	Description:	Optional--type in a brief description of the macro
Search for character string (use **@char** in this example)		F2
	-> Srch:	@char F2
Search backward for a blank line (i.e. for two hard returns together)		Shift-F2
(Note: WordPerfect automatically inserts the last string searched for when you initiate another search)	<- Srch:@char	Enter Enter F2
Initiate blocking		Alt-F4
Search forward for a blank line (i.e. for two hard returns together)		F2
	-> Srch:[HRt][HRt]	F2
Mark blocked text to be copied		Ctrl-F4 1 2
Move the cursor to the end of the document and copy the marked text		Home Home Down Enter
Terminate macro define		Ctrl-F10

Figure 7.9. A WordPerfect Macro to Find Blocks of Text Containing a Specified Character String and Copy Them to the End of the Document

5. Turn off the block mode.
6. Go to the end of the document.
7. Copy the blocked text to the current position.

This process will produce, at the end of the document, a copy of each paragraph containing the string specified in step 1. Within a secondary document for a specific code, it is the functional equivalent of searching for all paragraphs that contain two specific codes. Figure 7.9 shows how to create such a macro in WordPerfect.

Searches for combinations of codes or other specific strings can be extremely useful in the analytic process. In the sample data, for example, all the paragraphs related to collaboration were sorted by sex (i.e., by those coded @M and those coded @F) to facilitate looking for differences in the concept of collaboration between male and female academics. Reorganization of data in this way is governed by Boolean logic (after the 19th century English mathematician George Boole), which assigns specific definitions to *and*, *or*, and *not* to define all possible combinations of elements. Boolean combinations beyond the simple *and* are quite difficult to achieve using word processing software, and almost certainly not worth the effort required. For this and a number of other tasks, more specialized software is available and better suited to the task. In the conclusion, I outline the categories into which such software falls and describe their general characteristics.

Special-Purpose Software

Word processing programs are among the most mature and widespread applications available for PCs, and for this reason they provide an excellent starting point for applying computers to qualitative data. Beyond basic text manipulation, however, word processing software is limited as a tool for qualitative data analysis. Several circumstances may signal the need for more specialized software. First, as the volume of data grows, a word processor's search function becomes increasingly slow and cumbersome, particularly if data are contained in numerous files. A number of applications can search large amounts of data in multiple files quickly and easily. Second, specialized software is necessary to examine combinations of data categories (e.g., all text segments associated with male assistant professors talking about either mentors or protégés). Finally, virtually any quasi-statistical analysis will require software designed for that purpose. Tesch (1990) provides a thorough explanation of the purpose and functions of a variety of specialized software for qualitative data, and so I shall only briefly describe their general characteristics here. This software falls into three general categories.

Text retrieval software searches multiple files to find files, or parts of them, that match a search request. They allow the use of Boolean logical operators (*and, or, not*), a number of types of search terms and strategies (e.g., inexact, "fuzzy," search terms, proximity and similarity searches). Most can save search strategies for later use and can save reorganized text in separate files. Examples include: Dragnet, FYI 3000, Gofer, Magellan, Nota Bene, ZyIndex.

Text data base managers generally perform the same functions as text retrievers. They differ in that text retrievers operate on preexisting files usually created in a word processor; text data base managers operate on data base files that they create or import from other files. Examples include: Lotus Agenda, askSam, NoteBook II, Textbank.

Text analysis software facilitates particular kinds of qualitative analysis (primarily formal content analysis and the use of deductive protocols) by doing one or more of the following: (a) Concordances: lists of words used in a text, accompanied by their locations and some surrounding text; (b) Coding: assignment of codes to sections of text to allow later retrieval; (c) Statistical summaries: results of various counting operations on text, such as the number of unique words and the number of times each appears. Examples include: Clio, THE ETHNOGRAPH, Gator, Micro-OCP, QualPro, TEXTPACK, Word Cruncher.

The primary goal of this chapter has been to demonstrate the power and simplicity of using word processing software for text data management. Word processors are ubiquitous, and mastery of a few of their functions can greatly facilitate the analysis of text data. Moreover, understanding the logic of word processor-based text manipulation allows qualitative researchers to make well-informed decisions about when to use and how to select more specialized software.

PART IV

Special Cases of Analysis

8 Approaches to Audiotape and Videotape Analysis: Interpreting the Interactions Between Patients and Physicians

MOIRA STEWART

Overview

This chapter covers two main topics. First is an overview of approaches to the audiotape and videotape study of interactions between doctors and patients in primary care. Five approaches will be presented. Second is the description of one study of my own using audiotapes, illustrating an interpretive approach to the study of the relationship between patients and their doctors over time. Before dealing with the two main topics, background issues are presented.

Background

The conversation between the doctor and the patient is considered the backbone of the visit/consultation. During this encounter the patient explains the problems, perhaps expresses feelings, answers questions about the problems, and the physician in turn requests the information needed to assess the problems, answers the patient's questions, explains his or her interpretations of the problems, and suggests or negotiates a plan. In addition to the tasks of each specific consultation is the ongoing development of the doctor-patient relationship that takes place at each visit.

In Britain, physicians spend approximately "6 minutes with a patient" (Balint & Norell, 1976); in Canada, 8 minutes are spent for visits other than counseling and physical examinations (Stewart, Brown, & Weston, 1989); and in the United States, the time is 13 minutes (Greenfield, Kaplan, & Ware, 1988). During the brief time patients spend with their physician, much more happens than the verbal interaction. The physical examination entails the laying on of hands. Eye contact and facial expressions complement the verbal interaction. All of these facets are encompassed in what we call doctor-patient communication.

The medical profession in general, and the primary caregiver in particular, is interested in doctor-patient communication for several reasons. First, communication problems are relatively common. Half of patients' complaints and 80% of social problems are not known to the physician (Stewart & Buck, 1977). Agreement on the need for follow-up between doctors and patients is also quite low (66.4%) (Starfield et al., 1981). In addition, communication problems are serious not only in frequency but also in the intensity of patients' reactions of dissatisfaction. The majority of letters of complaint to Health Maintenance Organizations (R. Frankel, personal communication) and complaints to disciplinary bodies are due to communication breakdown between the patient and the physician (College of Physicians and Surgeons of Ontario, 1988).

Analysis Approaches

Most studies of doctor-patient interaction use recording devices as the primary data collection tool. As with the analysis of text, a number of different approaches may be taken to record data on patient-doctor interaction. An important distinction here is between the interpretive paradigm (naturalistic or constructivist inquiry) and the positivist paradigm (materialistic inquiry). This distinction has been elaborated in Chapter 1.

In addition to audio and video recordings, other sources of data on interactions include observation and interviews with participants. Only recordings, however, avoid a commitment to one paradigm or another at the data collection stage. Both observation and interviews can be conducted either within the interpretive paradigm (e.g., unstructured) or within the positivist paradigm (e.g., semi-structured and structured). In contrast, during data analysis usually one paradigm predominates—with statistical analysis of the structured data on the one hand and interpretive analysis of unstructured data on the other.

At least five approaches to the analysis of audio and video material concerning patient-doctor interaction are described in the literature. These include interpretive inquiry, structured coding, behavior checklists, participant feedback, and group process.

AN INTERPRETIVE STUDY

Frankel and Beckman (1989) observed that physicians interrupted their patients before they had an opportunity to fully express their concerns and problems. In addition they found that given sufficient time, the patient will mark the conclusion of his or her statement of problems.

This study of interruptions is a good example of constructivist research in which the purpose was to gain insights into the process of communication between patients and doctors. The investigators began by watching the beginning of videotaped interviews without knowing what they would see. When they noticed the interruptions, the authors turned to a structured analysis and began to count the seconds to the first interruption. In fact the doctors interrupted, on average, 18 seconds into the patients' story.

As the following interaction demonstrates, patients were found to indicate spontaneously the end of the description of their problems.

DOCTOR   What problems are you having?

PATIENT   My back has been hurting me, I've had headaches for three weeks, and recently I have been having a hurting in my chest which causes me to have to sit down after I've walked only half a block. (1.0 second pause)

DOCTOR   Go on.

PATIENT   That's all I wanted to talk about today.

In fact the authors then counted the seconds and found that no opening statement took longer than 150 seconds.

A STUDY USING STRUCTURED CODING

Kaplan, Greenfield, and Ware (1989) were to my knowledge the first to show that doctor-patient communication variables were related to patient recovery as assessed by physiologic outcomes. In their study, patients who had the lower blood glucose and lower blood pressure were those who were more controlling, expressed more emotion, gave less information, and were more effective in eliciting information from the doctor. The better patient outcomes were associated with doctors' behavior that was less controlling, showed more negative emotion, and gave more information (Greenfield, Kaplan, & Ware, 1988).

This study is an excellent example of a materialistic inquiry in which predetermined variables were measured and associated statistically. Kaplan et al. used a coding scheme to measure doctor-patient communication whereby each audiotaped utterance made by the patient and each by the doctor was coded. They then grouped certain kinds of utterances in order to obtain descriptions of interviews—for example, an effectiveness index.

A number of intricate coding schemes may be used for utterances/statements made by patients and doctors (Bales, 1950; Roter, 1977; Stiles, 1986). Roter's adaptation of Bales Interaction Process Analysis, for example, consists of 36 separate categories into which any one utterance of the physician or patient can be classified. A recent coding scheme developed for family practice is that of Callahan and Bertakis (1991). Somewhat different from coding schemes, which categorize utterances, are scoring techniques, which give a numeric score to each interaction. One such method is a patient-centered scale developed at The University of Western Ontario (Brown et al., 1986; Levenstein et al., 1986).

A STUDY TO EVALUATE
PHYSICIANS' INTERVIEWING SKILLS

Herro Kraan and colleagues have developed a 49-item checklist of behaviors, called the Maastricht History-taking and Advice Checklist (Kraan & Crijnen, 1987; Kraan et al., 1989). It focuses on trainable interview skills and has demonstrated reliability and validity.

The checklist contains six sublists:

1. Exploration of the reason for the encounter, 8 items
2. History-taking, 10 items
3. Presenting solutions, 11 items
4. Structuring the interview, 6 items
5. Interpersonal skills, 8 items
6. Communicative skills, 6 items

The evaluator is required to make a judgment whether the physician/ student has, for example, "asked the patient to give his opinion on the causes of the problem." The items contain only observable behaviors, thus making the checklist useful for videotape analysis.

A STUDY USING PARTICIPANTS AS EXPERTS

This method calls for interviews with participants of the interaction as they view the videotape of the interaction. What research method could be more truly qualitative than this? The interpretations come first from the participants. This data collection/analysis method can be used to generate statistical data but is used most often to generate interpretations. Originated by Jerome Kagan (1975) in the educational setting, it has been used in the primary care research setting by Frankel and Beckman (1982) and recently by Arborelius and Timpka (1990). Frankel and Beckman showed that comments by patients and physicians on the identical interactions agreed 60% of the time. In Arborelius and Timpka's study, physicians interpreted the key communication difficulty to be understanding what the patient meant and wanted.

STUDIES OF GROUPS REFLECTING
ON THE RELATIONSHIP

Finally I propose that a group process is another approach to enhance understanding of doctor-patient interactions. This approach may or may not use videotape or audiotape. The Balint groups in Britain (which gave rise to the famous books *The Doctor, His Patient and the Illness* [Balint, 1957], *Six Minutes per Patient* [Balint & Norell, 1976] and *Treatment or Diagnosis: The Study of Repeat Prescriptions in General Practice* [Balint et al., 1970]) are the best, and perhaps only, example of this approach with physicians. The format of these groups was a weekly presentation of a case and reflection by all group members. No chapter on doctor-patient interaction research in primary care would be complete without an acknowledgment of these groups' massive contribution to our discipline. Audiotaped transcripts of existing Balint groups would be a rich source of new insight.

Another example of insights from groups comes from the collaborative research of Milton Seifert (1987), whose stunning experiences with groups of once-desperate patients has led to an understanding of what works in the relationship between patients and doctors. These patients related to Seifert that the process that helped them recover was one of the doctor listening and caring, followed by the patient developing trust, and further, by the patient demonstrating a willingness to change.

An Interpretive Study of the Evolution of the Doctor-Patient Relationship Over Time

This final example is a study of my own, conducted in collaboration with the other members of the interdisciplinary team at the Centre for Studies in Family Medicine at The University of Western Ontario. The study arose out of my interest in one of the tenets of primary care and family medicine in Britain, Canada, and the United States—continuity of care. What do we know about the doctor-patient relationship in these settings of continuity? What do we know about ongoing relationships? In my view we know very little. All of the studies to date, including my own, have used the snapshot approach, audiotaping or videotaping one sampled visit and ignoring the fact that many visits preceded this one and that an opportunity exists for many more visits following the study visit. In addition most of the theoretical works on doctor-patient relationship imply the relationship is static and falls into one category or another. Some theoreticians, however, have recognized that different models might suit different circumstances (Szasz & Hollender, 1955).

METHODS

The study sought to describe ongoing and evolving doctor-patient relationships, using part of a unique and rich data set of interviews between doctors and patients in community family practices in

London, Ontario, Canada. These data were the transcripts from audio-tapes of all visits of seven patients and their family doctors for 1 year. The patients were eligible if they were female, 25-80 years old, and new to the family doctor's practice. Three doctors are represented in this data set, all with more than 2 years of experience in private practice. One was male, two were female. The seven patients had three to six visits during the year. When any eligible patient arrived at the doctor's office, the doctor asked permission to audio-tape all visits for 1 year. The overall refusal rate was 47%.

ANALYSIS

The qualitative analysis had three goals:

1. To describe the evolving relationship between the doctor and the patient with the ultimate goal of developing a typology of relationships
2. To identify turning points in the relationship. A *turning point* was defined as "a moment in the interaction which results in a change in the tone of the subsequent relationship."
3. To identify recurring themes in the relationships which might lead physicians and patients to better understand the process of developing a relationship

The qualitative analysis of the audiotaped visits proceeded in stages:

1. I listened to the audiotapes at the same time I proofread the transcripts and, at the end of listening to *each visit*, I wrote comments on the important aspects of the visit. I tried not to restrict my observations to the patient-centered concepts I have been working with for the past 5 years.
2. I listened and read a second time, but now to the complete set of audiotapes and transcripts for one patient and her physician in the order they occurred during the year. After reading a whole year's set, I described or characterized the relationship.
3. I presented my observations and characterizations to Drs. William Miller and Benjamin Crabtree, one a family physician and the other an anthropologist at the University of Connecticut. They commented on the relationships and on my interpretations.

4. I summarized the transcripts (5 pages down to 1 page), minimizing any interpretations, and I asked four colleagues—two academic family physicians, a nurse researcher, and a Ph.D. in social work—to read the summaries and to note the following: describe the relationships, identify any turning points, and identify themes arising from the sets of summaries. The purpose of these interpretations was to lend credibility to the results by guarding against any tendency on my part to see only what I wanted to see, "holistic fallacy," and to lend credibility by expanding the observations.

5. Working with my own interpretations and those of my six colleagues, I selected the descriptions and themes that were proposed by the majority, although the differing points of view and the vocabulary of the six will make an interesting future study of its own.

FINDINGS: RELATIONSHIPS OVER TIME

First, we could *not* identify clear turning points in the relationships from our analysis of the audiotapes and transcripts. Second, a very preliminary classification of types of doctor-patient relationships is suggested by the study. In general the relationships can be organized into three types (see Figure 8.1). The first kind of relationship can be described as *brisk, focused, trusting, straightforward,* and *unchanging.* This kind of relationship was revealed in two patients. The doctor's role in these relationships was traditional, and while almost no discussion of emotions was observed, a bit of social chat and laughter did take place. The agreement among all of the interpreters was complete on the nature of these two relationships.

The second general grouping of relationships also included two patients. These relationships were described as *tolerant, warm, trusting, complex,* and *evolving but stable.* Both of these relationships were developed very early, one at the beginning of the first interview, and the second just toward the end of the first interview. In contrast to the first kind of relationship, which was straightforward, this was rich and complex, hence the fat arrow in Figure 8.1.

The third kind of relationship included three patients. These relationships in general were interpreted as *unfocused, inconsistent,* and *unstable;* however, the relationships were quite different from each other. One was a relationship fraught with uncertainty and tension at the beginning, evolving to a more supportive, trusting relationship in the middle, and ending on a cool but cooperative note after six visits. A second was described as inconsistent, spotty, wandering,

1. Brisk, focused, trusting, straightforward, unchanging

2. Tolerant, warm, trusting, complex, evolving but stable

3. Unfocused, inconsistant, unstable

   a. uncertainty and tension⟶ cool but more collaborative

   b. inconsistent, businesslike but friendly

   c. lacking in structure, appropriate weaving back and forth
      between the medical and psychological

Figure 8.1. Description of Patient-Doctor Relationships

businesslike, and yet friendly at the same time. The last of these unfocused relationships was quite complex and interpreted differently by my colleagues. One said, for example, that the relationship was lacking in structure, while another suggested that an appropriate weaving back and forth occurred between the medical and psychosocial agendas.

Two examples illustrate the evolving but stable type of relationship between patients and doctors. The first example, Patient A, is one that was characterized as a basically stable relationship. Nevertheless this relationship evolved within that stability. The relationship moved from a beginning with *listening* and *caring*, through further revelations by the patient, to a third visit in which the patient complimented the doctor, and finally in the fourth visit, to evidence of a partnership between the doctor and the patient. The listening and caring portion of this relationship was illustrated by these quotes:

PATIENT   That's quite a smile, am I talking too much?

DOCTOR   No.

The patient then told long stories that were uninterrupted. The next phase of the relationship, labeled as "further revelations," was illustrated by these quotes:

PATIENT   I'm feeling sort of nervous. I just needed that reassurance. Can I call between visits?

DOCTOR   Yes.

The patient then told a long story that she concluded by saying, "That's what's been happening to me." The doctor affirmed her by saying, "Thank you for telling me."

The third phase of this relationship was illustrated when the patient *complimented the physician*—"The best thing you did was recommend toast." And later: "I'm glad we cleared up about the medications; I was worried."

The final visit illustrated a fuller *partnership*, which was demonstrated by these quotes:

PATIENT   OK that's the stomach. Have you any further comments?

DOCTOR   Sounds OK. (Laugh)

Later in the visit the doctor asked the patient, "What do you think the pain is?"

The second relationship that indicated some evolution was also characterized as basically stable. This relationship, however, started with *many revelations* by the patient (Patient B) and *affirmation* by the physician and moved through a series of visits that included discussion about job and some *storytelling* but no deep revelations. Then the final visit was characterized predominantly by *social talk*. The depth in this relationship seemed to become less and less as time went on. In the first visit the patient related a story about her teenage pregnancy and giving the baby up. The doctor replied, "That takes a lot of guts. Well, good for you." At the end of that visit the patient brought up a concern: "I didn't think I'd ever come to a lady doctor."

The doctor answered, "I know, my mother always took me to a male doctor too, but a doctor is a doctor."

In the second and third visits a discussion of job and family took place:

PATIENT   I got a job.

DOCTOR   Great.

PATIENT   My new job is linen services.

DOCTOR   Good for you.

PATIENT   I'm going to fitness now.

DOCTOR   Good for you.

PATIENT   My stepdaughter's now pregnant.

DOCTOR   It can happen to anyone.

The fourth and final visit of this relationship encompassed mostly social talk, some of which was repeated from the previous visit but forgotten by the doctor:

PATIENT   I'm working in linen services.

DOCTOR   Are you?

PATIENT   Didn't you know that? I didn't want to exercise anymore. It's got something to do with age.

DOCTOR   Don't talk to me about age.

PATIENT   I'll be thinking of you when I'm in Florida.

In summary, at least three types of relationships over time emerged, and they each could follow several paths. The two stable but evolving relationships illustrate the different paths taken. The first moved toward greater depth, understanding, and partnership, while the second evolved toward less depth.

FINDINGS: CONTEXT AND CONTINUITY

Two themes emerged from these data and deserve further comment. The first was that the *context* of the visit seemed to influence the evolution of the relationship. Five contextual factors influenced the seven relationships studied, and undoubtedly many others affect different doctor-patient relationships. The five revealed here include pregnancy, pressing clinical problem, pain, whether the patient was a health professional, and the physical examination. Other authors have written convincingly about the possibility of the social and clinical contexts of cases influencing doctors' decisions. All other things being equal, the same physician may make a different decision under differing conditions or contexts (Christie & Hoffmaster, 1986).

The second theme revealed by the qualitative analysis is *continuity* of care. We are cautioned in the literature to be aware of costs, as well as benefits, of continuity of care. Some of the accepted benefits include increased doctor's knowledge of the patient (McWhinney, 1975), and better patient compliance and satisfaction (Freeman, 1984, 1985). Arguments against personal continuity include patients becoming dependent on the doctor, and the physician relying too much on memory rather than keeping written notes (Freeman, 1985).

None of the seven patients studied showed evidence of an unhealthy attachment or dependence. Rather the deepening relationship and the mutual understandings that arose out of two relationships seemed comfortable for the patient and doctor alike. In my view this finding exemplifies the benefits of continuous personal relationships.

On the other hand, Patient B from above reveals to the doctor many problems at the first visit but reveals fewer and fewer problems as time goes on. She is perhaps an example of a second possibility in continuous relationships, namely that of an evolution toward complacency and staleness.

Another example of the pitfalls of continuous personal relationships between doctors and patients is demonstrated by the story from one of the relationship transcripts. In this instance the patient describes to her new doctor the rut that she and her previous doctor had fallen into, and she explains her reasons for leaving the previous doctor:

DOCTOR   What made you change doctors?

PATIENT   Well, I think it's become too, I don't know, on a too personal level. He can't seem to look at me objectively anymore.

DOCTOR   Uh huh.

PATIENT   He's seen me come through a lot. Some changes. And I find I'm changing but his ideas are not.

DOCTOR Uh huh.

PATIENT And it's making it difficult. I find that I've had some medical problems and I went to him and he maybe looked at me and said "Oh, it's your nerves." You know that type of thing. Because he knows so much about me. I lost my trust I think. And I feel guilty about it. And I really feel bad about it.

And later in the interview the doctor asks, "Any other health problems?"

PATIENT I had a lump in my breast last year. A cyst. And around two weeks ago I found a lump in here. So I went to see Doctor F and he checked my breasts and that lump and said I had another cyst. But the only thing that's scaring me is that my whole arm hurts . . . . I'm beginning to think I'm crazy.

(Later)

PATIENT Why do I feel so guilty about leaving Dr. F? I mean this is terrible.

DOCTOR Well, a lot of people do because there is a lot of loyalty. You've been through a lot with Dr. F.

PATIENT Yes, he's helped me tremendously in the last few years. Well I've been through a lot.

DOCTOR Uh huh.

PATIENT Everything, I've been there and I've gone through it in the last 12 years. He helped me through those times. But I think what's happened is somehow along the way he's missing the physical part of me. And my mind is well today and I'm getting stronger but my body is falling apart (laugh). And I'm afraid of the premenstrual syndrome.

DOCTOR A lot of the symptoms you've got are hard symptoms to sort out as you can imagine.

PATIENT Yeah.

DOCTOR The first step I'd like to do is do some blood work and see if that points us in any direction.

The relationship with the previous doctor got stuck in a groove that became unsatisfactory for the patient. When doctors and patients know each other for long periods of time (12 years in this example), it is likely the patient and the doctor will change. Their needs, expectations, and styles of interacting may change in a way that enhances the relationship, or they may grow apart.

We have perhaps taken for granted that continuity of care enhances the doctor-patient relationship. We have seen that while some relationships between patients and doctors are predictable and others unpredictable, some evolve with a sure sense of line and form.

Conclusion

The preceding study is the work of an epidemiologist conducting qualitative research. The epidemiologist in me is evident, as represented by the need to start with a hypothesis (that we would find turning points) and by the need for confirmation of interpretations from more than one person. Evident also is the previously hidden interpreter in me who recognized that the method of choice in this case was an interpretive one. I then had to come to terms with the felt need to crystalize all of the interpretations into one voice. The project represents the story of one researcher's foray, with the help of many esteemed colleagues, into an exciting and fruitful process of recorded discovery.

9 Historical Method: A Brief Introduction

MIGUEL BEDOLLA

Introduction

This chapter is about history and historical method. The implementation of historical method leads toward knowledge about history. The word *history*, however, is equivocal. It is employed in two senses that must be distinguished. In one sense, history is written about. In the other sense, history is written. The history that is written aims at expressing knowledge of the history that is written about. Historical knowledge is always about the past. Thus the historian needs an adequate theory about the nature of time—as a human reality and not as a physical one. Finally, historical knowledge is about the manner in which humans in the past have constructed their unique reality; it is about historical facts and their intelligible connections. Historical method is thus not only appropriate for questions about the past, but also for questions about what was happening then and about the manner in which humans constructed their reality. These are questions about historical facts or about their intelligible relations.

The designs used by historical method are flexible and open because the aim is to learn how past intentions were related to things and events due to their meaning and their value. Thus the basic design of historical method is similar to the design followed by an anthropologist

AUTHOR'S NOTE: I wish to express gratitude to Mr. Danny Jones and Dr. David Kronick of the Patrick Ireland Nixon Library of the University of Texas Health Science Center at San Antonio.

or any qualitative researcher who attempts to understand a culture. It is the design of an experience in which the historian learns about particular persons at particular times and places that present unique conditions and opportunities that were expressed in the construction of a unique historical reality (Lonergan, 1957).

Historical method is an adaptation of the procedures for learning. In general, historical method begins with a question that arises from historical data to which the historian previously has been alerted. The question initially leads the historian to the examination of the data from which the question emerged, and this, in turn, to new data. Suddenly and often unexpectedly an insight emerges as a tentative answer to the question. But the insight may be correct, probably correct, probably false, or false. Thus the historian must consider now the relation that exists between his or her insight and the data: Does the relation explain some of the data? Does it explain all of the data? Does it need to be supported by data that do not exist? The answers to these questions indicate whether the historian is in possession of what philosophers call a "virtual unconditioned" and/or how far he or she is from its possession. If all the existing data are explained, then the insight is in essence correct, and the historian is now in possession of knowledge that answers the question "correctly." This knowledge may be communicated.

Because historical method is an adaptation of the procedures of learning, the historian operates in the light of whole personal development. Learning moves the mind from data, to understanding, to judgment, to action. Historians have adapted these learning procedures and have transformed them into the four fundamental operations of historical method: (a) research on the remnants of the past that are available in the present; (b) interpretation of the results of the research; (c) judgment on the correctness of the interpretation; (d) the communication of the interpretation judged to be correct, usually in writing (Becker, 1959; Kragh, 1987).

At least two fundamental paradigmatic assumptions underlie what has been said about the method of history. The first assumption states: History that is written about is a human construction that results from human intentions and actions. This assumption is equivalent to saying a fundamental difference exists between nature and history, for nature is not the construction of human intentions and actions (Collingwood, 1969).

The second assumption is a consequence of the first. It is the assumption of a fundamental difference between written history and the natural and human sciences. The second assumption states: History that is written differs from natural science because history's object is a reality constructed by human intentions, decisions, and actions in the past. The objects of natural science are not constituted by human intention; the atom is not a construction of human intention. History differs from the positivist human sciences in that the results of history are descriptions and explanations about particular persons, actions, and things constructed, while the mind of the historian operates in the realm of meaning created by human intentionality. The results of the positivist human sciences, on the other hand, are arrived at while the mind of the researcher operates within a supposedly intentionless realm in which theory is constructed, and aims at results that are universally valid.

At this moment it is appropriate to introduce several semantic clarifications. The distinction between *historical data* and *historical facts* must be clear. Historical data, such as the text of Vesalius (1543), *De humani corporis fabrica libri septem*, are immediately available through the senses. Historical facts, on the contrary, are only available to the historian who arrives at correct understanding of his or her sources or to the reader who studies the communications of the historian and comes to judge that what is communicated is correct.

Historical fact and *historical experience* also must be distinguished. As noted above, historical data are here and now perceptible. The historian labors to ascertain their genesis and to evaluate their reliability. Insofar as the data are reliable, they yield information about the past. But the information they yield is as a general rule not historical knowledge but historical experience. The information has to be understood, and the understanding has to be judged correct in order to move from experience to knowledge. Thus historical experience regards the remnants of the past in whatever manner they happen to become available in the present. Historical experience still lacks the interpretive judgment that allows the historian to affirm the existence of unique historical facts and their intelligible relations. The process of obtaining the data and determining their reliability has to be followed by an interpretive process in which the historian pieces together the data that have been gathered and critically evaluated.

The notions of external and internal criticism now must be distinguished. *External criticism* yields critical editions of texts, ascertains their authors, and classifies historical sources (Levere, 1982). *Internal criticism* proceeds by the analogies of general psychology to reproduce the successive mental states of the source's author in order to determine (a) what the author meant or intended, (b) whether the author believed what was said or was committed to what was intended, and (c) whether the belief or commitment was justified.

Historical Method Illustrated

THE EXAMPLE

The curriculum of the medical school in the University of Texas Health Science Center at San Antonio includes a 6-week rotation in family practice during the junior year. One of the fundamental objectives of this rotation is to lead the students into discovering the uniqueness of family practice as a medical specialty. The students are led toward this discovery in a multitude of ways, including a lecture presented to them on the first hour of the first day. The lecture is entitled "Historical Significance of the Emergence of Family Medicine." This lecture derives from a larger investigation about the history of the doctor-patient relationship in which I have been involved for several years. The following is an abstract of that lecture:

The lecture explores the historical significance of the emergence of family medicine. It begins by stating that medieval medicine was Galenic and by explaining the relation between Galenic medicine and the medieval Celestial Principle (Thorndike, 1955). According to the principle, the contingency of human affairs was ruled by the positions and movements of celestial bodies. Physicians needed to be astrologers to understand the diseases of their patients (White, 1978). The emergence of an empirical ideal, and after a series of condemnations of astrology and Averroist philosophy, freed medicine from the authority of the Celestial Principle (Lonergan, 1985). One of the early manifestations of the manner in which the empirical ideal was appropriated by medicine is to be found in the performance of the first autopsies, procedures through which physicians, like Antonio Benivieni, searched for understanding about the causes of diseases within the bodies of their patients (Benivieni, 1960). After Benivieni, Vesalius studied the fabric of the human body and with the publication of his results the foundations of Galenic medicine began to crumble (Temkin, 1973; Vesalius, 1543). After Vesalius, it was Harvey who demonstrated Galen's lack of an empirical foundation (Harvey, 1928). But the most finished product of the empirical ideal was the science of mechanics as developed by Galileo. Guided by Bacon and Descartes, and expressed clearly by Boerhaave, medicine was now put under the authority of a Mechanical Principle: The body was to be understood as a machine; and health and disease, and their genesis, were to be understood in terms of physical and chemical realities acting upon the structure and function of the machine (Boerhaave, 1719; Boss, 1978; Descartes, 1986). With Morgagni was established the relation between changes in the machine and the signs and symptoms of disease; signs and symptoms that became increasingly perceptible to the increasing power of clinical observation (Auenbrugger, 1936; Foucault, 1975; Laennec, 1819; Morgagni, 1769; Reiser, 1979). The consequences of this were the surgicalization of medicine and the transformation of the patient into an object to be explored rather than a person with a clinical history (Gelfand, 1980; Lain-Entralgo, 1964). The clinical history lost its relevance. These transformations had a concrete expression in Charcot's attempt to understand hysteria as a disease of the patient's anatomy. Freud studied with Charcot in Paris; there he made two discoveries: the inadequacy of the viewpoint of his teacher and the notion of psychogenesis. With these discoveries he retrieved the possibility that medicine discover that the patient is, not just an object, but a human subject whose diseases derive their ultimate explanation from what they mean within a subject's history (Lain-Entralgo, 1964). Since then, two medical specialties have attempted to create a space-time within medicine for this subject: Psychiatry and Family Medicine. Psychiatry specializes in dealing with the diseases of the subject's psyche. Family Medicine specializes in dealing with frequent disease of any age or sex while treating the diseased individual as a subject whose subjectivity is put within the context of family dynamics. That is one of the unique characteristics of Family Medicine, and it is also one of the reasons the emergence of Family Medicine is historically significant.

GENERAL DESCRIPTION OF HISTORICAL METHOD

It was argued earlier that historical method is an adaptation of the procedures of learning. Because of this, the procedures of historical method are investigation, interpretation, judgment on the correctness of the interpretation, and communication of what has been judged to be correct or probably so. The starting point for the implementation of historical method is not some set of postulates or some generally accepted theory; it is all that the historian already knows and believes. Therefore depth of formal, cultivated knowledge and intelligence, breadth of experience, openness to all human values, and competent and rigorous training all contribute to increasing the historian's capacity to discover historical facts and their intelligible relations.

Investigation

Historical research may begin with the selection of an ideal type. An ideal type is not a description of reality or a hypothesis about reality; it is a theoretical construct in which possible events are related intelligibly to constitute an internally coherent system. Its utility is both heuristic and expository; that is, it can be useful inasmuch as it suggests and helps formulate hypotheses. Also, when a concrete situation approximates to the theoretical construct, the ideal type can guide an analysis of the situation and promote a clear understanding of it (Lonergan, 1972). The use of ideal types by the historian is justified because the past is assumed to be similar to the present, except in light of evidence of dissimilarity. The ideal type I have used in my investigations of the history of the doctor-patient relationship is Lain-Entralgo's structure of that relationship (Lain-Entralgo, 1964). This ideal type proposes that the relationship is structured by four "moments." The moments are cognitive, operative, affective, and ethico-religious.

Having chosen an ideal type, and in order to proceed from the present to the past described and explained in the abstract of the lecture, I began from what I already knew about Freud's contribution to medicine, about the nature of family medicine, and from the bits and pieces that I knew about the history of medieval and Renaissance medicine. Then I went to the sources of data about the past. I went to the Patrick Ireland Nixon Library of the University of Texas Health Science Center at San Antonio. There I found manuscripts, journals, scientific books, nonscientific books, and surviving physical objects (Knight, 1975). The study of these sources made available to me the data that allowed me to have the historical experience I needed. As with other qualitative research, historical research is concerned with assembling the information-rich data relevant to some particular question or problem—in my case the historical facts and their intelligible relations that help explain the emergence of family medicine as a specialty different from others.

The assembling of my data was facilitated by the multitude of persons, past and present, whose efforts are evident in the documents and organization of the Patrick Ireland Nixon Library of the University of Texas Health Science Center. In this library I was able to consult all of the sources that appear as references to the abstract of the lecture.

The historian's approximation to the sources, however, is selective (Kragh, 1987). Selection is the result of all that the historian already knows and believes. Thus I read Boerhaave because I knew he had been accused of being "Cartesian." I did not read anything by his contemporary, Baglivi, because nothing that I knew or suspected then, led me to believe he was important for the subjection of medicine to the mechanical principle. It is important to understand that because selection occurs, different histories are communicated (Braudel, 1980). These histories are not contradictory, not complete information, and not complete explanation. They are incomplete and approximate portrayals of an enormously complex reality constructed by persons whose awareness has reached varying levels of differentiation (Lonergan, 1972).

Interpretation

Interpretation follows investigation. Investigation makes available what remains from the past; interpretation attempts to understand what was meant or intended. The function of interpretation is to grasp meaning and intention in their appropriate context, in accordance with the proper mode and level of thought and expression, and in light of the circumstances and intentions of the author of the source. Because of this function, the process of interpretation has to confront the problems of modern epistemology, cognitional theory, and metaphysics.

Not every text stands in need of the same degree of interpretation. Because of this, at least two types of texts may be distinguished. Some texts are systematic in conception and execution, such as any mathematical text. And some texts are written in a common-sense mode, such as Harvey's (1928) introduction to De motu cordis et sanguinis. It is this latter type of text that requires more interpretation. It is because these texts are written in the mode of common sense that their interpretation is necessary and difficult. Common sense comes in many brands, each of them common only to the members of a particular cultural community, which have developed their particular mode in order to communicate with each other successfully. Thus the statements that have an obvious meaning for members of one community may be obscure to the members of an entirely different community. From the beginning of my investigation, I understood the importance of Harvey's work as an example of the appropriation of the empirical ideal by medicine. But it was not until near the end of the investigation that I understood what led Harvey to study the heart and to dedicate his book to the king of England. Had I been Harvey's contemporary and shared in his mode of common sense, his reasons for both would have been more obvious.

The historian generally does not belong to the community whose statements need to be interpreted. The historian has to transport these statements to the present. Because the horizon, values, interests, intellectual development, and experience of the historian may be different from those of the originating community, intersubjective, artistic, and symbolic components of the expressions encountered while doing historical research may be only partially understood or completely missed.

Finally, interpretation requires three basic exegetical operations: understanding the text, judging that one's understanding is correct, and stating what one judges to be the correct understanding of the text (Lonergan, 1972).

In order to understand a text, four conditions must be fulfilled. The first condition is to understand the object to which the text refers. Thus, in the case of the history of family medicine, I had to understand what a family is. The second condition is to understand the words employed in the text. Thus, even if I understand what a family is, I must understand the meaning of the notions implied by the words *family medicine* if I am going to understand the meaning of the Freudian notion of psychogenesis for the emergence of family medicine. The third condition is to understand the author of the words. Thus even if I understand what is meant by the words *psychogenesis* and *family medicine,* I must understand the intentions of Freud, as well as the intentions of those who constructed the specialty, family medicine. Was Freud attempting to go beyond mechanical determinism? Were the founders of family medicine attempting to move forward to a new specialty or to go back to the general physician of the past? To reach such understanding, one must learn about these persons. Sometimes this may happen only if one undergoes conversion into the persons' respective viewpoints. Thus the fourth condition to be fulfilled is that the historian must be willing to undergo conversion into the viewpoints of those being studied.

Historical Judgment

In order to judge the correctness of one's understanding of a text or a physical object, one must be aware of the context of whatever one happens to be researching. One must be aware of the hermeneutical circle (see Chapter 6; Gadamer, 1986). The historian must be aware also of the manner in which texts and objects fix the meanings of words and of how words fix the meanings of texts and objects. The historian must be alert to the relativity of the data available, to the possible relevance of more remote inquiries, and to the limitations placed on interpretations. In the case being analyzed, I had to know about the evolution of the doctor-patient relationship before Freud's introduction of the notion of psychogenesis. I had to know about the manner in which the sentences in the texts I consulted fixed the meaning of the word *psychogenesis* and about how the word fixed the meaning of the sentences. I also needed to know whether the data that I had were the data relevant to understanding the importance of the notion of psychogenesis for the emergence of family medicine. Finally, for my interpretation of the importance of Freud's notion for family medicine, I needed to know about the relevance of other inquiries, such as the study of the crisis suffered by physics as it moved from mechanical determinism, like that of Laplace, to the uncertainty of Heisenberg (Heisenberg, 1956; Laplace, 1956). Now as an investigation proceeds, insights accumulate and oversights diminish. This ongoing process, while it does not affect data inasmuch as they are or may be given, it does affect data enormously, inasmuch as the data are selected and combined, now this way and now that, in the ever larger and more complex structures that are finally affirmed to be the historical facts. This affirmation occurs when fewer and fewer questions are to be asked.

Judgment and the Communication of History

It is not sufficient to understand the data of history. The understanding has to be correct before it is communicated. Thus once I understood, led by the writings of Lain-Entralgo and Lonergan, the manner in which the Freudian notion of psychogenesis retrieved the possibility of discovering the patient as subject, I needed to ascertain that my understanding was correct before I communicated it to the students.

The function of the historian is not to describe, in all the detail possible, all of the meaningful human activities that occurred at a certain time and place in a certain sequence. The function is to understand as correctly as possible what was going on at that time and place, given the data available (Ricoeur, 1965), and when correct understanding has been achieved, to communicate it.

The history communicated after investigation, interpretation, and judgment may be basic, special, or general. *Basic history* tells where, when, who did what, who enjoyed a certain success, who suffered a failure, or who exerted a unique influence. Thus basic history describes as precisely as possible the relevant human activities in their temporal succession and geographic distribution. *Special histories* tell of specific movements. An example of this is the study I have been describing. *General history* is basic history complemented by all of the special histories. General history's intention is to offer a total view or some approximation of a total view. "It would express the historian's information, understanding, judgment and evaluation with regard to the sum of cultural, institutional, and doctrinal movements in their concrete setting" (Lonergan, 1972, p. 227).

The Contribution of History to Primary Care Research

Historical method as a contributor to primary care research is related to basic, special, and general history. Its fundamental concerns are at least twofold.

First, historical method is concerned with the history of all human activities related to health events whose nature is such that they must be attended by primary care specialists. This means, as can be inferred from what was stated above, a concern with the geographic location and temporal succession of all those activities that raise health issues that have a primary care solution. It seems, therefore, that the historian who sets out to deal with this concern must have also a good grasp of the methods of epidemiology (Brothwell, 1971).

Second, historical method is concerned with the history of the notion of primary care, the succession of events, and their geographic location, that led to the emergence and spread of the notion, its successes and failures, and the influences that have been exerted during this process.

While doing historical research, many pitfalls must be avoided. The naive notion that "texts and artifacts speak for themselves" and the idealist prejudice that all interpretation is subjective are two such pitfalls. The distinction between historical experience and historical knowledge also must be remembered. The naive notion reduces the work of the historian to that of a critical editor of texts. The idealist prejudice negates the possibility of historical knowledge. To forget the distinction between experience and knowledge leads to the disappearance of the difference between description and correct explanation.

Conclusions

Perhaps the fundamental tip to be passed along is that those who desire to do historical research must be ready to undergo conversion and to begin the arduous task of making explicit and appropriating the dynamic, self-assembling structures of their interior selves. A good start may be Philip McShane's *Wealth of Self and Wealth of Nations: The Self-Axis of the Great Ascent* (McShane, 1975). Those who are really ambitious and serious may want to read Lonergan's *Insight: A Study of Human Understanding* (1957). Only through this appropriation of self will historians be able to explain what it is they do when they claim to know history, why doing that is knowing history, and what it is they know when doing it. Only after becoming able to provide this explanation will those attempting to be historians know and communicate the difference between myth and history.

10 Philosophic Approaches

HOWARD BRODY

Introduction

For many, the juxtaposition of the terms *philosophy, research,* and *medical* might seem to be a sort of three-way oxymoron. Medical research is viewed often as involving only quantitative, biochemical, and physiological methods, perhaps branching out into epidemiology and biostatistics, but seldom so far afield as the humanities. Those who admit that qualitative methods might also be suitable for certain medical questions would wish ordinarily to expand the purview of "research" to include some of the social sciences, but even they might object to including philosophy. Moreover, to many who know little of the formal methods of study in philosophy, it would seem that philosophers do not really do *research* in any obvious sense. Philosophers may think and ponder and perhaps contemplate various body parts that shall here go unspecified—but nothing so systematic or rigorous as to deserve to be called "research."

It is obviously impossible in this chapter to outline the research methods of philosophy as a discipline. Accordingly I shall adopt a different route altogether. First I shall propose some specific similarities between philosophical inquiry and other qualitative methods. For this I shall use as a case study the exploration of the placebo effect. Next I shall suggest ways in which qualitative research meth-

---

AUTHOR'S NOTE: This work was supported in part through the Center for Meaning and Health, a collaborative enterprise of Michigan State University and the Fetzer Institute, Kalamazoo.

ods are especially useful for supplementing one particular subset of philosophical inquiries—medical ethics.

A political agenda underlies this approach to some extent. Interest in philosophy and humanities in medicine has grown markedly in the past two decades, so that almost all medical schools in the United States now offer some sort of course in medical ethics, and a good number of schools claim to have programs that teach aspects of "medical humanities," not ethics only. A majority of the scholars who now occupy positions in these programs are scholars with graduate degrees in the relevant humanities disciplines. A very few of them are physicians who have dual training in medicine and in humanities; and a slightly larger number are physicians with a well-developed interest in humanities but without formal training. Many of these latter contribute greatly to teaching humanities in medicine but produce little research. An informal survey of a number of physicians known to have a strong interest in humanities reveals many barriers to pursuing this as a specific career focus. One of the barriers is the lack of recognition, among those who award research seed money, released time, and other essential resources, that any sort of qualitative research, much less humanities research, counts as a valid use of those resources. A chapter like this cannot teach anyone how to do research in the medical humanities; but if it adds one small voice in favor of seeing humanities scholarship as a fully worthwhile pursuit for the physician investigator, then it will have served a useful purpose. The alternative is that all research in the medical humanities will be conducted by those with graduate degrees, most of whom are not physicians. As indispensable as their research contributions have been, I believe nevertheless that something will be lost if theirs are the only scholarly voices to be heard.

Philosophy as Qualitative Research

Qualitative research is a form of scientific investigation, and it may seem at first that whatever philosophy is, it cannot be science. For the most part, this is correct. But for my purposes in this chapter, it may be worth noting that science seeks to establish a particular hypothesis about the nature of the world as being worthy of belief. It does so by having developed rigorous methods both for suggesting plausible competing hypotheses, and for showing how those alternative hypotheses provide less satisfactory explanations of the phenomenon in question. No reason exists why philosophical inquiry cannot be turned toward precisely the same ends and why philosophical methods may not provide a high degree of rigor in identifying and in assessing alternative hypotheses.

Kuzel very nicely has applied the work of Guba, on qualitative or naturalistic modes of inquiry, to the research agenda of family medicine or primary care (Kuzel, 1986). Both the quantitative, positivist, or rationalistic method of research and the naturalistic or constructivist method seek the goal of trustworthiness of research findings. While the positivist or materialist paradigm seeks trustworthiness through such means as control and randomization, probabilistic sampling, replication, and objective instrumentation, the naturalistic paradigm seeks basically the same ends through different methods, which are better suited to a *human* subject matter. In this way both quantitative and qualitative methods are equally "scientific" and "rigorous" but via different routes. It is worthwhile to review some of the main methodological features of qualitative research to see whether analogies can be made with philosophical inquiry into medical issues.

If one looks carefully for these analogies, an interesting finding emerges—for some philosophical approaches turn out to be more closely allied with positivistic, quantitative methods than with naturalistic, qualitative methods. To the extent that analytic philosophy (at least until recently the dominant "school" among Anglo-American philosophers of the later 20th century) seeks truths that are logically necessary and independent of historical, cultural, and personal-psychological factors, it resembles positivist research much more than naturalistic research. Analytic philosophy is equally susceptible to the temptations to deny the "humanness" of the subject matter and to see the investigator not as a fellow human being who necessarily interacts with and alters the matter under study, but instead as an abstract reasoning machine. Indeed these aspects of analytic philosophy, as they have come to define the subject matter and the research agenda of medical ethics over the past 20-30 years, are coming increasingly under fire. Newer ethical approaches, which are more in tune with the life context within which actual ethical choices must be lived out, are being proposed as replacements or as supplements. By contrast, the phenomenological approaches to philosophy favored by the Continental school are more akin to naturalistic or constructivist research methodology.

It is instructive to compare three methods for seeking trustworthiness in qualitative research—triangulation, thick description, and reflexivity (Kuzel, 1986)—to methods that might be employed in philosophic inquiry. Research into the placebo effect provides a helpful clinical example for these comparisons. I might add that other important trustworthiness procedures exist, such as member checking and searching for disconfirming evidence (Kuzel & Like, 1991), which I will not address here.

Triangulation. The naturalistic investigator seeks trustworthiness in data collection by trying wherever possible to use multiple methods and divergent data sources. The process may be reiterated by checking the investigator's interpretations, at each step of the inquiry, with the respective data sources (member checks). Through cross-checking observations among divergent data sources, apparent differences eventually may resolve themselves, and a favored interpretation eventually may be constructed that coheres with all of the divergent data sources and that itself accounts for the differences observed earlier.

The analytic school of philosophy, influenced by Descartes' "*Cogito, ergo sum*," has for some centuries been in love with the idea that one should start reasoning from an indubitable truth, and so long as one uses sound logic at each subsequent step, one need never worry about falsity creeping into one's analysis. This approach proceeds linearly and sees no need for triangulation. But recently this "foundationalist" approach increasingly has come under attack from both inside and outside of the analytic school. Alternative approaches favor increased humility about the indubitability of any proposition and seek truth instead more pragmatically in the coherence among a wide variety of elements of reasoning (Rorty, 1979, 1982).

Consider how this might apply to philosophical inquiry into the placebo effect. The older analytic approach might suggest starting with one's favorite abstract proposition, possibly regarding the nature of the mind-body relationship, and proceeding to more specific conclusions by a process of linear deduction. The newer approach would sketch an agenda for testing one's new hypotheses and theories about placebo effect against a fairly wide array of divergent ideas and considerations:

1. Empirical data about human subjects' responses to placebos
2. Current scientific theories about neurophysiology
3. Philosophical theories about the mind-body relationship
4. Sociocultural and ethnographic inquiries into the nature of illness and healing
5. Philosophical theories about the nature of scientific inquiry in biology and medicine (including adequacy of research design, flaws or limitations in randomized double-blind trials, etc.)

Note that some of these considerations are expressed in very abstract or general terms and others in very concrete, specific terms. Ultimately a satisfactory theory of placebo effect will cohere meaningfully with all of these divergent considerations (Brody, 1980, 1985). Note that this is a long-term research agenda, since, without a doubt, one will be trying to hit a moving target. As new data are accumulated in empirical research or as theories of neurophysiology are modified, one will necessarily have to revise one's placebo theory in minor or even in substantial ways. This search for a coherent "fit" among divergent sorts of considerations is an application to medical science of a method labeled "wide reflective equilibrium" in social-political philosophy (Daniels, 1979).

Thick Description. For the naturalistic investigator, truths are usually local rather than universal. Research conclusions apply with confidence only to the particular group now under study and only at that particular moment in time. In order to judge how trustworthy would be any extension of those research conclusions to other, apparently similar groups, one must know in great detail the precise similarities and differences between these other groups and the group that has been studied. This knowledge requires a very detailed account of the context and the subjects of the study.

An example of a move toward "thick description" in medical contexts is the employment of a model like the hierarchy of natural systems, best known as the "biopsychosocial" model of Engel (1977). This model, it must be emphasized, is a broad approach to research that may prove more or less fruitful when applied to different problem domains; it is not a "theory" that can be "validated" or "invalidated" by specific factual findings (Brody, 1990a). In this way the biopsychosocial model may be seen as an example of philosophy of science; it is a theoretical effort to coordinate and integrate a set of divergent scientific observations and methods, rather than itself a scientific observation or method.

Philosophical inquiry into a complex phenomenon such as the placebo effect quickly reveals the paucity of thick description in the literature and the thinness of the descriptions that are offered from various disciplinary perspectives. For instance, studies into placebo and/or medication responses carried out by clinical pharmacologists, psychologists, sociologists, and anthropologists might each describe only a thin layer of the phenomenon observed, depending on the tools with which that investigator is most familiar. The clinical pharmacologist measures onset and duration of drug effects but says nothing about the personalities and the psychological reactions of the subjects. The psychologist addresses personality variables as measured by specific inventories and questionnaires but says nothing about the cultural belief systems regarding illness and medication that may be present among the subjects. One hopes that new studies into placebo effects, if informed by a thorough philosophical understanding of the issue, will be much "thicker" than most of the previously published work. One way to do this is to adopt more explicitly the biopsychosocial model as a guide to interdisciplinary cooperation within a research team (White, Tursky, & Schwartz, 1985).

Reflexivity. Since the naturalistic investigator is him- or herself the research "instrument," naturalistic inquiry cannot avoid observer bias by using the instrument to insulate the experiment from the preconceptions of the investigator. Instead open disclosure of preconceptions and assumptions that may have influenced data gathering and processing becomes an inherent part of the conduct of the inquiry.

While reflexivity as such is not usually an element of philosophical inquiry, philosophical methods may be extremely useful in identifying previously unexamined assumptions. It is in this sort of inquiry that the more traditional analytic techniques show their real strength. An example is the insistence on establishing clear definitions for key terms. Often it is through the exercise of clarifying definitions that one comes across unexamined preconceptions that are in need of further exploration.

For example, any philosopher tackling the problem of placebo phenomena would be tempted to start with the definition of *placebo* and *placebo effect*. Yet this exercise turns out to be much more convoluted than anyone would have expected at first glance. Many papers in medical journals refer to placebos as being "inert." Yet, if they were truly inert in the relevant sense, then obviously there would be no placebo *effect* in need of investigation. The question then turns into: In what sense (if any) are placebos inert, and in what sense are they active? Going a bit farther, one notices that many of the rough-and-ready definitions offered in the medical literature define the placebo effect as that which is *not* due to the pharmacologic or physiologic effect of medications. This definition naturally leads to a question of why placebo phenomena must be defined strictly in *negative* terms. Is this negative bent an outgrowth of our present scientific ignorance? Does it then mean that in the future no such thing as the placebo effect will exist, when scientific understanding of its underlying mechanisms has progressed sufficiently? Or does an attractive *positive* definition of placebo effect exist that may be offered as an alternative? (Brody, 1985; Grunbaum, 1985).

The point here in need of emphasis is that these questions are by no means "merely semantic." They strike to the heart of many important conceptual issues regarding the study of placebo phenomena. The investigator who does not take these questions seriously is at high risk of observing one sort of datum and thinking he or she is observing something else. For instance, if one is happy to define *placebo effect* as *not* the pharmacologic drug effect, one may note that subjects in the nondrug control group improved and call that a placebo response; but one may fail to note that some of these subjects may have improved because of the natural spontaneous remission rate of the disease itself, and others may have improved as a result of diet or exercise changes. It is hard to imagine that lumping together such disparate mechanisms will lead to a refinement in our understanding of how the placebo effect is produced.

Qualitative Research and Medical Ethics

Philosophers interested in medical issues have devoted most of their attention to ethical matters, rather than to the sorts of conceptual and scientific issues mentioned in the previous section. It is not possible in a chapter of this length to go into sufficient detail about the various methods of ethical inquiry. It may, however, be worth pointing out an important contribution that qualitative research more generally can make to our understanding of ethical issues in primary care. That is, I wish to shift my focus from philosophical research *as a form of* qualitative research to qualitative research *as an aid to* ethical research as one specific category of philosophical inquiry in medicine.

Purists of the analytic school would insist that ethics is the study of what ought to be, rather than of what is; therefore, scientific research of any sort is simply irrelevant to the discovery of ethical "truths." So long as one's ethical reflections are intended to help in practical problem-solving, however, one naturally wonders both how those problems are presently being solved and whether the behavior of the problem solvers will change after the appropriate sort of ethical input. Because most see medical ethics as primarily a practical or applied area of ethics, it is not surprising that a considerable body of empirical research has accumulated regarding ethical issues in medicine. This research is of variable quality. In some cases the poor quality of the research, in terms of its failure to address those aspects of the ethical problem that would seem to be of greatest interest, can be directly linked to reliance on quantitative or rationalistic methods.

Two examples—informed consent and orders not to resuscitate—illustrate the special contributions that properly designed qualitative research can make to ethical analysis.

Informed Consent

Informed consent has been studied widely as an ethical and legal issue. For some period of time, the literature was filled with one sort of empirical study almost to the exclusion of all others—studies of how well patients retained information after they had been "informed" by the physician. Many of these studies revealed a very poor retention of factual information some weeks after the "informed consent" session occurred. The investigators commonly interpreted this to mean that the whole concept of informed consent was basically flawed; if patients cannot remember what they have been told, why bother? These studies commonly were carried out by physicians, and many physicians resented informed consent as a lawyer's idea that had been inappropriately foisted onto medicine by meddlesome courts. That their studies purported to invalidate the usefulness of informed consent was therefore not surprising (for a comprehensive review, see Meisel & Roth, 1981).

What most of these studies simply assumed, and therefore failed to address in any meaningful way, was the simple equation of informed consent with information reception and retention. In other words the "informed" part was being addressed while the "consent" part was entirely lost sight of. It does not require too much philosophical skill to note that one's ability to participate meaningfully in a decision, to the extent that one wishes to do so, may require more or less information, depending on circumstances, and, once the decision is made, one has little reason to try to remember that information. Thus one could have been a very active and informed participant in a particular decision and still remember few of the relevant facts if quizzed 3 weeks later. Of course from a research standpoint it is fairly easy to quantify one's retention of facts and very difficult to quantify meaningful participation in a decision; so the adoption of quantitative research methods shifted the entire focus toward information retention. *It was a classic case of the measurable driving out the important.*

By contrast, some of the best research on informed consent was carried out by a multidisciplinary team at Pittsburgh, funded under a contract with the then-extant President's Commission for the Study of Ethical Problems in Medicine (Lidz et al., 1983). This research was a laborious participant-observer study carried on at several hospital sites over a period of months. The findings of those studies did indeed raise important challenges to the concept of informed consent but did so in a much more basic and sophisticated way than any of the earlier quantitative studies. For instance it turned out that virtually no physicians in the study showed an understanding of informed consent as a sort of participatory dialogue involving patients; instead they saw informed consent as a sort of legalistic mumbo jumbo that might protect the physician from a lawsuit but that could not possibly further the patient's own interests. Therefore, unsurprisingly, the way physicians behaved threw up numerous barriers to meaningful dialogue with patients about management decisions. On the other hand, the research also showed that patients do not place nearly as much value in participation in decision making as the notion of a "right" to informed consent would suggest. Indeed only about 10% of patients in that study indicated a real interest in participating in medical decisions even though they almost universally desired more information about their care than they had been provided. (Of course these patients may simply not have realized that participation in decisions was a practical possibility; later research has tended to indicate that increased participation leads to a variety of enhanced patient outcomes [Greenfield, Kaplan, & Ware, 1985].)

Resuscitation Issues

Another example of an ethical research area that can be enhanced by qualitative methods is the use of cardiopulmonary resuscitation and do-not-resuscitate (DNR) orders. Since resuscitation is a form of life-prolonging treatment, the ethical issues of DNR orders have been approached as an instance in the withholding of life-prolonging treatment, and various guidelines have been issued regarding patient consent. This includes turning for consent to family members only when the patient is incompetent to decide, and so forth. These guidelines also tend to stress that DNR should not be viewed as a sort of code word for withdrawing other forms of life-sustaining care; DNR refers simply to the nonuse of one technological intervention. By implication, withholding of other treatments such as ventilators, pressor agents, and so on would each require explicit patient discussion and consent (President's Commission for the Study of Ethical Problems in Medicine, 1983).

A substantial body of quantitative research has been conducted around DNR issues and has documented a number of worthwhile findings. The extent to which physicians comply with DNR orders (Quill, Stankaitis, & Krause, 1986), the increasing use of DNR orders in hospitals and nursing homes (Kamer et al., 1990), whether patients are asked directly or whether physicians bypass patients to speak to family members (Jonsson, McNamee, & Campion, 1988), how many patients desire DNR status and under what circumstances (Ebell, Smith, Seifert, & Polsinelli, 1990), and whether the patient or the physician typically initiates dialogue around DNR (Schmerling, Bedell, Lilienfeld, & Delbanco, 1988) are all matters that have received attention.

At the same time, very little qualitative research has been done on DNR orders. A pioneering though small-scale study by Ventres (1991) indicates that a number of questions surrounding DNR decisions will not be addressed very well unless qualitative methods are employed. For example, Ventres identified a wide array of factors influencing how the physician, the patient, and the family approach a DNR discussion; many of these factors create divergent viewpoints, which can make shared communication difficult. In particular, Ventres identified the importance of a number of physician emotional factors regarding the approaching death of the patient and issues of blame and guilt, which have been largely ignored in quantitative studies. Also, Ventres was able to show how a hospital form, designed to standardize DNR orders and to assist house staff in the process of obtaining patient consent, may actually have interfered with full communication of the more important patient and family values and tilted the discussion in a technological direction and away from important life issues.

In speaking up for the value of qualitative research methods in medical ethics, one need not neglect the importance of basic ethical principles and concepts of the sort that analytic philosophers identify and discuss. It is not possible to talk meaningfully about informed consent and DNR orders, much less design an informative research project, unless one thoroughly understands such basic ideas as patient autonomy. And yet abstract notions like autonomy, beneficence, and justice mean little until we learn how they become actualized and embodied by specific people in a specific social and cultural context. Qualitative research is very well designed to determine what those concepts actually mean to particular individuals within the fabric of their lives. To mention just one example, it has been suggested only recently that "autonomy" in an acute-care hospital and "autonomy" in long-term home care for chronic illness may be two quite distinct concepts (Agich, 1990).

Conclusion

The application of philosophical methods of inquiry to medical issues ordinarily will involve more formal study of the discipline than most primary care investigators will desire to obtain. This involvement means that for many of the sorts of studies indicated above, the primary care investigator will wish to collaborate with someone who has the requisite training and experience. The proliferation of medical ethics courses in medical schools and the increasing use of philosopher-ethicists as consultants in hospitals and medical centers makes it somewhat easier to identify such a collaborator.

Moreover, the occasional similarities between methods of philosophic inquiry and analysis and methods of qualitative research suggest an additional role for the philosopher as a possible consultant on the logic and clarity of the research design. For instance a philosopher might be helpful in detecting when the research question is not firmly linked to the initial hypotheses or when key terms have been defined inadequately. Such a collaboration can benefit both the qualitative investigator and the philosopher. The former will emerge with a tighter and better reasoned research design, while the latter may discover interesting conceptual problems in health care that are worthy of further reflection.

PART V

Putting It All Together: Completed Studies

11 A Qualitative Study of Family Practice Physician Health Promotion Activities

DENNIS G. WILLMS
NANCY ARBUTHNOT JOHNSON
NORMAN A. WHITE

Introduction

In prevention research, qualitative approaches often are viewed as a vehicle to generate hypotheses and to identify problems for later positivistic research (Willms et al., 1990). Alternatively, qualitative methods are employed after a basic science study has been conducted; at this latter stage they are used to identify appropriate strategies for disseminating the results of basic science research in the clinic or community (e.g., the results of a randomized, controlled clinical trial). Countering this "handmaiden" role in primary prevention research, we believe that qualitative methods are also relevant in their own right. They are a useful method for interpreting the response

AUTHORS' NOTE: We acknowledge and are grateful for the financial support of the Ontario Ministry of Health (Research Grant #02030), which permitted us to conduct this research. In addition we wish to thank our research team for their contribution to the study: the co-investigators—J. Allan Best, Elizabeth A. Lindsay, J. Raymond Gilbert, Douglas M. C. Wilson, D. Wayne Taylor, and Joel Singer; the research staff—Kenneth Friesen, Alan Harkness, Mane Arratia, Karen Sykes, and Diana Tuttleman.

of persons and communities to critical events (e.g., the response of physicians, as a subculture, to allegations of extra-billing), and identifying the social-cultural meanings of these "events-that-happen" by casting problems, purposes, and intentions in a new light. In short, qualitative studies enable investigators to examine and explain problems and events *from the perspective of the actor*—his or her experiences, understandings, and interpretations of events and "events-that-happen." The nondirective methods of participant observation, semistructured interviews, and focus groups are commonly used means of uncovering these understandings. We describe these three methodologies, as well as the preliminary results of our recent study of the health promotion activities of a group of family practice physicians.

Background

From a primary care perspective, physicians' offices are an obvious setting for initiating, negotiating, and maintaining health promotion advice. The family practice physician who treats entire families and establishes a history of care with related family members is in an advantaged position to authoritatively negotiate competing notions of risk, explanations of disease etiology, and life-style strategies for disease prevention. Stated differently, the family practice physician is situated professionally to mediate scientific (biomedical explanations), professional (clinical/biomedical capabilities and contingencies), and popular (individual/social-cultural expectations) realities (Kleinman, 1980; Kleinman, Eisenberg, & Good, 1978; Stein, 1985) for the patient and his or her support group.

Relatively little, however, is known about the strategies or methods employed by physicians in delivering motivational messages to their patients. What we do know is that physicians involved in health promotion activities differ considerably in their effectiveness as advice givers (Ewart, Wood, & Li, 1982). The reasons for these differences are many: the issue of whether a physician personally exemplifies a healthy life-style; differences between the physician and patient in the perception, assessment, and explanation of clinically presented problems (Kleinman, 1980); a professionally ineffective relationship established between physician and patient, predicated on either interpersonal or social-cultural differences (Kleinman,

1980; Willms, Kottke, Solberg, & Brekee, 1986). We do know, for example, that physicians utilize subjective, as well as objective, assessments in the clinical encounter (Hahn, 1985; Stein, 1985).

In the present study, we sought to learn from exemplary family physicians—those who were especially motivated and involved in health promotion work in their practices—how it is that they are effective as health promoters. Specifically we attempted to generate a description of the strategies, models, and approaches employed by this group of family practice physicians as they engaged in health promotion interventions—in particular, smoking cessation counseling. In addition to characterizing and typifying their work and experience as health promoters, we attempted to identify modifiable barriers in family practice medicine that currently impede the effective dissemination of health promotion advice.

Design and Methods

Twelve family practice physicians from the Kitchener-Waterloo area of southern Ontario, Canada, were recruited to participate in the study. The research involved (a) *interviews with physicians* to learn their views and experiences of health promotion work in family practice; (b) *interviews with patients* to elicit their perspectives on the physician-patient clinical encounter; (c) *physician focus group interviews* in which we brought the physicians together in small groups to refine critically these views; and (d) an ethnographic *participant observation* substudy of 4 of the 12 physicians who agreed to have one of the researchers spend approximately 4 half-days in each of the clinics, observing the full range of clinical strategies used by the physicians in their day-to-day practice (see Figure 11.1).

The triangulation of research methods and data entry points (physician interviews, focus groups with physicians, patient interviews, and participant observation of physician-patient encounters) is helpful in qualitative research to confirm the reliability and validity of the interpretations (Jick, 1979). Where convergence exists in understandings between these different methods, the data are viewed as being the most reliable; differing viewpoints, while valid on an individual basis, contribute to the refinement of problems identified, hypotheses generated, and explication of social-cultural meanings.

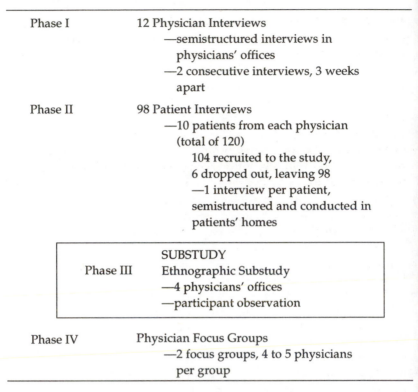

Phase I	12 Physician Interviews
	—semistructured interviews in physicians' offices
	—2 consecutive interviews, 3 weeks apart
Phase II	98 Patient Interviews
	—10 patients from each physician (total of 120)
	104 recruited to the study, 6 dropped out, leaving 98
	—1 interview per patient, semistructured and conducted in patients' homes

SUBSTUDY
Phase III   Ethnographic Substudy
—4 physicians' offices
—participant observation

| Phase IV | Physician Focus Groups |
| | —2 focus groups, 4 to 5 physicians per group |

Figure 11.1. Phases of the Qualitative Research Study

The 12 family practice physicians who agreed to participate in the study were motivated to do health promotion work in their practice, were involved currently in some form of health promotion work, and already had established their own individualized strategies for engaging in health promotion activities. Motivation was determined by the physicians' interest in participating in this form of intensive and intrusive research, which required a substantial time commitment on their part.

The qualitative or field research style was selected as the research strategy. While knowledge, attitude, and practice (KAP) surveys and structured interviews direct the researcher into the general area of how a problem is perceived intellectually, qualitative field research illuminates the context for these cognitive perceptions. Through observation of physician practice and the elicitation of physician and patient-driven stories and narratives, the researcher identifies and uncovers the constraints and contingencies that limit effective prevention and health promotion. Furthermore, while KAP surveys can be administered easily to a broad cross-section of participants, qualitative field research requires a limited number of participants and uncovers a personal and social world of "lived experience" (cf. Schutz, 1973) that elucidates how these professional health promotion choices are made, on what basis they are made, and what the perceived outcomes will be both personally and for their patient population. We originally hoped to work with 15 physicians; 12 agreed to participate fully in the study.

The Research Process

PHASE I: PHYSICIAN INTERVIEWS

In Phase I of the study, we sought to generate physicians' general impressions of how it is they engage in health promotion activities in their practice. This more general discussion was designed (a) to earn the cooperative interest of the physician in the study; (b) to elucidate perceptions of barriers to health promotion work, such as time, cost, training, and patient's world-view; (c) to determine how it is the physicians have overcome these problems to become more effective.

Physicians were interviewed on two separate occasions before they began to recruit patients for smoking cessation counseling and participation in the study (Phase II). The interviews were scheduled 2-3 weeks apart and were conducted in each physician's office by an experienced member of the research team. Each interview lasted approximately 1-11/2 hours. During these sessions the physicians were interviewed using semistructured, open-ended interviewing techniques (Agar, 1980; Pelto & Pelto, 1978), and each received an honorarium for his or her time. A set of questions was developed to elicit physicians' statements regarding (a) their personal interest in health promotion and professional experience, (b) their perception of their patient population, (c) the place of health promotion in family practice, and (d) the barriers to doing clinical preventive medicine. These questions served to guide the interview process rather than dictate it. The following is a sample of some of the questions used in the first interview:

1. How would you describe your practice?
2. What kind of patients do you normally see?
3. How do you define, or think about, the notion of health promotion?
4. Do you normally provide health promotion advice? In what instances would you do this? To whom? Can you give examples?
5. How would you go about advising someone to stop smoking?
6. How do you communicate the element of risk to a patient who will not stop smoking?
7. Does your approach change relative to age or sex?
8. Keeping in mind the topic of health promotion, are there any cases that have posed a moral problem or dilemma for you, anything in approaching or dealing with patients that you found or still find difficult? For example, some doctors report that they find it difficult to counsel someone to quit smoking while still smoking themselves.
9. Do you as a doctor have the right or responsibility to try to change a patient's behavior?
10. How do you think your patients perceive you?
11. How do other doctors differ from you in their attitudes to health promotion?

Permission was obtained from each of the physicians to audiotape the interviews. The tapes then were transcribed onto a microcomputer to facilitate analysis. Field notes were written by the field researchers after each interview. We recommended that the field notes be divided into three content areas: (a) a subjective description of the events of the interview, as well as description of the setting, mood, and degree of rapport established; (b) a list of key words that emerge in the interview (e.g., "too busy, one voice, life-style," etc.); and (c) a list of questions that should be asked of those physicians to advance emerging explanations of health promotion work in their practices. The transcripts, as well as the field notes recorded by the interviewer following each session, proved useful in developing questions for the second set of physician interviews. These questions were tailored to each physician and were designed to follow up or explore in more detail issues raised in the first interview.

PHASE II: PATIENT INTERVIEWS

While the purpose of Phase I was to determine physicians' general perceptions of health promotion work, our intention in the second and third phases of the study was to study the actual methods, approaches, and strategies used. We expected to learn about (a) areas of agreement and disagreement between patient and physician, (b) the kind of recommendations and advice offered to patients and the advice's perceived appropriateness, (c) differing perceptions of risk, and (d) significance and meaning attributed to physician interventions. We garnered this information through patient interviews (Phase II) and participant observation of the interactions of four physicians with patients in the clinical setting (Phase III).

Each of the 12 physicians was asked to recruit 10 smokers to the study. These patients agreed to discuss quitting with their physicians and to be interviewed by one of the members of the research team following the visit. Patients were advised that their participation in the study did not necessitate an actual decision to quit on their part and that the information they volunteered would be confidential and would not be reported back to the doctor.

Physicians were given control over which patients they selected for recruitment. They were encouraged, however, to identify both "difficult" and "easy" patients. Physicians were asked to counsel and advise these patients to quit smoking in their usual fashion and during normally scheduled office hours.

While physicians selected patients to participate in the study, actual recruitment was done by receptionists in the physicians' offices. These receptionists were trained in a standardized recruitment procedure, and a highly specific patient recruitment log was developed to assist them in the process. Each receptionist/nurse was asked to recruit 2 patients per week until a total of 10 patients were recruited to the study.

Within 48 hours after the first physician visit, patients were contacted by a member of the research team to schedule a home or workplace interview. Again permission to audiotape the session was obtained from each participant, and a set of questions designed to elicit their perceptions of the physician counseling procedure was used to guide the interview. The following is a sample of some of the questions used in the patient interviews:

1. Can you recall some of the things Dr. _____ talked about or told you about your smoking?
2. Did he or she ask you to try to quit smoking?
3. Did he or she suggest how you could do this? How?

4. Do you agree with what he or she told you?

5. Do you think he or she adequately understands your views and opinions concerning smoking? Do you think he or she adequately understands why you smoke? Do you think he or she sufficiently understands what quitting would involve for you?

6. How much help do you think your physician can be to your quitting attempt?

7. How do you feel about Dr. _____ talking to you about your smoking and these things? Do you mind? Are you appreciative? Does it bother you? Why?

8. Does he or she explain things sufficiently?

9. Do you find it easy to talk and discuss matters with him or her?

Field notes were written up by the interviewer after each session, and 20% of the audiotapes were transcribed. Because it was too costly to transcribe all of the interviews, each interviewer was expected to evaluate and grade his or her interviews according to the following subjective criteria: (a) the degree to which new information was presented, (b) the qualitative depth and richness of interviewees' responses, and (c) the variability in forms of explanation. Yes and no answers to questions were graded low, while responses with "thick description" were graded high and recommended for transcription.

In total, 104 patients were recruited to the study. Of these 104 individuals, 6 dropped out. Of the remaining 98 participants, 43% had smoked for 10-19 years; 34.7% were between the ages of 30 and 39 years; and 68.4% were married. Also, 63 of the participants were females, and 35 were males.

PHASE III: ETHNOGRAPHIC SUBSTUDY

The ethnographic substudy, or participant observation component, was initiated while the physicians were recruiting patients for smoking cessation counseling. Four of the 12 physicians agreed to participate in the substudy; in these physicians' clinics Dennis Willms spent approximately 2 half-days per week for a period of 2 weeks observing the range of clinical strategies used in their day-to-day practice. The investigator was present in each physician's clinic on the half-days that the first four patients recruited were scheduled to see the physician. At the physician's professional discretion the investigator observed additional physician-patient encounters in which health promotion advice may or may not have been offered. The investigator was introduced to the patient as a researcher interested in studying physician-patient interactions, and the individual's consent for the investigator to be present was obtained. Over 100 patient encounters were observed, and a physician encounter record was completed for each (see Figure 11.2).

PHASE IV: PHYSICIAN FOCUS GROUPS

In the fourth and final phase of the study, each of the 12 doctors was invited to participate in a focus group discussion with 5 of their colleagues who also had participated in the study and 3 members of the research team. Nine of the 12 physicians took part in two focus group discussions. These were designed to permit the physicians to critically develop, refine, and test each other's assessments of health promotion work. With this method of gathering information, we moved out of the domain of individual experience to the shared and consensual agreement of physicians as a professional group, thus allowing us to substantiate further the generalizable findings of the study.

In sum, five sets of data were collected over the course of the study: (a) texts of physician interviews comprising over 700 pages of verbatim discourse, (b) texts of patient interviews totaling approximately 250 pages, (c) field notes from both the patient and physician interviews, (d) texts of the two focus group interviews, and (e) over 100 patient encounter records from the substudy.

Analysis and Interpretation

We approached these five data sets with three goals. The first was to identify emergent themes and issues and to develop a coding scheme that would be applied to the transcribed text of patient and physician interviews. This application would allow for any helpful quantification of some of our results, as well as easy retrieval of verbatim statements by physicians or patients around specific points. The verbatim quotations would be used subsequently to illustrate our conclusions. The codes also would allow us to look for relationships/ patterns among various themes. Our second goal was to compile, from the texts of field notes and the interviews, a case study for each

Physician #: _____		Date: _____
Patient #: _____ Age: _____		Sex: _____
Occupation: _____		Visit #: _____
Brought to Clinic by Family/Friend: _____		

PHYSICIAN	**PATIENT**

Entering Examination Room
t¹

BEHAVIOR (1)

DISCOURSE (2)

**PREVENTION/
HEALTH PROMOTION (3)**

t²
Exiting
Examination
Room

Prescription (s): New _____ Renewed _____   Comments:
Other Recommended Therapies: _____
Referral (s): _____
Follow-up Requested: Yes _____ No _____

1. In this space, the researcher records the behaviors and actions of the physician and patient.
2. In this space, the researcher documents the discourse between the physician and patient in the examination room.
3. In this space, the researcher documents any references in the discourse to health promotion or disease prevention.

Figure 11.2. Physician/Patient Encounter Record

physician which would capture that individual's style and method of
delivering health promotion advice. Our third goal was to generate

10000	PHYSICIANS' COMMENTS
10200	Health Promotion: Definition and Activities
10301	Definitions: Health promotion, disease prevention
10302	Content areas of health promotion and disease prevention (eg.,smoking cessation, weight loss, alcohol reduction)
10303	Approaches to health promotion: methods of health promotion
10304	Comments and analysis of effecitveness at health promotion, disase prevention, lifestyle counseling
10305	Explanatory models: health, disease, smoking
10306	Factors that encourage/discourage doing health promotion

Figure 11.3. Examples of Coding Scheme

a set of hypotheses and questions for future research using both the case studies and the identified themes and issues.

CODING OF VARIABLES AND EMERGENT THEMES

The texts of field notes and interviews with the physicians and patients were read by several members of the research team. Each team member constructed a preliminary list of issues and themes that then were compared, discussed, and reworked. The result was a 5-digit coding scheme (see Figure 11.3). The first digit indicates the source of the comments. The digit 1 refers to physician comments, 2 to patient comments, and 3 to the researchers' comments. The second and third digits specify a particular domain of comments, such as "Physician-Patient Relationships." The fourth and fifth digits indicate a specific theme within a domain. For example, the code number 10601 was applied to physicians' statements (as indicated by the initial digit 1) regarding "Elements/ingredients/components in the physician-patient relationship necessary to induce change toward better health in a patient." This was one of two themes relating to physicians' statements within the domain of comments on "Physician-Patient Relationship" (as indicated by the second and third digits 06). A list of thematic categories is shown in Figure 11.4.

Using a specialized software package, Ethnographic Theme Search (ETS), designed for use in a previous study (Willms et al., 1990), we

10000	PHYSICIANS' COMMENTS
10100	Clinic/Practice/Work Environment
10200	Resources (external to practice)
10300	Health Promotion: Definitions and Activities
10400	Patients
10500	Physicians
10600	Physician-Patient Relationship
10700	Reflecting/Philosophizing on Health Promotion
10800	Life History: At Home
10900	Life History: At University
11000	Life History: At Work
11100	Training
20000	PATIENTS' COMMENTS
20100	Physician's Interventions
20200	Past Interventions
20300	Perception of Physician's Interventions
20400	Philosophizing about Physician's Interventions
20500	History of Smoking
20600	Risk Perception
20700	Quitting Smoking
20800	History of Patient-Physician Interactions
20900	Patient-Physician Relationship
21000	Philosophizing about Doctors
21100	Experiences with Other Doctors
21200	Life History
30000	RESEARCHER'S COMMENTS
30100	Comments on the Participant
30200	Comments on the Interview
30300	Comments about Doctors
30400	Comments on Smoking/Quitting
30500	Comments on Important Events in the Participant's Life

Figure 11.4. General Headings for the Coding Scheme

retrieved "discrete units of text." Each consisted of the interviewer's question and the coded response of the participant under a particular rubric such as "Approaches to health promotion: methods of health promotion" (10303). Additionally ETS allowed us to retrieve discrete units of text that contained co-occurrences of codes. For example, we could search for co-occurrences of particular codes such as 10303 (see above) and 10107, "Length of time at this practice," using the "Text" function. This capability allowed us to investigate suspected relationships between themes and to discover unanticipated relationships. The "Quantification" function of ETS provided us with descriptive statistics of the co-occurrences.

CASE STUDIES/PROFILES

In order to preserve the idiosyncratic, personal details of the physicians' work experience as they emerged from their discourse on individual methods, as well as to preserve their styles and approaches to health promotion, case studies ranging in length from 5-20 pages were written for each of the 12 physicians. These case studies are a compilation of relevant quotes organized around the following subjects: description of practice and patient population, health promotion strategies, and barriers and frustrations to doing health promotion.

Generally the case studies begin with a description of the physician's practice and patient population, which includes details relating to type of practice, other health professionals and support staff employed, kinds of patients seen most frequently, and areas of practice the physician considers to be of a health promotion nature. For example, Dr. Dyck (a pseudonym) shares office space with two other physicians who graduated from a university in southern Ontario the same year he did. Each of the three physicians has his or her own solo practice, although they fill in for each other during vacations. They share one full-time nurse between them. Dr. Dyck describes his practice as a "fairly overall general practice." Although the other two doctors have not done obstetrics for a number of years, he continues to do so. "We do a lot of baby care," he says, "a lot of well female exams." He notes, "The opportunity to do preventive medicine is fairly high here."

A large portion of the case study is devoted to a summary of the various methods, approaches, and "tricks" the physician described using, as well as any comments on when and in what contexts he or she employs certain strategies. Dr. Dyck, for example, in attempting to convey the hazards of smoking, tends to "use a number of his own experiences" recounting incidents of smoking patients who died of cancer. He says that he makes use of his patients to help him. One woman patient became an "expert on crib death" after losing her own child. He refers couples whose infants have a higher risk to this lady. His office nurse is an ex-smoker, and he sometimes refers patients who want to quit smoking to her. She is "glad to talk to them about how she quit and the difference it's made."

Accompanying the description of the physician's health promotion strategies is a summary of the physician's thoughts on the problems and frustrations of doing health promotion work. In Dr. Dyck's case, he says the most frustrating aspect of doing preventive medicine and health promotion is the "time element." Only a certain amount of time is allotted for each patient visit, and you have to "prioritize it; you have to deal with immediate physical complaints, and you may have to call them back to deal with some of the other problems." He often schedules another appointment to deal with health promotional issues, especially when he is "highly concerned . . . that is, the patient is 100 pounds overweight, smoking and drinking."

Another problem he encounters is that "many patients can't see a connection between stress and their 'physical symptoms.' " He uses popular analogies to try to explain this to them. For example, he asks them what their stomach felt like just before they had to make their first speech in class and then tells them, "The same thing can happen if you're under stress at work, only it might affect your heart, your stomach, your bowels, your kidneys." Dr. Dyck says that much of his patient counseling revolves around stress-related issues.

Each of the case studies is complemented by a physician profile drawn from the texts of field notes and interviews with the patients (see Figure 11.5). Similar to the case studies, the physician profiles are a compilation of relevant quotes relating to the patients' expectations of their physician, their perceptions of his or her intervention, and his or her rapport with the patient. Figure 11.5 contains two excerpts from the patient interviews for Dr. Dyck.

HYPOTHESES AND PROBLEMATICS

Our analysis of the case studies, the physician profiles, and the identified themes and issues suggested a number of hypotheses and questions for further investigation. These covered a range of areas, including organization of health care delivery, the patient-provider relationship, physician roles, patient expectations, and competing definitions or notions of health. For example, with respect to patients' expectations, we found that patients generally are looking for

Dr. Dyck obviously adapts his style to suit each patient's idiosyncrasies, so that he can suitably impress them with his advice and effect their compliance. For instance, with one younger patient who is a fairly new mother, his emphasis on encouraging her to quit smoking i son the health of her young son and the importance of providing a good enviroment for him. And he has been successful in impressing upon the woman that it is her responsibility to do something about this in such a way that she can reflect upon his suggestion and make her decision. "He always suggest. . .but he doesn't push. . . so that I don't feel that i'm being forced" (1102 p. 5). "I think people are responsible for themseleves. . . I think a doctor maybe should tell them. . . the facts. . . (and) offer as much help as he can" (1102 p. 8). This is exactly what Dr. Dyck has done in her situation. "He's giving me pretty well the information I wanted. . . gave me the booklet" (which she has read), has suggested that the patient "try to plan that you're not going to be around smoking people. . . don't go to parties" (1102 p. 5).

In general, the patients feel that the doctor understands them and their predicaments well. They have a great deal of confidence in him and his capabilities and it seems as if they feel a real sense of partnership with Dr. Dyck, which has obviously been developed through the years. Dr. Dyck's use of humor as a means of gaining a sense of intimacy with his patients seems to prove a very effective approach, since it is appreciated even by those patients who do not wish to listen to his advice and make serious lifestyle changes. "I don't want to quit, to go through that misery. . .I'd rather go through childbirth again rather than the pain of quitting smoking" (1005 p. 4). "He doesn't hassle me . . . he says, 'You shouldn't be smoking, you've got emphysema!' (1005 p.1), but he knows I'm addicted. That's about it (p.3) . . . he's a character, he's easy to get along with . . . he's more approachable than some doctors are . . . he's got all of our trust" (1005 p. 6). They also recognize that in treating physical ailments, the patient's "state of mind" becomes a most important element since "40, 50, 60, or 70% of it is in the mind" (1006 p. 31).

Figure 11.5. Physician Profile

a physician who understands their subjective complaints, offers helpful advice and counsel, and perhaps most important, treats them as subjects, moral agents, in control of their own bodies and not as objects of experimentation. Patient expectations may be related to how patients are empowered to become more involved in their own health and well-being. They also raise the question of how physicians can learn to attribute more power in decision making to patients and their families so that the process becomes one of negotiation between the physician's expert opinion and the patient's autonomy and self-directedness, and how family and community supports can be brought to bear on the process of healing.

Another set of questions that emerged from our analysis concerns the extent to which physicians adopt an almost monochromatic professional persona. Is it fair to say that a physician is not permitted to allow personal life to emerge in professional life and work? Do persons who become physicians adopt a cultural image of "physician-like ness" and the characteristics and traits that support the personification of the ideal physician? Are physicians expected to present themselves as always being on an even keel, a presentation of professionalism that epitomizes stability, security, invulnerability, and unalterability?

In this respect, the presented image of invulnerability may be seen as analogous to the position of the indigenous healer in traditional societies. It attributes to them a source of power. They are on the margins of society—mysterious, aloof, different, not an average person—and therefore seemingly not as dependent on others, more powerful, and having more control. We ask ourselves whether there are times when physicians must become "vulnerable" so as to heal? Our data would suggest such times exist. Rules and a framework are lacking, however, for directing these shifts in power and authority.

Our data also suggest that perhaps a new specialty is emerging, as yet only informally, among physicians relating to health promotion. For example, Dr. Meyers and Dr. Phillips (pseudonyms) are recognized by other physicians in their communities as "experts" in dealing with smoking cessation and depression, respectively. Other physicians refer patients to them for counseling. It remains unclear to what extent this change is externally or internally driven. For example, to what degree has the emergence of "expert opinion" among physicians interested in life-style issues been brought about because certain life-style behaviors are being medicalized unnecessarily.

Conclusions

This chapter provides an overview of steps taken in systematically conducting a qualitative research study. While much more detail could have been presented in elucidating each phase of the project and our interpretation of results—the harsh light, soft focus of ethnography (Peacock, 1986)—our wide-angle lens provided a general view of the landscape of qualitative research methods and focused on necessary anchors for entering the field so as to see and to understand more clearly. We have covered a range of qualitative concerns: (a) the issue of problem formulation; (b) the qualitative or field research design, with consideration given to issues of reliability and validity through time and method triangulation; (c) the identification of emergent issues and themes; and (d) the generation of problems and hypotheses.

12 Doctor-Caregiver Relationships: An Exploration Using Focus Groups

DAVID L. MORGAN

Introduction

This chapter describes two studies that used focus groups as part of an ongoing research program on how older adults cope with caregiving for an older family member with Alzheimer's disease (A.D.) or a similar memory disorder. The overarching questions guiding both studies were (a) How do people come to understand the demands of caregiving? and (b) How do they obtain the skills to cope with these demands? Until recently (Pearlin, Turner, & Semple, 1989), caregivers' coping strategies have received little attention. The part that physicians play in either creating problems or aiding coping has received even less attention.

The topics for the studies were two different turning points within the longer "career" of family caregiving for people with A.D. Taken in the order they were done, the first study concerned the later phases of caregiving, and the turning point was the possibility of placing the family member with A.D. in a nursing home or similar formal care setting. The second study investigated the earlier phases of caregiving, and the turning point was the presentation of the family member for expert diagnosis. Each study included an interest in the ways that caregivers accessed health care as part of their efforts at coping, as well as the possibility that the health care system itself would present problems that required further efforts at coping.

The fact that both research projects involved the exploration of relatively unknown aspects of caregivers' experiences and decision making meant that qualitative methods were an appropriate choice for gathering the data. In each case the ultimate goal was to uncover caregivers' experiences, feelings, and beliefs in ways that would be useful to the researchers but to do so with a minimum of direction from the researchers; consequently, focus groups (Basch, 1987; Krueger, 1988; Morgan, 1988) were a particularly effective means of gathering the data. As exploratory research, each study sought to discover the caregivers' perspectives on institutionalization and diagnosis, rather than to presume the researchers already knew what the appropriate questions were. Allowing the caregivers to describe their situation to their peers, and the researchers' listening to how they made comparisons between their own experiences and those of outwardly similar others, provided a sense of how much similarity and diversity existed among the caregivers in each study.

Although both studies used focus groups to investigate the general topic of transitions in the careers of A.D. family caregivers, numerous differences existed in the research designs of the studies. This chapter thus begins with a brief overview of each study. Following that, the bulk of the chapter describes reasons for the research designs in the two studies. Next, I consider the set of decisions that went into the construction of the focus groups in each study.

After the discussion of the research design decisions in these studies, the chapter concludes with a discussion of the analysis of one aspect of the data produced—the doctor-caregiver relationship (Morgan & Zhao, 1991). It should be clear from the outset that the topic of caregiver-physician relationships had not entered our minds when we undertook the first study. Nor did we make it the crux of the second study, although we were well aware of its importance by the time we undertook that work. Instead, we extracted this topic from the caregivers' broader discussions of the transitions they experienced. Because of the wide range of topics that we covered in each study, concentrating on this specific topic helps demonstrate how our design decisions, both large and small, influenced the actual data we obtained. Hence the strategy for this chapter is to present the complete set of design decisions for both studies, but the analysis strategy for a more limited segment of the projects.

In spirit this chapter falls somewhere between two polar extremes for presenting decisions about research design and analysis. At one extreme are prescriptive accounts of how research design and analysis *should* be done. This approach provides general decision rules that have relatively little to do with the realities of any particular research project. I have not followed this approach here because I already have presented an abstract discussion of research design decisions for focus groups elsewhere (Morgan, in press). At the other extreme are personal, even confessional, accounts of how design decisions actually *are* made (cf. Hammond's [1964] classic collection, *Sociologists at Work*). This approach provides a detailed description of the unavoidable realities that affect the course of a particular research project, with less attention to what this experience implies for research in general. In the present case this approach would be premature, as we still have too little sense of how to do focus groups, let alone how to do them "in spite of ourselves." Overall, the basic intent of this chapter is to provide a didactic discussion of the decisions that were involved in collecting these two different sets of focus group data, as well as a concrete sense of the efforts that were necessary to analyze such data.

Research Overview

THE FIRST STUDY:
IS FORMAL CARE THE END OF CAREGIVING?

In this study, our research team investigated the experiences of caregivers who had placed their cognitively impaired family member in a nursing home or other similar formal care facility. In this case a large literature already existed on home-based caregiving for family members with A.D., as well as an emerging finding (e.g., Pratt, Wright, & Schmall, 1987) that caregivers who had placed their family member in formal care were no less burdened than those who performed their caregiving in the community. Consequently we needed to collect data that not only paralleled earlier work on caregiving in the community but also explored the ways in which caregiving in formal care settings departed from experiences in the community. In practice this meant that we divided our data collection efforts between survey instruments that replicated previous work, and focus groups that examined caregivers' experiences in a relatively unstructured fashion. The study was financed by a grant for $49,000 from the Andrus Foundation and had a 1-year time frame (for a more detailed description of the data collection and analysis, see Morgan, 1989).

We recruited our participants to provide an adequate number of observations within each cell of a 2x2 design, in which half the caregivers were community-based and half were formal-care-based, and half were caring for a spouse and half were caring for a parent. All of the participants were screened to ensure they had substantial involvement in caring for a family member with severe cognitive impairment. Given that there was no basis for selecting a representative sample, we recruited the participants from several different sources in order to reduce the bias that would result from using any single source. Our final data set consisted of 30 transcripts from a total of 179 caregivers.

The data were collected from groups of caregivers who typically met in sites associated with a group or organization. The participants first spent 45 minutes on a self-administered questionnaire with assistance from the project staff. After that, they participated in tape-recorded focus groups for another 45 minutes. In each group, we began with two basic questions: (a) What kinds of things made caregiving either easier or harder? and (b) How did the caregiving at home differ from caregiving in nursing homes? In the early portion of the study, longer discussions of these two questions constituted the entire focus group. Later we shortened the discussion of the first question to introduce a subsequent set of more specific questions, including ways in which other people (including health care professionals) could be helpful in decisions about the move to formal care. In each case, we ended with a discussion of the things that participants would recommend to other caregivers, a topic that was designed to conclude the groups on a relatively positive note.

We conducted our analysis of the focus group transcripts using *THE ETHNOGRAPH* software package (Seidel, Kjolseth, & Seymour, 1988). The initial coding used simple, manifest content categories based on the major domains within the survey: social networks, areas of involvement in caregiving, and burdens associated with caregiving. The social networks codes consisted of a list of possible relationships, including a general code for health care professionals, in which each mention of a given type of relationship was flagged, along with a code about whether the relationship was mentioned in a positive, negative, or neutral fashion. For involvement we located instances of 10 areas of caregiving activity that had been included in the questionnaire. For burdens we located 4 areas that also paralleled scales in the questionnaire.

The overall plan for the study involved a comparison between home-based and formal-care-based caregiving, and a comparison between the survey data and the focus group data. Within this larger design, the purpose of the focus groups was to help us learn about the caregivers' experiences without the researcher-imposed questioning that was inherent in our survey. In collecting and analyzing the focus group data, our goal was to maximize the breadth of things we would hear at the expense of not hearing about any of them in depth. This meant that in most groups, we did not ask explicit questions about the doctor-caregiver relationship, although the general questions that we asked allowed this topic to occur within any of the groups.

THE SECOND STUDY:
WHEN DO FAMILIES SEEK EXPERT DIAGNOSIS?

Our second study was not designed as a follow-up to the first. Instead we wished to investigate a specific issue related to the earlier rather than the later phases of the caregiver's career: When do families first seek expert diagnosis for age-related memory problems such as Alzheimer's disease? In this case, very little prior research existed about the circumstances that led families to seek expert diagnosis for A.D., although an extensive literature did exist on the general question of seeking medical care (see review in Becker & Maiman, 1983). Hence our objective was to discover why families sought diagnosis at different points and to do so in a theoretically informed fashion. In particular our contacts with a diagnostic clinic showed that initial work-ups were divided evenly between patients with mild and severe cognitive impairment. In seeking to understand why families sought expert diagnosis at different levels of symptom severity, our research goals were largely exploratory but narrowly defined. The study was financed by a grant for $13,000 from the Alzheimer's Disease Center of Oregon and had a 1-year time frame (for a more detailed description of the data collection and analysis, see Morgan, Wheeler, & Boise, 1991).

We began with medical records from a neuropsychological testing unit at a medical center that specialized in A.D. and other age-related cognitive impairments. Our case selection criteria included a diagnosis for a progressive dementia in which no evidence was found of seeking a second opinion. For each "positive" diagnosis, the medical record contained a score on the Mini-Mental State Exam (Folstein, Folstein, & McHugh, 1975), and we divided the available cases at the midpoint to distinguish between patients with higher and lower levels of impairment. We then used the records to determine which patients had family caregivers, and contacted these caregivers, first by mail and then by phone. We recruited caregivers associated with 38 patients and interviewed them in three groups in which the family members had a higher level of impairment at the time of diagnosis and three groups in which the family members had a lower level of impairment.

The focus groups were the basic source of data in this study and lasted approximately 1 1/2 hours per group. Before the start of each discussion, the participants completed a brief questionnaire, including a history of their caregiving experience and a checklist of their family member's symptoms. In the focus groups our questions followed a "history-taking" approach. We began by asking what were the earliest symptoms that the caregivers could recall, with whom they first discussed these symptoms, and how the symptoms had changed since the beginning. A second block of questions asked how they first decided to contact a doctor or other health professional about the symptoms and how they arrived at this diagnostic unit. Finally we asked about several topics from the Health Beliefs Model (e.g., benefits and barriers, triggers to action, etc.) and about advice they would give to other families facing similar decisions.

The general analytic strategy relied on *THE ETHNOGRAPH* and a predetermined content analysis using manifest coding categories. We used the same set of relationship codes as in the previous study to record all positive and negative mentions of other people and groups, including health care professionals. We also coded all mentions of specific symptoms, using the list of symptoms from the questionnaire as a starting point, and then expanding it substantially after preliminary coding on the first half of the interviews. We also used broad codes to capture transcript segments that contained elements of the Health Beliefs Model.

The overall plan for the study centered on the comparison between the groups in which the families presented their patients for diagnosis at higher and lower levels of impairment. Although the brief survey provided quantitative data on the differences between these two categories of caregivers, the principal objective of the study was to use the focus groups for a detailed exploration of these issues. In contrast to the first study, this research emphasized depth rather than breadth, and in this case, elements of the doctor-caregiver relationship were part of the topics that we investigated in depth.

The Decision to Use Focus Groups

COMPARED WITH SURVEYS

Both of these studies were multimethod and used surveys in conjunction with focus groups. The relative importance of the surveys was, however, quite different between the two studies. In the first study on the transition to formal care, half of the data collection time was given over to the survey, and the entire project, including the focus groups, would have been done rather differently if the survey had not been included. In the second study on diagnosis seeking, the survey played a largely secondary role, and little would have been done differently if it had been omitted.

For the first study, the combination of the survey and focus groups reflected our dual goals of creating a continuity with previous research on home-based caregivers and exploring the less well-understood experiences of caregivers in formal care settings. This meant that the survey portion of the project would address the traditional topics in the caregiving literature in the most direct way possible, replication using closed-ended items. Once we were certain that many of the core topics in the literature would be covered in the questionnaires, we were able to design a less structured data collection strategy for the focus groups, based on an open solicitation of things that made caregiving either easier or harder and differences between caregiving in the home and in formal care settings.

In the second study, we used a survey only as a supplement to the basic data provided through the focus groups, and the principal value of this survey material was to provide strictly comparable data across all of the participants in this study. Although we could have used a survey-based strategy by adapting previous studies based on the Health Beliefs Model to this specific situation, we elected not to because we felt that imposing a "top-down" adaptation of existing materials would be less revealing than a "bottom-up" exploration of the potentially very different situation that we were studying. One of our long-range goals was to use these discussions to generate questionnaire items for subsequent surveys, with the assurance that such questions would be well grounded in the participants' own beliefs and experiences. The value of this exploratory approach was demonstrated by the fact that even though we combined several popular symptom checklists to arrive at our survey instrument, we still had to expand the number of categories substantially in our content analytic coding in order to capture the range of symptoms that caregivers discussed in the focus groups.

COMPARED WITH PARTICIPANT OBSERVATION

Both of these studies would have been difficult to pursue with observational methods because the topics involve an extended time period, a shifting cast of characters, and a diffuse range of settings. Indeed most qualitative work on caregiving has been based on interviewing (but see Gubrium, 1986, for an observational study of an ongoing support group). The emphasis on transitions in these studies would have created another problem for observation, as we would have needed to locate families before they decided either to move to a nursing home or to seek diagnosis. If we were to drop the emphasis on transitions, however, then it would be quite possible to observe the activities of families in nursing homes and expert diagnostic units. Indeed both of these studies could be followed usefully by in-depth observations. For the move to formal care, our data point to the importance of observations of the relationships that form between staff and families (Duncan & Morgan, 1990). For diagnosis seeking, we would like to have observational records of caregiving families' encounters with medical providers, including encounters with family physicians in the general community (Morgan & Zhao, 1991).

COMPARED WITH INDIVIDUAL INTERVIEWS

Individual qualitative interviews are often the best alternative to focus groups, and that is the case in these two studies, as either of them could have been done using individual rather than group interviews. The difference between these two methods would have been greater for the first study, due to the need for a relatively large

N arising from the 2x2 design in the survey. The mechanics of collecting and analyzing well over 100 individual interviews would have been daunting indeed. We could have resolved this by interviewing only a subset of the survey participants, but such interviews would have complicated our design and limited the available data. The price we paid for not doing individual interviews was the lack of a continuous account of each caregiver's experiences, especially for the half of our sample who already had made the transition to placing their family members in formal care. As a step toward resolving this desire for more detailed data on families' continuous experiences, we have just completed doing follow-up individual interviews with 10 caregivers who made the transition from home-based to formal-care-based caregiving since the original study.

In the study on diagnosis seeking, the major advantage of group rather than individual interviews in such exploratory work was that they stimulated the thinking of the participants. In this case the caregivers tended to have a version of their diagnosis "story" that they were ready to tell, but often this story was reworked in comparison with the other stories in the group. For example, after hearing the accounts of other caregivers, it was common for participants to go back and amend their report of their family member's first symptom to something they had "forgotten all about until now." In this study, as in the previous one, an advantage of individual interviews would have been the ability to obtain greater detail on the history of each individual family. Note, however, that this detail would have come at the expense of collecting and analyzing essentially six times as many transcripts. In the present case, we were more interested in the overall comparison of cases with higher and lower symptom levels, rather than in detailed histories from individual families.

In both studies another advantage of working with individual interviews would have been to expand the range of caregivers we could reach. By interviewing them individually at times and locations that suited their convenience, we could have included caregivers who had trouble getting to a group meeting—for example, those with severe respite needs. In addition, in the second study, using groups led us to exclude several cases in which the medical record and nursing notes indicated that caregivers had problems such as substance abuse, intermittent psychiatric hospitalization, and lawsuits over custody of the family member with A.D. Even so, our groups revealed several instances in which factors related to "dysfunctional families" had a major impact on the timing of diagnosis, and we believe that area deserves further study. Thus individual interviews have an advantage over group interviews when some of the categories of participants are not good candidates for group discussions, as well as in the more general circumstance in which the participants have difficulty traveling to a researcher-designated meeting place.

OVERALL IMPLICATIONS

In the first study, much of the decision about which qualitative method to employ was determined by our earlier decision to pair a survey with qualitative data. This pairing made focus groups a particularly efficient and effective choice. Certainly the broader topic of differences between caregiving at home and in nursing homes could be studied by any of these methods; however, focus groups do have unique advantages for the combination of survey and qualitative data. It is also true, however, that a major reason we felt able to include the survey was because we knew it could be paired with the focus groups. Thus each of our decisions about methods influenced the other, as is inevitable in a complex project such as this.

In the second study, the major influence on the design was its exploratory objective. In addition, the fact that we wanted to compare those who had sought diagnosis in the presence of either more or less severe symptoms made it reasonable to assemble groups in each category and let them describe the elements of their shared experience. In addition, we envisioned this study as paving the way for a later project based on surveys of a similar population. Planning on a more quantitative approach in our subsequent research actually encouraged us to be more exploratory in the present project, as we knew that the value of the data in that latter project would depend on the insights from this one. Thus research design decisions are often not fully describable within the limits of a single study, as they may depend on the way that any one study fits within an ongoing series of interrelated investigations.

Making Design Decisions for Focus Groups

In discussing the design of research that uses focus groups, I have suggested that a typical project can be described in terms of four

Table 12.1 Design Dimensions for Focus Groups

Rules of Thumb Structure	First Study (Formal Care) Structure	Second Study (Diagnosis) Structure
Moderate to high in questioning strategy Moderate to high in group dynamics	Low to moderate in questioning strategy Low in group dynamics	Moderate to high in questioning strategy Moderate to high in group dynamics
Group Size	*Group Size*	*Group Size*
6-10 participants	4-8 participants	4-8 participants
Composition	*Composition*	*Composition*
Participants should be homogeneous Participants should be strangers	Participants were mixed on 2 dimensions Many participants were already acquainted	Participants were homogeneous Participants were strangers
Number of Groups	*Number of Groups*	*Number of Groups*
4-6 groups	30 groups	6 groups

rules of thumb: (a) groups are highly structured, (b) groups have 6-10 participants, (c) groups are composed of homogeneous strangers, and (d) the total project consists of 4-6 groups (Morgan, in press). The point is not, however, that these rules of thumb should govern the design of focus groups but that conscious decisions should be made about why the research will match or depart from the rule of thumb for each of these four dimensions. As Table 12.1 shows, the first study departed from the norm in several ways, while the second study nearly matched the typical pattern. The following section reviews the decisions that led to these two particular configurations.

STRUCTURE

The fundamental design issue with regard to the amount of structure in a focus group is the extent to which the researcher controls both the content of the questions and the group dynamics of the discussion. The decision about structure in the first study is particularly notable because that project departed from the rule of thumb by using groups that were relatively unstructured in both content and dynamics. The unstructured content meant that we provided the participants with a small number of relatively general questions that were intended to produce relatively lengthy and wide-ranging discussions. The unstructured dynamics meant that the member of the research team who met with each group did not actually "run" the group; instead, the groups were largely "self-managed" (Morgan, 1988).

The basic reason for selecting unstructured groups in this study was that we already had a highly structured view of the caregivers' experiences from the survey. To match that data with a more exploratory view, we began by asking the caregivers to discuss things that had made their caregiving either easier or harder for at least half of the available 45 minutes before turning to the question of how caregiving differed between care at home and in formal settings. As the study progressed, we moved to the second question somewhat earlier so that we could introduce several more specific issues at the end of the discussion. The reason for this shift toward more structure was the large number of groups we were interviewing. Once we had collected a sufficient volume of exploratory data, it was more effective to collect further data on specific topics. By placing these additional questions near the end of the interview, we assured a basic comparability across the experiences of those who participated in the earlier and later groups. This shift toward a more structured questioning strategy in the later groups also demonstrated the value of concurrent collection and analysis.

Our management of group dynamics remained unstructured throughout the first study. In particular each focus group had a member of the research staff who explained the goals of the discussion, posed the first question, and then moved aside from the table to take notes. The fact that the "moderator" was not present at the table meant that it was up to the group to conduct their own discussion. On rare occasions the group would direct questions about their task to the staff member; on still rarer occasions it was necessary for the staff member to refocus the group on the discussion topic. As the allotted time for a given question expired, the staff member would break gently into the discussion and provide the next topic.

The second study used a highly structured questioning strategy that was paired with a high degree of control over group dynamics. With regard to the questions, the guide we constructed began by asking about the earliest symptoms and worked forward in time to the contact with the specialized diagnostic unit that served as the recruitment source. Because we had a clear goal of determining what led our two categories of participants into diagnosis at different times, we used this "history-taking" format to ask questions about factors that influenced decision making at each step. Thus the more structured questioning strategy was based on a common set of experiences that could be probed for each participant, as well as a clear sense of what questions the research should address.

These groups were also relatively structured with regard to the moderator's role in managing group dynamics. The reason for this decision was our desire to get comparable data from the separate groups of caregivers with more and less impaired family members. In practice, this structure amounted to having predetermined probes that were intended to keep the discussion on track, as well as questions to those participants who did not volunteer answers. The tactic of directing questions to less verbal participants was used also to control any tendency of more active participants to dominate the discussion.

The differences in the kind of data that resulted from these two approaches to group structure were most apparent in the analysis phase of the research. The analysis was more time consuming in the first study because the participants in each group were able to cover whatever topics they wished in whatever order they wished. We reduced some of the work involved in coding such unstructured data through our commitment to using predetermined, content analytic code categories that matched our survey instruments. This commitment did not, of course, resolve the larger task of exploring topics that were not in the questionnaire. In the second study, we also used our questionnaire as a starting point in coding activities (e.g., the symptom checklist), but the largely exploratory nature of that study meant that more of the coding system had to be generated from the transcripts themselves. In the second study, this process was facilitated by the more structured nature of these groups, as we were able to compare what was said in response to each question across all of the groups. Overall, this linkage between the design of the focus groups and the analysis of the data they produced provides an important illustration of the kinds of planning that need to go into one's choices about not only group structure, but also each of the other design dimensions in Table 12.1.

GROUP SIZE

In both studies the size of the groups was somewhat smaller than the rule of thumb. This was due largely to recruitment constraints in each setting, although the nature of these constraints was quite different. The first study was influenced strongly by the fact that most of the data collection sessions utilized naturally occurring sites such as support groups and adult day-care centers. Under these circumstances a distinct uncertainty arose about the number of participants who would show up for each session. We knew from the beginning that we would be lucky if some of our sites produced as many as 6 participants, while others could easily generate more than 20. We thus decided to standardize on the low end of the size range and to run multiple, smaller groups at larger sites, setting 4 as a minimum size and 8 as a maximum. A further factor in the determination of group size for this study stemmed from our 2x2 design, based on home-based and formal-care-based caregivers and spouses and children. At the larger sites, we would examine the distribution of these characteristics to determine whether it would be possible to create homogeneous groups. For example, rather than simply dividing 12 participants into 2 groups of 6, we might split them 7 and 5 if the smaller group were "pure" with regard to one of our design categories.

In the second study the most important influence on the decision about group size was the limited number of participants available for the total study. The size of these groups was basically a function of the number of participants available divided by the number of groups desired. Even with these constraints, we were able to produce the data that we wanted by using a design that combined smaller groups with more structure in order to produce a large amount of preselected information from each participant. In both studies the key point is that design decisions often represent a compromise between the purposes for which one needs the data and other priorities imposed by the research setting.

GROUP COMPOSITION

Table 12.1 indicates that two major aspects of composition that had to be taken into account were whether the groups are homogeneous and whether the participants were acquainted previously. With regard to prior acquaintance, our ability to recruit strangers in both studies was determined almost entirely by our research sites. In the first study the use of naturally occurring research sites such as support groups ensured that some of the participants would be acquainted. Our recruitment processes in that study, however, also used mailing lists to bring in additional participants, so most groups contained both acquaintances and strangers. Interestingly, analysis of the discussions indicates a definite effort to include the strangers in the group. We speculate that this downplaying of prior acquaintance was partially due to the large number of support group participants in this study, as they maintained a norm of being open to strangers. This would not necessarily be the case with other recruitment bases. In the second study our use of medical records ensured that most participants would be strangers. The key issue is not, however, simply matching a rule of thumb; instead, it is making an informed design choice. In particular, strangers often have difficulty generating a discussion when they have a low level of shared involvement in a topic, but that was not a problem in this study.

In deciding about homogeneity, the question is always—homogeneous with regard to what criterion? In the first study, we screened to ensure that all the participants had major involvement in caring for a family member who had advanced impairments due to A.D. or a similar condition. Seen in this light, the participants were quite homogeneous. At another level, however, most groups contained a mix between home care and formal care and between spouses and children. Although it might have been desirable to have pure representations of our design categories (e.g., children with parents in formal care), this presentation would have been quite difficult because our naturally occurring research sites often contained an unpredictable mix of the four design categories.

The question that arises in this circumstance is an empirical one: What was the effect of mixing different categories of caregivers, as opposed to running perfectly matched groups? Fortunately we have the data to address this issue since we were able to sort out "pure groups" at some of the larger sites. Our final data thus consists of both "mixed" and "matched" groups, although the former clearly predominate. We are presently in the process of comparing the content in these different types of groups in order to move beyond our preliminary sense that mixing had relatively few effects.

In the second study the decision to create homogeneous groups of caregivers according to higher and lower levels of patient impairment was straightforward, since the major research question was how these two categories differed. If differences between these two sets of experiences truly did exist, then interacting with peers should do the most to reveal the shared experiences within each category. Overall, in this study and the previous one, our decisions about group composition reflected a reasonably comfortable compromise between the constraints posed by the setting and our research questions.

NUMBER OF GROUPS

In both studies, the decision on the number of groups was linked to considerations that already have been raised. In the first study, the need to recruit a large a number of participants for the survey and the desire to have a relatively small group size led to a total of 30 groups. Although this decision led to an unusually large number of groups, studies that use unstructured questioning strategies to produce data on the broader range of topics often require more groups to yield sufficient data on a given topic. In this case the advantage of running a larger number of unstructured groups resulted in the availability of reasonable amounts of data on doctor-caregiver relationships even though this was not a preplanned element of this study.

In the second study our goal of comparing caregivers who sought diagnosis in the presence of higher and lower levels of impairment was a major influence on our decision about the number of groups. The simplest rule of thumb is that the minimum number of groups in each category should equal that for a self-contained study of that category, namely four groups. As I have noted already, this was not possible because we were limited by the number of cases available and our desired group size. The result is that we had fewer groups in each sample segment than one would desire typically in a study devoted to that category alone. In practice this meant we concentrated on locating aspects of diagnosis seeking that were clearly different between caregivers with more and less impaired family members. Given the frankly exploratory nature of this study, the inability to characterize each category precisely or to detect small differences between the categories was not a major problem, but it would be a more severe limitation in a study that was intended to be definitive rather than exploratory.

SUMMARY

Looking across the four design dimensions for these two studies reveals the interconnectedness of the decisions that one must make in designing focus group research. In the real world these decisions cannot be made independently and then assembled in a "Tinkertoy fashion" into a completed design. Nor is the final design a pure application of methodological guidelines to the research question at hand, as one must always work within the constraints imposed by the research setting and such resources as time, money, and staff. But even these considerations are not sufficient to describe the process of making design decisions, as one also must take into account how the data will be analyzed. In the next section, I turn to questions about how the design of these studies affected the data that were available on doctor-caregiver relationships, along with a description of the analysis procedures for these data.

Analysis Decisions: Doctor-Caregiver Relationships

AVAILABLE DATA

In our report on the discussions of doctor-caregiver relationships in these studies (Morgan & Zhao, 1991), we distinguished two reasons for comparing these data sets. First, the separate studies tapped decisions that occurred in the earlier and later phases of caregiving, so a comparison could reveal substantive differences in the factors that affected this relationship across the longer career of A.D. caregiving. Second, because the two studies both used focus groups but used different approaches to locating and interviewing the caregivers, we can be more certain that results that were consistent across the studies were not due to unique features of either research design. In other words, differences in the research design could have produced differences in the data on doctor-caregiver relationships in each study.

In the first study, one portion of the data on doctors came from the unstructured discussion of what makes caregiving easier and what makes it harder. Because each group was free to pursue its own definition of what made things easier or harder, some groups contained extensive discussions of doctors, while others had hardly any. This difference allowed us to put the topic of doctor-caregiver relationships in perspective by seeing that it occurred often enough to be of interest to these caregivers but not so often that it was a dominant issue. Another portion of the data on doctor-caregiver relationships in this study came from later groups, in which we asked global questions about the caregivers' contacts with doctors, nurses, and other health care professionals. In these sessions extensive discussion often occurred regarding doctor-caregiver relationships, indicating that these caregivers did have readily available responses to this topic, once it was raised. Comparing these two ways of eliciting the data, we found no differences between the kinds of things that were mentioned when members of the group spontaneously introduced the topic versus when we did.

Practically speaking, this research design had both positive and negative effects on our ability to address questions about the doctor-caregiver relationship. On the positive side, one of the advantages of these less structured focus groups was that the information about doctor-caregiver relationships came to us with minimal direction from the researchers, so we can determine the range of things that interested caregivers from their point of view rather than our own. On the negative side, the fact that doctor-caregiver relationships were only a secondary topic of this study meant that we did not collect a notably large volume of data on this topic. Further, the data that we got were not systematic in nature.

One particular advantage of engaging the participants' perspective was that it allowed new research topics to emerge. In fact we first became interested in doctor-caregiver relationships while working with codes that captured mentions of emotional burden. We were surprised by how many of the mentions of emotional burden involved negative interactions with doctors and just how vehement some of these remarks were. One direct result of this discovery was that we made the doctor-caregiver relationship a more prominent feature of our next study.

Because the second study emphasized depth over breadth, the doctor-caregiver relationship was one area for which we had a large amount of data. In line with our "history-taking" emphasis, we asked first about contacts with physicians and then about the role that doctors played in the ultimate referral to the expert diagnostic unit. Thus we were still able to produce the data on the specific topic of doctor-caregiver relationships while giving only minimal direction with regard to our interest in this issue.

Once again this strategy had its positive and negative aspects. On the positive side was the large volume of data that we produced on doctor-caregiver relationships without specifically cuing the participants about our interest in this topic. On the negative side we heard only about aspects of this relationship that occurred within the narrow framework of decisions about diagnosis seeking. Also these data were limited by the specific source that we used to generate the sample. In particular we cannot say anything about cases that did not proceed to expert diagnosis or that did so within some totally different framework, such as a prepaid plan or the Veterans Administration system. In addition this was a relatively elite unit, and this affected the kind of cases that it attracted.

Overall, the two studies did a reasonable job of compensating for each other's weaknesses. The fact that the first study produced a relatively small volume of data was matched by the large amount of discussion on doctor-caregiver relationships in the second study. And the limitations in the second study that were due to concentrating only on diagnosis and using a limiting sampling source were matched by the unstructured nature of the first study and its diverse sample sources. Taken as a set, the two studies met many of the methodological objections that would apply to either one taken alone.

ANALYSIS STRATEGY

The approach we used in comparing the data from the two studies was to apply a single content analytic coding system to both data sets. Although considerable debate has occurred over the meaning of *qualitative content analysis* (Altheide, 1987; Berelson, 1952; Mostyn, 1985; Starosta, 1984), we take it as a hallmark of this approach that the codes are developed from the data. We used a template analysis style (see Chapter 5). We began the development of our coding system by working with the manifest content codes (the template) that we had used in an initial round of coding. In both data sets, we had included codes that captured each mention of health professionals, along with an additional code if the mention contained a positive or negative evaluation. We used the search procedure in *THE ETHNOGRAPH* (Seidel, Kjolseth, & Seymour, 1988) software to print out each transcript segment in either study that contained a clearly positive or negative mention of health professionals and used these passages to develop our code categories.

Next, two analysts (Morgan and Zhao) divided the set of segments from the first, less structured study, and each separately applied an open coding approach (Strauss & Corbin, 1990) to half of the material. We used the less structured data for this purpose because the goal at this point was to capture as many themes as possible in this material; therefore, we started with the broader range of topics that were discussed in the first study. Comparing the coding of two independent analysts also helped ensure that we would consider a broad range of possibilities.

In order to group the open codes into themes, we entered all of our codes into a powerful outlining program on a microcomputer, using only a division between positive and negative mentions at the first stage. Working within first the positive and then the negative mentions, we grouped together all codes that we agreed were virtually identical in content. We then put tentative labels on these thematic groups and used the outlining software to rearrange the themes into a preliminary coding system that placed related groups of codes under larger headings.

At each stage of this process, we worked on the positive and negative mentions separately, so we actually produced a two-part coding system. Although our ultimate intention was to produce one set of code categories for both positive and negative mentions, we accomplished this by unifying the two separate code systems. The advantage of starting with separate systems was that it alerted us to themes that the caregivers discussed in an almost entirely negative or positive fashion. Because contrasts between positive and negative aspects of the doctor-caregiver relationship were of particular interest to us, we were able to construct a final coding system that allowed for this possibility.

To build the final coding system, I took the tentative codes and tested them on a subset of the segments from the second, more structured data set. Based on this testing, we first expanded and refined the initial theme set so that it would describe both data sets, and then we consolidated the positive and negative themes into a single system. This system assigned a three-part code to each relevant segment. The first portion of the code distinguished the substantive content; the second portion noted which category of provider was involved; the third portion of the code captured whether the particular combination of substantive content and provider was mentioned positively or negatively. In general, such a three-part coding system, based on mentions of actions, actors, and evaluations, seems to have promise as a generic basis for the development of more specific coding systems.

Although the code categories for the type of provider and for positive or negative content were straightforward, the coding system for the substantive content was moderately complex. One group of codes was related to mentions of the more interpersonal aspects of doctor-caregiver relationships (i.e., the doctor's attitude, the relationship between the doctor and the A.D. care receiver, etc.). Another group of codes was related to aspects of the care that was provided (i.e., the doctor's competence, the quality of advice and information, etc.). For this second group of substantive codes, whenever the mention involved a specific quality-of-care issue, the code reflected what this issue was (e.g., ability to diagnose, advice about home care, etc.).

In designing the coding system, we erred on the side of creating more codes than we might actually be able to fill, so that we would be sure to have information on any category that the caregivers mentioned often enough to merit attention. We collapsed code categories after the final counting so that we preserved any category that occurred at least 10 times in one of the two studies. The result was a set of six substantive topics (plus six specific quality-of-care issues) and four categories of providers, along with our fundamental distinction between positive and negative mentions.

The next step was to apply these codes to the material in the original transcript segments. Given that the manifest content coding simply had located passages involving mentions of health professionals, our more detailed coding often involved the application of multiple code sets to a single passage. For example, one transcript segment might contain not only several descriptions of contacts with a community physician, but also a comparison of this relationship to subsequent contacts with a specialist. Thus the number of codes that we ultimately generated was much larger than the number of transcript segments with which we started.

We summarized our analysis through a comparison of positive and negative mentions across the two studies. For example, we found that the caregivers were more likely to mention specialists positively and community physicians negatively, and this difference was stronger in the study on diagnosis seeking than in the study on moves to formal care, although it was clearly present in both studies. A finding such as this illustrates the strength of having the two data sets based on different samples and different designs. On the one hand, it would be possible to dismiss such a finding from the study on diagnosis because many of these caregivers had sought the expert unit as a direct result of their dissatisfaction with community physicians. On the other hand, the fact that the diagnosis study simply generated a stronger version of a pattern that was present also in the community-based study gives us more faith that this was a reliable result and not an artifact of a particular research design.

In a quasi-statistical content analysis, the location of such "findings" would be the endpoint in the analysis, but in our template-style content analysis, it provided a set of empirical patterns that we then pursued in the transcripts. Given the richness of our qualitative data, we were not satisfied by merely demonstrating these were the patterns in the data; we also wished to give an account of why these patterns occurred. To do so, we reexamined the transcript segments involved in the production of strong contrasts between positive and negative mentions to determine the sources of these differences. At the same time, we also searched for quotations that provided clear illustrations of these points and used them to illustrate our arguments. Overall, our analysis strategy fits well with the general approach that Tesch (1990) describes: first a decontextualization of our selected subject matter in the coding and counting phase of our analysis, and then a recontextualization of this material in our efforts to account for why we found the patterns we did.

Conclusions

In many ways the core argument in this chapter has been that research design is a crucial issue not only in focus groups but also in qualitative research more generally. Although this argument is not particularly novel (cf. Marshall & Rossman, 1989), it is still not entirely uncontroversial. It is important, however, not to confuse the qualitative sense of design as reasoned choices between clearly understood alternatives with the experimental design view that the researcher must specify all research procedures before the beginning of data collection and follow them in an unalterable course. Virtually all qualitative research is based on a set of initial and emergent design choices.

It is certainly possible to design research, using focus groups, that emphasizes a more emergent approach than we used in these two studies. In particular, one could begin with groups that were largely unstructured in both questioning strategy and group dynamics and then use these discussions as the basis for further groups that pursued emergent issues in a more structured fashion. One could also purposely vary other elements of the design to find out whether different aspects of a topic came up in discussions among strangers or acquaintances, in homogeneous or heterogeneous groups, or in large or small groups. For some research questions, the appropriate approach to design is indeed to prespecify the various dimensions of the data gathering and analysis strategy; for other research questions, a more open-ended approach is appropriate.

For focus groups, social scientists and health researchers only recently have begun to explore the issues involved in designing research that uses this method. Even in this brief time, self-conscious methodological experimentation already has become a hallmark of our approach to focus groups (McQuarrie, 1990). In the long run, however, such methodological experimentation will be of little value if it is not tied to practical application, and that has been the overriding goal of the present chapter.

PART VI

Summary

13 Qualitative Research: Perspectives on the Future

STEPHEN J. ZYZANSKI
IAN R. McWHINNEY
ROBERT BLAKE, JR.
BENJAMIN F. CRABTREE
WILLIAM L. MILLER

Introduction

What does it all mean? We have built our craft and reached the edge of the river. We are now ready to slip into the mainstream of primary care research. But how will we find the water? How does qualitative research fit into the present and future realities of primary care?

In this summary chapter, qualitative research in primary care is examined from three different perspectives. Stephen Zyzanski looks at qualitative research through the eyes of family systems theory, psychometrics, and the dominant research paradigm. Ian McWhinney shares his perspective as a family physician, academic leader, and visionary. Robert Blake reveals his personal journey and his perspectives as a family physician, as an epidemiologist, and as a journal editor.

A Psychometrician's Perspective

The approach I took in assessing qualitative methods was a pragmatic one. I looked carefully at the details of conducting qualitative

231

research. My aim was to point out the practical issues so that investigators would have a good sense of what was involved. My approach to assessing these methods is to evaluate their strengths and weaknesses as to general approach, basic design, the nature of the data, and analysis.

GENERAL APPROACH

Turning first to the overall general approach, three strengths come to mind. First, qualitative methods are the methods of choice for investigating certain types of problems such as building rapport for sensitive topics, in-depth inquiries, and investigating new areas. Second, as Miller and Crabtree (Chapter 1) have pointed out, quantitative researchers often research the wrong problem or research a problem that is not worth solving. It also has been said that clinicians ask the right questions, wrong, and researchers the wrong questions, right. In many ways qualitative research attempts to set this straight—to ask the right questions, right. Third, many quantitative researchers know very little about qualitative methods. For example, I was not aware of 16 strategies for purposive sampling. Thus a lot of knowledge exists concerning these techniques for us to learn. Unfortunately, many quantitative researchers think qualitative research is the inclusion of an open-ended question or two in a study. This book illustrates what a simplistic notion that is.

One major weakness of qualitative research in general concerns the confusing vocabulary and conceptual tradition-based jargon used by the various qualitative methods. For example, what are in vivo or axial codings, and what constitutes exegetical operations? Many of the approaches also seem to blend together and are hard to follow, especially by those not trained in these specific traditions.

DESIGNS

Qualitative research designs are best characterized as unique and flexible. They are evolving constantly throughout the research process. One concurrently frames and reframes not only the research question, but the sample selection, the analysis, and the theory construction. This flexibility maximizes the likelihood of gathering data rich in detail. Still it is often difficult to communicate the iterative nature of the qualitative research process. Such methods as participant observation and hermeneutics demand a lot of the researcher in terms of time and energy. Historical research is heavily dependent on the experience and skill of the historian. Thus qualitative research designs are often very labor intensive, intrusive, and require a substantial time commitment from those involved.

The specific content of qualitative data is very different from quantitative data with words, behaviors, actions, and practices serving as the data. Some forms are highly specialized, such as participant observation field notes. Such notes contain the all-important reflective part that includes analysis, method, conflicts, clarifications, and also frame of mind. In hermeneutics, both verbal text and actions are analyzed for meaning. But this mixture of verbal and nonverbal behavior could make it difficult to identify common themes across modalities.

Quantitative measures often wash out the gestalt and richness of data derived from qualitative sources. For example, the coronary-prone Type A behavior pattern started with detailed clinical observations from multiple settings. The psychologist who developed the Type A scale was a participant observer who took excellent field notes, which he converted into items and then into scales. In the quantification process, a lot of the richness was lost or could not be measured —for example, the stylistics of a Type A's response. Qualitative approaches therefore preserve the rich detail and thereby generate more themes than corresponding quantitative approaches. Still, with many themes it may be difficult to tell which are highly redundant and which are unique.

Sample size recommendations for qualitative research tend to be small, 6-8 subjects for homogeneous samples and 12-20 for maximum variations or when testing for disconfirmation. Sample size is not the determinant of research significance in a qualitative study; the major concern is with information richness. Still the small sample size and the likelihood that it is a biased sample can cause major problems in establishing the trustworthiness of the data. It also may cause difficulties in getting articles accepted for publication in journals accustomed to larger sample quantitative studies.

DATA

Qualitative data collection techniques are as varied as their methods. Logs, diaries, jottings, journals, memos, notes, field notes, and reflective notes are just some of the procedures used. In historical research and participant observation, the researcher is the main instrument for both data collection and analysis.

Most of these techniques, however, are both time and labor intensive. The Long Interview, for example, takes about 1 year to develop, administer, and analyze data from 8 subjects. Participant observation requires prolonged periods of intensive social interaction between the researcher and subjects and can take more than a year to complete. The reflective part takes about 3-6 hours to record for each hour of participant observation. Thus this level of involvement makes it very difficult for researchers to participate in multiple qualitative projects simultaneously.

Sampling of subjects in qualitative studies tends to be purposive rather than random. The aim is to illuminate the study question, and the concern is with information richness, not representativeness. Kuzel (Chapter 2) has identified four purposive sampling strategies relevant for primary care research. These include maximum variation sampling, critical case sampling, theory-based sampling, and selecting confirming and disconfirming cases. Kuzel also provided an outline of characteristics of qualitative sampling that was very useful. It included (a) a flexible sampling design, (b) sample units selected serially, (c) sample continuously adjusted by concurrent development of theory, (d) selection to the point of redundancy, and (e) a search for negative cases for greater breadth and strength.

Overall, the purposive sampling strategies seem to be well thought through. A major concern would have to be the number of subjects needed to reach a point of redundancy. Given the considerable effort involved, one quickly could reach a stage at which available resources would make it impossible to continue.

The equivalent terms for *reliability* and *validity* for qualitative data are *credibility, dependability,* and *confirmability.* These are generally verified by using triangulation, reflexivity, and independent audits. Where convergence exists in understanding between different methods, the data are viewed as being more reliable and valid. Brody (Chapter 10) describes five methods for seeking trustworthiness in qualitative research. They are triangulation, thick description, reflexivity, member checking, and searching for disconfirmations. These methods bear strong similarities to quantitative methods for establishing reliability and validity.

Some problems inherent in these approaches include inter-observer variations and observer bias, especially for techniques in which the researcher is both data collector and data analyst. Also, as one makes samples more homogeneous, the reduced variability generally tends to reduce reliability. Similarly, a small number of descriptors for a theme will generally be less reliable than a large number, and a thick description will be more reliable still. Triangulation is a form of replication. Still, when this is not achieved, the implication that observer bias and unreliability contributed to this lack of triangulation cannot be ignored.

ANALYSIS

Data analysis for qualitative research is not a linear but an iterative process. Analysis starts shortly after the first data are collected and proceeds simultaneously with data collection. Computer programs now exist that make the analysis tasks much easier. Many word processors have data management functions that can do the essential tasks of data entry, data identification, and data manipulation. Finally, special-purpose software is also commercially available for text retrieval, data base management, and a variety of analysis functions. These are essential programs since qualitative research often results in large volumes of verbal text that must be coded, sorted, interpreted, and summarized, using text-based analysis techniques.

As useful as these programs are, qualitative data is labor intensive to analyze. Transcribing tapes is time consuming. The software used to do it can be expensive and can require significant amounts of training time. When the researcher is the instrument of analysis, the process requires looking at one's self as intensely as one looks at the events observed. This is a complex process of assessing one's own bias. Bogdewic (Chapter 3) said it well: "Who you are and what you see cannot be separated, only understood."

Although generalizability is not an aim of qualitative research, I still worry about the validity of themes based on very small sample sizes. Themes that apply to a wide spectrum of patients would have considerable utility. Since qualitative research cannot avoid observer bias, one also worries about how the bias enters the process. Would another qualitative researcher come up with the same insights? Interpretations?

Sample response bias can be another problem. In Stewart's (Chapter 8) study, patients were asked whether audiotapes of their visits could be made, and 47% refused. Data from only the compliers are likely to provide us with a limited picture. Finally, in Willms et al.'s (Chapter 11) study, only 20% of the audiotapes were transcribed because it was too costly. These examples illustrate the financial and labor investment involved in analyzing such data.

CONCLUSION

In conclusion, I find much that is attractive in qualitative research. To study and construct complex family variables is difficult. I believe that we can learn to study and measure complex family variables better through the use of qualitative techniques. But I also think the best way to proceed at this point is first to use a multimethod approach, a mixture of qualitative and quantitative methods. In this way we can gain valuable experience with selected qualitative methods. Second, since qualitative training is intensive and goes well beyond the acquisition of clinical interviewing skills, selected individuals should receive formal training in the qualitative methods best suited for primary care research. The recommendations of Miller and Crabtree are important starting points here, and so is the material from this book. Even for these methods, however, important questions remain. For example, can some methods be shortened and still provide valid results? Who should be trained in qualitative methods? Should they be experienced clinicians or young junior faculty? And last, it initially may be very difficult to obtain research funding for qualitative research designs that evolve as you go. Basically you are saying to the reviewers, "Trust me to do it right." Reviewers generally have a difficult time approving studies that rely heavily on "to be done" issues.

One needs also to keep in mind that these methods are time and labor intensive, not easily generalized, and currently not widely accepted in medicine. The plethora of terms is a further barrier to comprehending the methods and findings of qualitative research.

Finally I like to think of the end result of a qualitative study not as an end but as a beginning. I anticipate quantitative follow-up for many of the discoveries of qualitative research. I envision quantitative measurement applied to important themes and many new concepts tested for predicted validity. From these efforts finally may come the tools to conduct valid family-based research.

A Family Physician's Perspective

Medicine is one of those sciences valued both for its application to human problems and for the intrinsic interest of its subject matter. As an applied science, it uses knowledge from a number of independent sciences, including physics, chemistry, anatomy, physiology, and pharmacology. Its own status as an independent science, however, rests on a body of knowledge gathered by observation of sick people. This is a descriptive science, based on the observation and recording of symptoms, signs, and pathological appearances, and on the ordering of these observations into categories with explanatory and predictive power. As an applied science, medicine uses experimental methods to evaluate its techniques. These methods rely heavily on quantification. As a descriptive science, medicine uses the methods of the taxonomist, and these make very little use of quantification. At most it involves the counting of categories and their components, and this comes only after the taxonomists have done their work of describing a species or a disease.

I say this to make the point that **qualitative research is not new to medicine.** On the contrary, medicine has been built on it. Our clinical categories often are based on descriptions of qualities—color, texture, shape, smell, rhythm, pitch, and so on. Sweet diabetes (mellitus) was recognized because Thomas Willis tasted the urine in 1674. Roseola infantum is recognized by its color, and a pleural effusion by its dullness when percussed. I will call this qualitative research, Q1. Q1 has concentrated mainly on the physical phenomena of illness, either reported by the patient or observed by the physician and pathologist. The personal context of the illness, its meaning for the patient, has been excluded. Q1 has followed the dominant scientific paradigm by regarding medical scientists as detached observers acquiring impersonal knowledge of processes external to themselves. Q1 medical science, for all its benefit to us, has been a dehumanized science. This book is an invitation to medicine to move on to another phase, Q2, to become one of the sciences of the human spirit. It would be unwise for medicine to refuse this invitation. As A. N. Whitehead (1948) wrote: "There is a nemesis . . . which waits upon those who deliberately avoid avenues of knowledge" (p. 17).

LEVELS OF KNOWLEDGE

When we move from knowledge of the external world to knowledge of the meaning of experience, we move up a step in the hierarchy of knowledge. The traditional wisdom of all philosophies and religions recognizes three levels of knowledge: the physical, the mental, and the transcendental or contemplative. In the language of the Christian tradition, these are the three ways to knowledge: the eye of the flesh, the eye of the mind, and the eye of contemplation. For knowledge of the external world, we use our five senses—the eye of the flesh. Knowledge of the inner lives of others, however, can be gained only by a dialogue between people, in the course of which the meaning of utterances and actions are explored, refined, and verified—the eye of the mind. The eye of the mind is concerned with what Wilber (1983) calls "the nature, structure, and meaning of intelligibilia"—language, logic, value, ideas, images, and symbols. It is true that our five senses can help us in this form of inquiry. In trying to understand the meaning of a gesture, for example, we can observe the behavior of people making the gesture in different contexts. We can make inferences about its meaning by comparing how the gesture is used in different contexts. We may understand the gesture intuitively because it is a gesture we make ourselves. To verify its meaning, however, we have at some stage to enter into a dialogue with people making the gesture. Engel (1980) uses the example of the "giving up" gesture to illustrate the scientific nature of the knowledge of patients' behavior. What he does not go on to say is that we are talking here about a different form of inquiry from that conventionally understood as scientific, a form in which the subject matter is intelligibilia. The differences in these two forms are not those of rigor; they are equally rigorous, though obviously having different canons of verification.

In intersubjective inquiry, the main research instrument is the investigator herself or himself. Just as investigators in an empirical science have to learn the use of their instruments, both material and conceptual, so those in qualitative inquiry have to prepare themselves rigorously for the work. According to the ancient *principle of adequatio,* a field of knowledge is open only to those who are prepared to receive it. The observer of the external world must train the senses; the inquirer into the mental-phenomenological world, as Wilber calls it, must train the inner person. This training requires rigorous self-examination, as well as the mastery of interpersonal skills and techniques of text analysis.

An awareness of the different levels of knowledge, and the avenue appropriate to each level, is crucial for an understanding of mental-phenomenological inquiry. The levels, however, should not be looked on as strictly demarcated from each other. I have mentioned already that direct observation can contribute to an understanding of human behavior. Even quantification and formalization are not limited to the first level. Answers to questions about the meaning of experience can be scored and counted.

A PATIENT WITH MACULAR DEGENERATION

To exemplify some of these points, consider an article by Dr. Stetten (1981), describing his experience of progressive loss of vision and the medical care he received:

> Through all of these years and despite many encounters with skilled and experienced professionals, no ophthalmologist has at any time suggested any devices that might be of assistance to me. No ophthalmologist has mentioned any of the many ways in which I could stem the deterioration in the quality of my life. Fortunately, I have discovered a number of means whereby I have helped myself, and the purpose of this essay is to call the attention of the ophthalmological world to some of these devices and, courteously but firmly, to complain of what appears to be the ophthalmologist's attitude: "We are interested in vision but have little interest in blindness." (p. 458)

Although the physicians he saw were experts in their field and skilled clinicians, they showed no interest in or knowledge of the devastating experience he was living through. How could these physicians have gained this kind of knowledge? What kind of research could have furnished it?

In diagnosing macular degeneration, the physician uses knowledge derived from medical science, much of it qualitative. First is the early history of some impairment of vision. This history is obtained by doctor and patient entering into a dialogue about the patient's sensations. The result is a qualitative description of the patient's experience, arrived at by a person-to-person process. This description is often referred to as subjective data, as contrasted with the objective data gained by the use of sensory perception. I think this description is an error. The data about a person's experience of loss of vision, verified intersubjectively and verifiable by different observers, has an objective existence independent of both doctor and patient.

Next is the knowledge gained from examination of the fundus. This knowledge is described as objective, which is sometimes taken to mean "impersonal." Yet the person of the observer always enters into the knowledge. An ophthalmologist usually "sees" more in the fundus than the internist or family physician. The knowledge gained through our senses is influenced by the training of our perceptions. Like our knowledge of the patient's experience, it is both subjective and objective. Having obtained a history and examined the fundus, the physician can map the visual fields. Here again the knowledge gained depends partly on interpretation. The point at which the object ceases to be seen is recorded when observer and patient have agreed that this point has been reached. This agreement is a personal judgment on the part of both.

The knowledge gained so far enables the clinician to diagnose the patient's problem as macular degeneration. Because other physicians have studied the pathology of the retina and have followed patients' loss of vision for a period of years, the physician can make inferences about what is happening in the retina and about the prognosis. Note that these observations on the pathology and natural history of the disease are largely qualitative.

So far, then, medical knowledge has thrown a good deal of light on the patient's condition. It has, for example, enabled the physician to predict the course and outcome, and perhaps, by intervention, to arrest its progress. It has done so by a process of abstraction. From the patient's total experience, it has abstracted data on visual loss and the appearance of the retina. The abstraction makes it possible to generalize the knowledge to all patients with the condition. In this case, however, it was little help to the patient. Knowing his diagnosis and prognosis did not help him prepare for this dreaded experience. To help the patient in this way requires in the physician a different kind of knowledge—a knowledge of what it is like to go blind. Since we are talking about the meaning of a human experience, this knowledge cannot be gained or validated through our sensory perceptions alone, as can be done with the appearance of the fundus.

We could try quantitative methods in this search for meaning, but they are unlikely to get us very far. We could, for example, devise a quality-of-life questionnaire and index. This questionnaire would give us a quality-of-life score at different stages of the illness and in different groups of patients. We could quantify the helpfulness of various resources: "On a scale of 1 to 5 rate the helpfulness of the following: talking books, large type books, Braille books." I suspect we would look at the results and say to ourselves, "How does that help us care for this patient who is going blind?" For this we need much deeper insight into the meaning of experience, and this can be gained only person-to-person. I have said already that the person of the knower enters into all types of knowledge, even knowledge we think of as objective. Participation by the knower in the search for knowledge, however, occurs in degrees. In the science of human experience, the participation is at its highest. As Michael Polanyi (1962) said, "As we ascend to higher manifestations of life, we have to exercise ever more personal faculties—a more far-reaching participation of the knower" (p. 347).

The meaning of human experience, moreover, is unlikely to be universal. The meaning of blindness probably will vary with age, sex, occupation, education, intelligence, culture, and so on. Common factors in the experience may exist, but powerful generalizations are an unlikely outcome of this kind of research. We are sometimes asked, "How can you generalize from a small sample?" This question misses the point. The purpose of qualitative research is explanation and understanding, not prediction. Generalization requires abstraction, and we have deliberately eschewed abstraction in the interests of enriching our knowledge. Abstraction leaves out the context, and we have chosen deliberately to take the context into account.

Qualitative research enriches our knowledge of particulars rather than giving us large generalizations. In the hierarchy of sciences, those that produce generalizations tend to be placed at the top and valued more highly than sciences whose generalizations are more limited. As Gorovitz and MacIntyre (1976) have observed, this is entirely a matter of value. A mechanistic, technological culture like ours will place a higher value on knowledge that gives us power, over knowledge that gives us wisdom. But as William James (1958) said: "[A] large acquaintance with particulars often makes us wiser than the possession of abstract formulas, however deep" (p. ix).

Having said this, generalizations can be made from qualitative research, though they are not the lawlike generalizations we associate with deductive scientific methods. In her study of dying patients,

Kübler-Ross (1969) evolved a typology of responses—the stages of dying. This typology helped bring together her observations, make them accessible to us, and give us a language to describe them. On the other hand, it was misunderstood by some people who treated the stages of dying as a law of life, a process through which all patients should be encouraged to pass.

The knowledge we gain from qualitative research enriches our imagination. When we look at Stetten's experience, what strikes us is the poverty of imagination shown by his doctors. They seemed unable to picture for themselves the experience he was living through. To be a healer for a person faced with a devastating illness requires imagination.

The sciences of the spirit speak to a different part of us than the sciences of nature. They answer different questions; they give us a different kind of knowledge. Each is appropriate for its purpose, but we must not expect one to fulfill the purposes of the other. If our need is for meaning, then we need a science of the spirit; a science of nature will not help us.

A Family Physician/Epidemiologist Editor's Perspective

Providers of primary health care confront a variety of clinical challenges in their day-to-day work. In the process of addressing these challenges, they collect and assess information from an array of sources and engage in a complex cognitive and social process of analysis, integration, synthesis and communication in an effort to meet health care needs. Primary care providers draw on the products of the research traditions identified by Miller and Crabtree in Chapter 1. Clearly the application of research strategies encompassed in the experimental style and survey style has yielded knowledge of great value to patient care in the primary care setting. These styles are what come to mind when most primary care providers think of clinical research.

Through a complementary mix of theory, methods, and illustrative examples, the contributors to this volume have identified the many ways in which qualitative research models may be of value to primary care practitioners. Many of the questions that challenge such providers on a day-to-day basis are not amenable to solution by epidemiologic or quantitative strategies. Epidemiology is very helpful in identifying hypertension as a risk factor for cardiovascular disease and in demonstrating the efficacy of antihypertensive medications. Epidemiology is of much less value in explaining why a hypertensive patient does not comply with therapeutic recommendations. Quantitative methods are relatively impotent in elucidating the complex confluence of psychological, cultural, and social factors that leads a person to seek medical attention for a particular problem at a particular time from a particular health professional. Patient noncompliance and health-seeking behavior are just two of the many important primary care issues that are amenable to qualitative research.

The discussions of underlying theory and conceptual frameworks and the descriptions of qualitative methods contained in this book suggest parallels between the processes of qualitative investigation and the processes of primary care. Several contributors have emphasized that qualitative research does not involve the imposition of a specified design structure on the study situation or material. Rather the design emerges from their work in a complex process of discovery, which is iterative, recursive, and circular. This process is well illustrated in Addison's (Chapter 6) description of his study of residents and his "flash of clarity" regarding survival as an organizing theme in their professional lives. Similarly, in approaching patients with undifferentiated complaints and illnesses, primary care providers frequently employ an unstructured circular approach that is sensitive to emergent information and themes. The traditional medical sequence of history, physical examination, and laboratory investigation is frequently modified and truncated in response to the unfolding patient narrative. Thus flexibility and adaptability characterize both the work of the primary provider in patient care and the work of the qualitative researcher in the processes of discovery and interpretation.

Other similarities exist between qualitative research and primary care. In many forms of qualitative inquiry, the investigator serves as a research instrument, becoming immersed in the phenomena under study. Similarly the primary care physician is involved intimately in a relationship with the patient, and this relationship may be a major component of the therapeutic intervention. In contrast to the epidemiologist who is distanced from the study subjects, the qualitative researcher and the primary care provider are irrevocably entwined in the webbing of action and meaning.

Given some degree of synergism between primary care and qualitative research, why is this research paradigm not highly valued by many primary care providers, particularly physicians? The explanation for this apparent paradox involves the dominant research paradigm in medicine. This way of thinking about discovery and the pursuit of knowledge is quantitative, reductionistic, and rationalistic. Emphasis is placed on precise measurement—counting events and persons, numerical scores, aggregation, comparison of groups, and statistical analyses. Complex phenomena and behaviors are conceptualized and defined as variables to be measured, manipulated, and analyzed to reveal some generalizable truth.

In some respects this paradigm and the ensuing research models have served medicine and the patients it seeks to help well. The paradigm, however, has exerted a very pervasive, controlling influence on the thinking of many health care providers about science and what constitutes legitimate scientific inquiry and methodology. The standards of quality and credibility espoused by the prevailing paradigm are applied frequently to qualitative research in a way that devalues and discredits that research. Many primary care providers thus have a very limited appreciation of the potential of qualitative research strategies to assist them in their care of patients. This book should go far in removing such limitations.

Several of the common concerns expressed by primary care providers about qualitative research are addressed directly by the material in this book. Qualitative research is criticized frequently as lacking rigor, as being subjective rather than objective, as producing "soft" results, and as lacking generalizability beyond the individuals and circumstances of the study. These criticisms are based on assumptions and conceptualizations that define major fundamental differences between qualitative approaches and quantitative approaches to research.

The issue of generalizability is raised frequently in critiques of qualitative research. In epidemiology, generating a sample that is representative of some larger population to which the findings will be extrapolated is an important goal. The basic concepts of generalizability and representativeness, however, are challenged by the theoretical underpinnings of qualitative research. Generalizability and representativeness imply a single reality that is independent of context and that applies in most or all circumstances. This notion of reality is rejected by most of the theory and conceptual frameworks that underlie qualitative inquiry. Rather than a single reality that exists in all circumstances and contexts, much qualitative research is based on the view that multiple realities exist. A frequent question posed by a qualitative researcher is, Whose reality is this? In Willms et al.'s (Chapter 11) study of the health promotion activities of family practice physicians, Dr. Dyck's reality regarding the dangers of cigarette smoking may differ dramatically from the reality of his patient who smokes to reduce stress.

The qualitative researcher is not particularly bothered by a lack of generalizability. He or she is under no illusion that his or her observations and interpretations necessarily apply to other persons, events, or contexts. Rather he or she endeavors to construct as thick and detailed a description as possible of his or her particular setting and circumstances so that others who encounter his or her description can determine its possible applicability to their setting and circumstances. While epidemiology seeks the logic of generalizability, qualitative research acknowledges the possibility of concept applicability or transferability but makes no claim that this necessarily occurs. The logic of concept applicability should certainly not be alien to the experiences of primary care physicians. Physicians do not care for samples of patients who are selected randomly from some larger population. Rather they care for patients who have particular demographic, social, and cultural characteristics that significantly influence the illnesses they experience, their interpretations of and behavioral responses to their illnesses, and their acceptance of treatment. Thus epidemiological findings, no matter how generalizable to some referent population, should be subjected to the filter of local realities before being applied to a specific practice setting. Similarly the extent to which Addison's (Chapter 6) finding that survival is an organizing theme for a group of residents is applicable to any other group of residents can be determined only on an individual basis by those involved in a particular residency drama.

The closely related objection that qualitative research lacks rigor, is subjective, and yields "soft" information can be considered also in the light of conceptualizations, descriptions, and analyses provided in this book. The notion of rigor in scientific inquiry has been addressed comprehensively by Ratcliffe and Gonzales-del-Valle (1988). In general, rigor in scientific investigation is heavily determined by the standards, criteria, and rules created within the prevailing quantitative, rationalistic paradigm. Thus the extent to which studies are considered rigorous is determined by the extent to which perceived sources of random and systematic error are controlled or minimized. Rigor is defined by adherence to preestablished protocols of methodologic conduct and by compliance with rules of evidence. Rigor is achieved as the researcher moves from an attitude of subjectivity to an attitude of objectivity in relation to the phenomena and material being studied.

No doubt exists that if rigor is defined in terms of quantitation, control of extraneous factors, and objectivity, most qualitative research will fail the test of rigor. These criteria for rigor, however, place undue constraints on the scientific pursuit of new knowledge, insights, and understanding. Does not scientific rigor exist in the elaborate processes of qualitative inquiry described by the contributors to this book? Bogdewic's detailed description of participant observation, Crabtree and Miller's description of the template approach to text analysis, Morgan's use of focus groups, and Willms's use of multiple methods to explore physician health promotion activities represent clear and impressive examples of a type of rigor that is meaningful and important to primary care providers.

The insistence on rigor and objectivity in scientific inquiry reflects a deeper need on the part of both doers and users of research for the methods employed, the results found, and the interpretations made to be somehow accurate and credible. Within the quantitative research paradigm, this need is addressed by efforts to validate instruments and to minimize random and systematic errors. In qualitative research a multiplicity of strategies is available to enhance the believability and trustworthiness of findings. These strategies are well illustrated in this book and include maintaining a detailed and accurate paper trail, verification by research participants, triangulation, and reflexivity. With such methods the consistency and coherence of emergent findings can be assessed and the credibility of evolving interpretations can be determined in an attempt to achieve some degree of trustworthiness. Subjectivity of the investigator is not incompatible with trustworthiness of the findings and, if the findings are trustworthy, subjectivity is a strength rather than a perceived weakness.

The perception that the "soft" information provided by qualitative inquiry is inferior to the "hard" data produced by quantitative approaches is based on a particular way of thinking about evidence that should be challenged. What constitutes "hard" and "soft" data? The common perception is that the measurement of blood pressure results in "hard" data, while the thick description of the dynamics of a doctor's relationship with a hypertensive patient yields "soft" data. Is this value judgment appropriate?

Morgan was interested in exploring, from the caregiver's perspective, the residential transition of an Alzheimer's patient from the home to the nursing home. During the course of studying, he gradually discovered that the caregiver-physician relationship was an extremely important component in the transition. This was not a preexisting hypothesis or even a hunch. Rather it emerged during the course of the study. With the focus group approach, Morgan was able to accumulate extensive descriptions of caregiver attitudes and feelings about the role of physicians in the care of Alzheimer's patients. This rich, in-depth material offers fertile opportunity for understanding elements of the caregiver-physician relationship. Is this "soft" data generated during the course of this study really inferior to a numerical score representing caregiver satisfaction with the physician role as calculated from responses to an index of satisfaction? The "soft" information provided by qualitative inquiry has the potential to describe the phenomenon of interest in all its complexity and ambiguity with appropriate consideration of context and attention to the meaning of events and experiences for participants. The preference for "hard" data over "soft" data runs the significant risk (to paraphrase Brody) of measuring the less important at the expense of understanding the more important.

Recognizing the value of qualitative research for the work of primary care requires some transcending of the principles and standards embodied in the prevailing quantitative paradigm. Notions of generalizability, rigor, research objectivity, and "soft" versus "hard" data should not constitute obstacles to the conduct and use of qualitative research. These issues are important because they do reflect a reality for many primary care providers. Part of the process of intellectual growth is to reconstruct this reality in the light of new knowledge and understanding. The contents of this book provide a basis for this process of reconstruction.

Summary

What are your experiences? What are your patients' experiences? What are the dilemmas and puzzles in these experiences? What are the researchable questions embedded in these stories? This is where primary care research begins and to where it must always return. The authors of this book have shared their knowledge and experience of qualitative methods. These methods expand and enrich primary care investigators' ability to answer more of the questions that matter. A multimethod primary care research craft is now in the river. It is time to steer our craft with qualitative and quantitative oars. The qualitative methods presented here provide yet another view into the water. What makes this view special is that it not only shows us more of the river bottom, but it keeps us in the stream, and if the sun is before us, it reflects ourselves. Turn your global eye toward home, step down the ladder, and join in the dance. The questions and hopes of primary health care depend on seeing how like our patients we are.

References

Addison, R. B. (1984). *Surviving the residency: A grounded interpretive investigation of physician socialization.* Unpublished doctoral dissertation, University of California, Berkeley.

Addison, R. B. (1989). Grounded interpretive research: An investigation of physician socialization. In M. J. Packer & R. B. Addison (Eds.), *Entering the circle: Hermeneutic investigation in psychology* (pp. 39-57). Albany: State University of New York Press.

Agar, M. H. (1980). *The professional stranger: An informal introduction to ethnography.* Orlando, FL: Academic Press.

Agar, M. H. (1986). *Speaking of ethnography.* Newbury Park, CA: Sage.

Agich, G. J. (1990). Reassessing autonomy in long-term care. *Hastings Center Report, 20*(6), 12-17.

Allen, M. N., & Jenson, L. (1990). Hermeneutical inquiry: Meaning and scope. *Western Journal of Nursing Research, 12*(2), 241-253.

Altheide, D. L. (1987). Ethnographic content analysis. *Qualitative Sociology, 10,* 65-77.

American Academy of Family Physicians. (1991). *Directory of family practice residency programs.* Kansas City, MO: Author.

Arborelius, E., & Timpka, T. (1990). General practitioner's comments on video recorded consultations as an aid to understanding the doctor-patient relationship. *Family Practice, 7*(2), 84-90.

Auenbrugger, L. (1936). *On percussion of the chest* (J. Forbes, M.D., Trans. [1824]). Baltimore: Johns Hopkins University Press.

Babbie, E. R. (1979). *The practice of social research* (2nd ed.). Belmont, CA: Wadsworth.

Bales, R. F. (1950). *Interaction process analysis —A method for the study of small groups.* Cambridge, MA: Addison-Wesley.

Balint, E., & Norell, J. S. (1976). *Six minutes per patient.* London: Neuthen.

Balint, M. (1957). *The doctor, his patient and the illness.* London: Pitman.

Balint, M., Hunt, J., Joyce, D., et al. (1970). *Treatment or diagnosis: A study of repeat prescriptions in general practice.* Toronto: J. B. Lippincott.

Bargagliotti, L. A. (1983). The scientific method and phenomonology: Toward their peaceful coexistence in nursing. *Journal of Nursing Research, 5,* 409-411.

Barker, R. G. (1968). *Ecological psychology: Concepts and methods for studying the environment of human behavior*. Stanford, CA: Stanford University Press.

Bartz, R. (in preparation). *Social context and the doctor-patient relationship: A comparative study of the care of type II diabetes*.

Basch, C. E. (1987). Focus group interview: An underutilized research technique for improving theory and practice in health education. *Health Education Quarterly, 14*, 411-448.

Bateson, G. (1979). *Mind and nature: A necessary unity*. Toronto: Bantam.

Becker, C. L. (1959). What are historical facts? In H. Meyerhoff (Ed.), *The philosophy of history in our time: An anthology* (pp. 120-139). Garden City, NY: Doubleday Anchor Books.

Becker, H. S., Geer, B., Hughes, E., & Strauss, A. (1961). *Boys in white: Student culture in medical school*. Chicago: Chicago University Press.

Becker, M. H., & Maiman, L. A. (1983). Models of health related behavior. In D. Mechanic (Ed.), *Handbook of health, health care, and the professions* (pp. 539-563). New York: Free Press.

Bee, R. L., & Crabtree, B. F. (1992). Using ETHNOGRAPH in fieldnote management. In M. S. Boone & J. Wood (Eds.), *Computer applications in anthropology* (pp. 91-112). New York: Wadsworth.

Benivieni, A. (1960). On the secret causes of diseases (excerpt). In L. Clendening (Ed.), *Source book of medical history* (pp. 239-240). New York: Dover.

Benner, P. (1984). *From novice to expert: Excellence and power in clinical nursing practice*. Menlo Park, CA: Addison-Wesley.

Benner, P. (1985). Quality of life: A phenomenological perspective on explanation, prediction, and understanding in nursing science. *Advances in Nursing Science, 8*, 1-14.

Berelson, B. (1952). *Content analysis in communication research*. Glencoe, IL: Free Press.

Berelson, B. (1971). *Content analysis in communication research* (2nd ed.). New York: Free Press.

Bernard, H. R. (1988). *Research methods in cultural anthropology*. Newbury Park, CA: Sage.

Bernstein, R. J. (1976). *The restructuring of social and political theory*. Philadelphia: University of Pennsylvania Press.

Bernstein, R. J. (1983). *Beyond objectivism and relativism: Science, hermeneutics, and praxis*. Philadelphia: University of Pennsylvania Press.

Birdwhistell, R. L. (1970). *Kinesics and context*. Philadelphia: University of Pennsylvania Press.

Blackman, B. I. (1987). *Qualpro text database and productivity tool (User's Manual)*. Tallahassee, FL: Impulse Development Company.

Blake, R. L., & Bertuso, D. D. (1988). The life space drawing as a measure of social relationships. *Family Medicine, 20*, 295-297.

Bleicher, J. (1980). *Contemporary hermeneutics: Hermeneutics as method, philosophy and critique*. London: Routledge & Kegan Paul.

Bleicher, J. (1982). *The hermeneutic imagination: Outline of a positive critique of scientism and sociology*. London: Routledge & Kegan Paul.

Bloom, S. W. (1963). The process of becoming a physician. *Annals of the American Academy of Political and Social Science, 346*, 77-87.

Blumer, H. (1969). *Symbolic interactionism*. Englewood Cliffs, NJ: Prentice-Hall.

Boerhaave, H. (1719). *A method of studying physick.* London: Printed for C. Rivington at the Bible and Crown, in St. Paul's Churchyard.

Bogdan, R. C. (1972). *Participant observation in organizational settings.* Syracuse, NY: Syracuse University Press.

Bogdan, R. C., & Biklen, S. K. (1982). *Qualitative research for education: An introduction to theory and methods.* Boston: Allyn & Bacon.

Bogdewic, S. P. (1987). *On becoming a family physician: The stages and characteristics of identity formation in family medicine residency training.* Unpublished doctoral dissertation, University of North Carolina, Chapel Hill.

Borkan, J. M., Quirk, M., & Sullivan, M. (in preparation). *Finding meaning after the fall: Injury narratives from elderly hip fracture patients.*

Borman, K. M., Lecompte, M. D., & Goetz, J. P. (1986). Ethnographic and qualitative research design and why it doesn't work. *American Behavioral Scientist, 30,* 42-57.

Bosk, C. L. (1979). *Forgive and remember: Managing medical failure.* Chicago: University of Chicago Press.

Boss, J. (1978). The medical philosophy of Francis Bacon (1561-1626). *Medical Hypothesis, 4,* 208-220.

Braudel, F. (1980). History and sociology. In F. Braudel (Ed.), *On history* (pp. 64-82). Chicago: University of Chicago Press.

Brewer, J., & Hunter, A. (1989). *Multimethod research: A synthesis of styles.* Newbury Park, CA: Sage.

Briggs, C. (1986). *Learning to ask.* Cambridge, UK: Cambridge University Press.

Brody, H. (1980). *Placebos and the philosophy of medicine.* Chicago: University of Chicago Press.

Brody, H. (1985). Placebo effect: An examination of Grunbaum's definition. In L. White, B. Tursky, & G. Schwartz (Eds.), *Placebo: Theory, research, and mechanisms* (pp. 37-58). New York: Guilford.

Brody, H. (1990a). The validation of the biopsychosocial model. *Journal of Family Practice, 30,* 271-272.

Brody, H. (1990b). *Stories of sickness.* New Haven, CT: Yale University Press.

Brothwell, D. (1971). Disease, micro-evolution and earlier populations: An important bridge between medical history and medical biology. In E. Clarke (Ed.), *Modern methods in the history of medicine.* London: Athlone Press of the University of London.

Brown, J. B., Stewart, M. A., McCracken, E., et al. (1986). The patient-centered clinical method 2. Definition and application. *Family Practice, 3,* 75-79.

Burkett, G. L. (1990). Classifying basic research designs. *Family Medicine, 22*(2), 143-148.

Burkett, G. L. (1991). Culture, illness, and the biopsychosocial model. *Family Medicine, 23,* 287-291.

Callahan, E. J., & Bertakis, K. D. (1991). Development and validation of the Davis Observation Code. *Family Medicine, 23,* 19-24.

Caputo, J. D. (1987). *Radical hermeneutics: Repetition, deconstruction, and the hermeneutic project.* Bloomington: Indiana University Press.

Cassell, E. J. (1985). *Talking with patients* (2 vols.). Cambridge, MA: MIT Press.

Chenitz, W. C., & Swanson, J. M. (Eds.). (1986). *From practice to grounded theory: Qualitative research in nursing.* Menlo Park, CA: Addison-Wesley.

Christie, R. J., & Hoffmaster, C. B. (1986). *Ethical issues in family medicine.* New York: Oxford University Press.

Colaizzi, P. (1978). Psychological research as the phenomonologist views it. In R. Vale & M. King (Eds.), *Existential-phenomonological alternatives for psychology* (pp. 48-71). New York: Oxford University Press.

College of Physicians and Surgeons of Ontario. (1988). *Annual Report.* Ontario, Canada: Author.

Collingwood, R. G. (1969). *The idea of history.* London: Oxford University Press.

Coward, D. D. (1990). Critical multiplism: A research strategy for nursing science. *Image, 22,* 163-167.

Crabtree, B. F., & Miller, W. L. (1991). A qualitative approach to primary care research: The long interview. *Family Medicine, 23*(2), 145-151.

Crabtree, B. F., & Miller, W. L. (1992). The analysis of narratives from a long interview. In M. Stewart, F. Tudiver, M. Bass, E. Dunn, & P. Norton (Eds.) *Tools for primary care research* (pp. 209-220). Newbury Park, CA: Sage.

Daniels, N. (1979). Wide reflective equilibrium and theory acceptance in ethics. *Journal of Philosophy, 76,* 256-82.

Denzin, N. K. (1989a). *Interpretive interactionism.* Newbury Park, CA: Sage.

Denzin, N. K. (1989b). *Interpretive biography.* Newbury Park, CA: Sage.

Descartes, R. (1986). *Meditations on first philosophy* (Sixth Meditation). London: Cambridge University Press.

Diers, D. (1979). *Research in nursing practice.* Philadelphia: J. B. Lippincott.

Dobbert, M. L. (1982). *Ethnographic research: Theory and application for modern schools and societies.* New York: Praeger.

Douglas, M. (1982). *Natural symbols: Explorations in cosmology.* New York: Pantheon.

Dozor, R. B., & Addison, R. B. (in preparation). *Toward a good death: An interpretive investigation of how family practice residents work with dying patients and their families.*

Dreyfus, H. L. (1986). Why studies of human capacities modeled on ideal natural science can never achieve their goal. In J. Margolis, M. Krausz, & R. M. Burian (Eds.), *Rationality, relativism and the human sciences* (pp. 3-22). Dordrecht, Holland: Martinus Nijhoff.

Dreyfus, H. L. (1991). *Being-in-the-world: A commentary on Heidegger's being and time, Division I.* Cambridge, MA: MIT Press.

Duncan, M., & Morgan, D. L. (1990). *Sharing the caring: Interactions between family and staff.* Paper presented at the meetings of the Gerontological Society of America, Boston.

Ebell, M. H., Smith, M. A., Seifert, K. G., & Polsinelli, K. (1990). The do-not-resuscitate order: Outpatient experience and decision-making preferences. *Journal of Family Practice, 31,* 630-636.

Eibl-Eibesfeldt, I. (1989). *Human ethology.* New York: Aldine de Grayter.

Ellen, R. F. (1984). *Ethnographic research: A guide to general conduct.* New York: Academic Press.

Engel, G. L. (1977). The need for a new medical model: A challenge for biomedicine. *Science, 196,* 129-136.

Engel, G. L. (1980). The clinical application of the biopsychosocial model. *American Journal of Psychiatry, 137,* 535.

Epstein, R. M. (in preparation). *HIV and primary care: The physicians' perspective.*

Erickson, F. (1977). Some approaches to inquiry in school-community ethnography. *Anthropology and Education Quarterly, 8*(2), 58-69.

Ewart, C. K., Wood, J., & Li, V. C. (Eds.). (1982). *Factors determining physician's influence against smoking.* Baltimore: The Johns Hopkins Medical Institutions.

Fay, B. (1987). *Critical social science.* Ithaca, NY: Cornell University Press.

Fetterman, D. M. (1989). *Ethnography: Step-by-step.* Newbury Park, CA: Sage.

Field, P. A., & Morse, J. M. (1985). *Nursing research: The application of qualitative approaches.* Rockville, MD: Aspen.

Folstein, M. F., Folstein, S. F., & McHugh, P. R. (1975). Mini-mental state: A practical method of grading the cognitive state of patients for the clinician. *Journal of Psychiatric Research, 12,* 189-198.

Foucault, M. (1975). *The birth of the clinic: An archeology of medical perception* (A. M. Sheridan Smith, Trans.). New York: Vantage Books.

Frankel, R. M., & Beckman, H. B. (1982). Impact: An interaction-based method for preserving and analyzing clinical transactions. In L. S. Pettigrew (Ed.), *Straight talk: Explorations in provider and patient interactions* (pp. 72-85). Louisville, KY: Humana.

Frankel, R. M., & Beckman, H. B. (1989). Evaluating the patient's primary problem(s). In M. Stewart & D. Roter (Eds.), *Communicating with medical patients* (pp. 86-98). Newbury Park, CA: Sage.

Freeman, G. (1984). Continuity of care in general practice. *Family Practice, 11*(4), 245-252.

Freeman, G. (1985). Priority given by doctors to continuity of care. *Journal of the Royal College of General Practitioners, 35,* 423-426.

Friedrichs, J., & Ludtke, H. (1974). *Participant observation: Theory and practice.* Westmead, UK: Saxon House.

Gadamer, H. G. (1976). *Philosophical hermeneutics.* Berkeley: University of California Press.

Gadamer, H. G. (1986). *Truth and method.* New York: Crossroad.

Garfinkel, H. (1967). *Studies in ethnomethodology.* Englewood Cliffs, NJ: Prentice-Hall.

Geer, B., Haas, J., ViVona, C., Miller, S., Woods, C., & Becker, H. (1968). Learning the ropes: Situational learning in four occupational training programs. In I. Deutscher & E. Thompson (Eds.), *Among the people: Encounters with the poor* (pp. 209-233). New York: Basic Books.

Geertz, C. (1973). *Interpretation of cultures.* New York: Basic Books.

Geertz, C. (1983). *Local knowledge: Further essays in interpretive anthropology.* New York: Basic Books.

Gelfand, T. (1980). *Professionalizing modern medicine: Paris surgeons and medical science and institutions in the eighteenth century.* Westport, CT: Greenwood.

Gillespie, G. W., Jr. (1986). Using word processor macros for computer-assisted qualitative analysis. *Qualitative Sociology, 9*(3), 283-292.

Giorgi, A. (1970). *Psychology as a human science: A phenomonologically based approach.* New York: Harper & Row.

Gladwin, C. H. (1989). *Ethnographic decision tree modeling.* Newbury Park, CA: Sage.

Glaser, B. C. (1978). *Theoretical sensitivity.* Mill Valley, CA: Sociology Press.

Glaser, B., & Strauss, A. L. (1967). *The discovery of grounded theory.* New York: Aldine.

Gluckman, M. (Ed.). (1963). *Essays on the ritual of social relations.* Manchester, UK: Manchester University Press.

Goetz, J. P., & LeCompte, M. D. (1984). *Ethnography and qualitative design in educational research.* Orlando, FL: Academic Press.

Gorovitz, S., & MacIntyre, A. (1976). Toward a theory of medical fallibility. *Journal of Medical Philosophy, 1,* 51-71.

Greenfield, S., Kaplan, S., & Ware, J. E. (1985). Expanding patient involvement in care: Effects on patient outcomes. *Annals of Internal Medicine, 102,* 520-528.

Greenfield, S., Kaplan, S., & Ware, J. E. (1988). Patient participation in medical care: Effects on blood sugar and quality of life in diabetes. *Journal of General Internal Medicine, 3,* 448-457.

Gregor, S., & Galazka, S. S. (1990). The use of key informant networks in the assessment of community health. *Family Medicine, 22,* 118-121.

Grunbaum, A. (1985). Explication and implications of the placebo concept. In L. White, B. Tursky, & G. Schwartz (Eds.), *Placebo: Theory, research, and mechanisms* (pp. 9-36). New York: Guilford.

Guba, E. G. (1990). *The paradigm dialog.* Newbury Park, CA: Sage.

Guba, E. G., & Lincoln, Y. S. (1989). *Fourth generation evaluation.* Newbury Park, CA: Sage.

Gubrium, J. F. (1986). *Oldtimers and Alzheimer's: The descriptive organization of senility.* Greenwich, CT: JAI.

Gumperz, J. J., & Hymes, D. (Eds.). (1972). *Directions in sociolinguistics: The ethnography of communication.* New York: Holt, Rinehart & Winston.

Habermas, J. (1968). *Knowledge and human interests.* Boston: Beacon.

Habermas, J. (1977). A review of Gadamer's truth and method. In F. R. Dallmayr & T. A. McCarthy (Eds.), *Understanding and social inquiry* (pp. 335-363). Notre Dame, IN: University of Notre Dame Press.

Hahn, R. A. (1985). A world of internal medicine: Portrait of an internist. In R. A. Hahn & A. D. Gaines (Eds.), *Physicians of western medicine: Anthropological approaches to theory and practice* (pp. 51-111). Dordrecht, Holland: D. Reidel.

Hall, E. T. (1974). *Handbook for proxemic research.* Washington, DC: Society for the Anthropology of Visual Communication.

Hammersley, M., & Atkinson, P. (1983). *Ethnography: Principles in practice.* New York: Tavistock.

Hammond, P. E. (1964). *Sociologists at work: Essays on the craft of social research.* New York: Basic Books.

Harris, M. (1966). The cultural ecology of India's sacred cattle. *Current Anthropology, 7,* 51-66.

Harvey, W. (1928). *Exercitatio anatomica de motu cordis at sanguinis in animalibus.* With an English translation and annotations by C. Leaky. London: Bailliere, Tindall & Cox.

Heidegger, M. (1927/1962). *Being and time.* New York: Harper & Row.

Heisenberg, W. (1956). The uncertainty principle. In J. Newman (Ed.), *The world of mathematics* (pp. 1051-1055). New York: Simon & Schuster.

Helman, C. G. (1990). *Culture, health and illness.* Boston: Butterworth-Heinemann.

Helman, C. G. (1991a). The family culture: A useful concept for family medicine. *Family Medicine, 23,* 376-381.

Helman, C. G. (1991b). Research in primary care: The qualitative approach. In P. Norton, M. Stewart, F. Tudiver, M. Bass, & E. Dunn (Eds.), *Primary care research: Traditional and innovative approaches* (pp. 105-127). Newbury Park, CA: Sage.

Houts, A., Cook, T., & Shadish, W. (1986). The person-situation debate: A critical multiplist perspective. *Journal of Personality, 54,* 53-107.

Howe, K., & Eisenhart, M. (1990). Standards for qualitative (and quantitative) research: A prolegomenon. *Educational Researcher, 5,* 2-9.

Husserl, E. (1931). *Ideas: A general introduction to pure phenomenology.* New York: Humanities Press.

Jaeger, R. M. (1988). *Complementary methods for research in education.* Washington, DC: American Educational Research Association.

James, W. (1958). *The varieties of religious experience: The Gifford Lectures on natural religion delivered at Edinburgh in 1901-1902.* New York: New American Library.

Jick, T. D. (1979). Mixing qualitative and quantitative methods: Triangulation in action. *Administrative Science Quarterly, 24,* 602-611.

Johnson, J. C. (1990). *Selecting ethnographic informants.* Newbury Park, CA: Sage.

Jonsson, P. V., McNamee, M., & Campion, E. W. (1988). The "do not resuscitate" order: A profile of its changing use. *Archives of Internal Medicine, 148,* 2373-2375.

Jorgensen, D. L. (1989). *Participant observation: A methodology for human studies.* Newbury Park, CA: Sage.

Junker, B. H. (1960). *Field work: An introduction to the social sciences.* Chicago: University of Chicago Press.

Kagan, N. (1975). *Interpersonal process recall: A method of influencing human interaction.* Mason, MI: Mason Media.

Kamer, R. S., Dieck, E. M., McClung, J. A., et al. (1990). Effect of New York State's do-not-resuscitate legislation on in-hospital cardiopulmonary resuscitation practice. *American Journal of Medicine, 88,* 108-111.

Kaplan, S., Greenfield, S., & Ware. J. (1989). Impact of the doctor-patient relationship on the outcome of chronic disease. In M. Stewart & D. Roter (Eds.), *Communicating with medical patients* (pp. 228-245). Newbury Park, CA: Sage.

Kelsey, J. L., White, A. A., Pastides, H., et al. (1979). The impact of musculoskeletal disorders on the population of the United States. *The Journal of Bone and Joint Surgery, 61-A*(7), 959-964.

Kirk, J., & Miller, M. (1986). *Reliability and validity in qualitative research.* Newbury Park, CA: Sage.

Kleinman, A. (1980). *Patients and healers in the context of culture.* Berkeley: University of California Press.

Kleinman, A. (1983). The cultural meanings and social uses of illness. *Journal of Family Practice, 16,* 539-545.

Kleinman, A. (1988). *The illness narratives: Suffering, healing, and the human condition.* New York: Basic Books.

Knight, D. (1975). *Sources for the history of science: 1660-1914.* Ithaca, NY: Cornell University Press.

Konner, M. (1987). *Becoming a doctor: A journey of initiation in medical school.* New York: Viking Penguin.

Kotarba, J. A. (1983). *Chronic pain: Its social dimensions.* Newbury Park, CA: Sage.

Kraan, H. F., & Crijnen, A. A. M. (1987). *The Maastricht history-taking and advice checklist: Studies of instrumental utility.* Amsterdam: Lundbeck.

Kraan, H. F., Crijnen, A., & Zuidweg, J. (1989). Evaluating undergraduate training: A checklist for medical interviewing skills. In M. Stewart & D. Roter (Eds.), *Communicating with medical patients* (pp. 167-177). Newbury Park, CA: Sage.

Kragh, H. (1987). *An introduction to the historiography of science.* Cambridge, UK: Cambridge University Press.

Krueger, R. A. (1988). *Focus groups: A practical guide for applied research.* Newbury Park, CA: Sage.

Kübler-Ross, E. (1969). *On death and dying.* New York: Macmillan.

Kuzel, A. J. (1986). Naturalistic inquiry: An appropriate model for family medicine. *Family Medicine, 18,* 369-374.

Kuzel, A. J., Engel, J. D., Addison. R. B., et al. (1990, May). *Standards for qualitative inquiry.* Workshop presented at Annual Meeting of the Society of Teachers of Family Medicine, Seattle.

Kuzel, A. J., & Like, R. C. (1991). Standards of trustworthiness for qualitative studies in primary care. In P. Norton, M. Stewart, F. Tudiver, M. Bass, & E. Dunn (Eds.), *Primary care research: Traditional and innovative approaches* (pp. 138-158). Newbury Park, CA: Sage.

Laennec, H. (1819). *De l'auscultation mediate ou tratie du diagnostic des maladies des poumons et coeur* (tome premier). Paris: Brosson et Chaude.

Lain-Entralgo, P. (1964). *La relacion medico-enfermo: Historia y teoria.* Madrid: Revista de Occidente.

Laplace, P. S. De. (1956). Concerning probability. In J. Newman (Ed.), *The world of mathematics* (pp. 1325-1333). New York: Simon & Schuster.

Last, J. M. (Ed.). (1983). *A dictionary of epidemiology.* New York: Oxford University Press.

Lather, P. (1986a). Research as praxis. *Harvard Educational Review, 56*(3), 257-277.

Lather, P. (1986b). Issues of validity in openly ideological research: Between a rock and a soft place. *Interchange, 17,* 63-84.

Levenstein, J. H., McCracken, E. C., McWhinney, I. R., et al. (1986). The patient-centred clinical method. I. A model for the doctor-patient interaction in family medicine. *Family Practice, 3*(1), 24-30.

Levere, T. H. (Ed.). (1982). *Editing texts in the history of science and medicine.* New York: Garland.

Levi-Strauss, C. (1963). *Structural anthropology.* New York: Basic Books.

Levkoff, S. E., Cleary, P. D., Wetle, T., & Besdine, R. W. (1988). Illness behavior in the aged: Implications for clinicians. *Journal of the American Geriatrics Society, 36,* 622-629.

Lidz, C. W., Meisel, A., Osterweis, M., et al. (1983). Barriers to informed consent. *Annals of Internal Medicine, 99,* 539-543.

Light, R., & Pillemer, D. (1982). Numbers and narrative: Combining their strengths in research reviews. *Harvard Educational Review, 52,* 1-23.

Lin, N. (1976). *Foundations of social research.* New York: McGraw-Hill.

Lincoln, Y. S., & Guba, E. G. (1985). *Naturalistic inquiry.* Newbury Park, CA: Sage.

Lindemann, E. C. (1924). *Social discovery.* New York: Republic.

Lofland, J. G., & Lofland, L. H. (1984). *Analyzing social settings.* Belmont, CA: Wadsworth.

Lonergan, B. (1957). *Insight: A study of human understanding.* New York: Philosophical Library.

Lonergan, B. (1972). *Method in theology.* New York: Herder and Herder.

Lonergan, B. (1985). Aquinas today: Tradition and innovation. In S. Crowe (Ed.), *A third collection: Papers by Bernard J. F. Lonergan, S. J.* (pp. 35-54). New York: Paulist Press.

Lorenz, K. (1966). *On aggression*. London: Methuen.

Malinowski, B. 1961. *Argonauts of the western Pacific*. New York: E. P. Dutton.

Manning, P. K. (1987). *Semiotics and fieldwork*. Newbury Park, CA: Sage.

Mansfield Software Group. (1987). *Kedit user's manual, Version 3.52*. Storrs, CT: Author.

Marchand, L. (1991, May). *Infant feeding choices: Understanding the decision-making process*. Paper presented at the 19th Annual Meeting of the North American Primary Care Research Group, Quebec, Canada.

Marshall, C., & Rossman, G. B. (1989). *Designing qualitative research*. Newbury Park, CA: Sage.

Marvel, M. K., Staehling, S., & Hendricks, B. (1991) A taxonomy of clinical research methods: Comparisons of family practice and general medicine journals. *Family Medicine, 23*(3), 202-207.

Mausner, J. S., & Kramer, S. (1985). *Epidemiology: An introductory book* (2nd ed.). Philadelphia: W. B. Saunders.

McCarthy, T. (1978). *The critical theory of Jurgen Habermas*. Cambridge, MA: MIT Press.

McCracken, G. (1988). *The long interview*. Newbury Park, CA: Sage.

McGoldrick, M., & Gerson, R. (1985). *Genogram in family assessment*. New York: W. W. Norton.

McLaughlin, M. L. (1984). *Conversation: How talk is organized*. Beverly Hills, CA: Sage.

McQuarrie, E. F. (1990). Review of focus groups as qualitative research and the long interview. *Journal of Marketing Research, 27*, 114-117.

McShane, P. (1975). *Wealth of self and wealth of nations: The self-axis of the great ascent*. Hicksville, NY: Exposition Press.

McWhinney, I. R. (1975). Continuity of care in family practice. *The Journal of Family Practice, 2*, 373- 374.

McWhinney, I. R. (1989). *A textbook of family medicine*. New York: Oxford University Press.

McWhinney, I. R. (1991). Primary care research in the next twenty years. In P. Norton, M. Stewart, F. Tudiver, M. Bass, & E. Dunn (Eds.), *Primary care research: Traditional and innovative approaches* (pp. 1-12). Newbury Park, CA: Sage.

McWilliam, C. L. (1991, May). *Discharging elderly patients from hospital to home: The qualitative challenges*. Paper presented at the 19th Annual Meeting of the North American Primary Care Research Group. Quebec, Canada.

Mehan, H., & Wood, H. (1975). *The reality of ethnomethodology*. New York: John Wiley.

Meisel, A., & Roth, L. H. (1981). What we do and do not know about informed consent. *Journal of the American Medical Association, 246*, 2473-2477.

Merriam, S. B. (1988). *Case study research in education*. San Francisco: Jossey-Bass.

Miles, M. B., & Huberman, A. M. (1984). *Qualitative data analysis: A sourcebook of new methods*. Beverly Hills, CA: Sage.

Miller, W. L., & Crabtree, B. F. (1990). Start with the stories. *Family Medicine Research Updates, 9*, 2-3.

Miller, W. L., & Crabtree, B. F. (1992). Depth interviewing: The long interview approach. In M. Stewart, F. Tudiver, M. Bass, E. Dunn, & P. Norton (Eds.), *Tools for primary care research* (pp. 194-208). Newbury Park, CA: Sage.

Mishler, E. G. (1984). *The discourse of medicine: Dialectics of medical interviews*. Norwood, NJ: Ablex.

Mizrahi, T. (1986). *Getting rid of patients: Contradictions in the socialization of physicians.* New Brunswick, NJ: Rutgers University Press.

Moerman, M. (1988). *Talking culture: Ethnography and conversation analysis.* Philadelphia: University of Pennsylvania Press.

Morgagni, G. (1769). *The seats and causes of diseases investigated by anatomy* (In 5 books, containing a great variety of dissections with remarks. Translated from the Latin of John Baptist Morgagni, by B. Alexander. 1st English ed.). London: A. Miller and T. Cadell, his successor.

Morgan, D. L. (1988). *Focus groups as qualitative research.* Newbury Park, CA: Sage.

Morgan, D. L. (1989). *Caregivers for elderly Alzheimer's victims: A comparison of caregiving in the home and in institutions.* Final Report to the AARP/Andrus Foundation, Portland, OR.

Morgan, D. L. (1992). Designing focus group research. In M. Stewart, F. Tudiver, M. Bass, E. Dunn, & P. Norton (Eds.), *Tools for primary care research* (pp. 177-193). Newbury Park, CA: Sage.

Morgan, D. L., Wheeler, P., & Boise, L. (1991). *The family's role in early diagnosis and service utilization.* Final Report to the Alzheimer's Disease Center of Oregon.

Morgan, D. L., & Zhao, P. P. (1991, February). *The doctor-caregiver relationship: Managing the care of family members with Alzheimer's disease.* Paper presented at the Qualitative Health Research Conference, Edmonton, Canada.

Morse, J. M. (1986). Qualitative and quantitative research: Issues in sampling. In P. L. Chinn (Ed.), *Nursing research methodology* (pp. 181-193). Rockville, MD: Aspen.

Mostyn, B. (1985). The content analysis of qualitative research data: A dynamic approach. In M. Brenner, J. Brown, & D. Canter (Eds.), *The research interview: Uses and approaches* (pp. 115-145). New York: Academic Press.

Moustakas, C. (1990). *Heuristic research: Design, methodology and applications.* Newbury Park, CA: Sage.

Mumford, E. (1970). *Interns: From students to physicians.* Cambridge, MA: Harvard University Press.

Murdock, G. P., Ford, C. S., Hudson, A. E., et al. (1950). *Outline of cultural materials* (3rd ed.). New Haven, CT: Human Relations Area Files.

Newman, M. (1991, May). *The emotional impact of mistakes upon family physicians.* Paper presented at the Annual Spring Conference of the Society of Teachers of Family Medicine, Philadelphia.

O'Connor, P. J. (1990). Normative data: Their definition, interpretation, and importance for primary care physicians. *Family Medicine, 22,* 307-311.

Oiler, C. (1982). The phenomenological approach in nursing research. *Nursing Research, 31*(3), 178-181.

Packer, M. J., & Addison, R. B. (1989). *Entering the circle: Hermeneutic investigation in psychology.* Albany: State University of New York Press.

Palmer, R. E. (1969). *Hermeneutics: Interpretation theory in Schleiermacher, Dilthey, Heidegger, and Gadamer.* Evanston, IL: Northwestern University Press.

Patton, M. Q. (1980). *Qualitative evaluation methods.* Beverly Hills, CA: Sage.

Patton, M. Q. (1990). *Qualitative evaluation and research methods* (2nd ed.). Newbury Park, CA: Sage.

Peacock, J. L. (1986). *The anthropological lens: Harsh light, soft focus.* Cambridge, UK: Cambridge University Press.

Pearlin, L. I., Turner, H. A., & Semple, S. J. (1989). Coping and the mediation of caregiver stress. In E. Light & B. Lebowitz (Eds.), *Alzheimer's disease and family stress: Directions for research* (pp. 198-217). Washington, DC: National Institute of Mental Health.

Pelto, P. J., & Pelto, G. H. (1978). *Anthropological research: The structure of inquiry* (2nd ed.). New York: Cambridge University Press.

Penayo, U., Jacobson, L., Caldera, T., & Burmann, G. (1988). Community attitudes and awareness of mental health disorders: A key informant study in two Nicaraguan towns. *ACTA Psychiatry Scandinavian, 78*, 561-566.

Pfaffenberger, B. (1988). *Microcomputer applications in qualitative research.* Newbury Park, CA: Sage.

Polanyi, M. (1962). *Personal knowledge: Towards a post-critical philosophy.* Chicago: University of Chicago Press.

Pratt, C., Wright, S., & Schmall, V. (1987). Burden, coping, and health status: A comparison of family caregivers to community dwelling and institutionalized Alzheimer's patients. *Journal of Gerontological Social Work, 10*, 99-112.

President's Commission for the Study of Ethical Problems in Medicine. (1983). *Deciding to forego life-sustaining treatment.* Washington, DC: Government Printing Office.

Quill, T. E., Stankaitis, J. A., & Krause, C. R. (1986). The effect of a community hospital resuscitation policy on elderly patients. *New York State Journal of Medicine, 86*, 622-625.

Rabinow, P., & Sullivan, W. M. (Eds.). (1979). *Interpretive social science: A reader.* Berkeley: University of California Press.

Ratcliffe, J. W., & Gonzalez-del-Valle, A. (1988). Rigor in health-related research: Toward an expanded conceptualization. *International Journal of Health Services, 18*(3), 361-391.

Reiser, S. J. (1979). The medical influence of the stethoscope. *Scientific American, 240*, 148-166.

Richardson, L. (1990). *Writing strategies: Reaching diverse audiences.* Newbury Park, CA: Sage.

Ricoeur, P. (1965). *History and truth.* Evanston, IL: Northwestern University Press.

Ricoeur, P. (1979). The model of the text: Meaningful action considered as a text. In P. Rabinow & W. M. Sullivan (Eds.), *Interpretive social science: A reader* (pp. 73-101). Berkeley: University of California Press.

Ricoeur, P. (1981). *Hermeneutics and the human sciences.* Cambridge, UK: Cambridge University Press.

Rorty, R. (1979). *Philosophy and the mirror of nature.* Princeton, NJ: Princeton University Press.

Rorty, R. (1982). *Consequences of pragmatism.* Minneapolis: University of Minnesota Press.

Rosner, T. T., Namazi, K. H., & Wykle, M. L. (1988). Physician use among the old-old: Factors affecting variability. *Medical Care, 26*(10), 982-990.

Roter, D. (1977). Patient participation in patient-provider interaction. *Health Education Monographs, 5*, 281-315.

Sanjek, R. (Ed.). (1990). *Fieldnotes: The makings of anthropology.* Ithaca, NY: Cornell University Press.

Schatzman, L., & Strauss, A. L. (1973). *Field research: Strategies for a natural sociology*. Englewood Cliffs, NJ: Prentice-Hall.

Schein, E. H. (1987). *The clinical perspective in fieldwork*. Newbury Park, CA: Sage.

Schmerling, R. H., Bedell, S. E., Lilienfeld, A., & Delbanco, T. L. (1988). Discussing cardiopulmonary resuscitation: A study of elderly outpatients. *Journal of General Internal Medicine, 3*, 317-321.

Schutz, A. (1973). *Collected papers: The problem of social reality*. The Hague: Martinus Nijhoff.

Schwartz, M. S., & Schwartz, C. G. (1955). Problems in participant observation. *American Journal of Sociology, 60*, 343-354.

Seidel, J. V., Kjolseth, R., & Seymour, E. (1988). *THE ETHNOGRAPH: A user's guide (Version 3.0)*. Littleton, CO: Qualis Research Associates.

Seifert, M. (1987, May). *How do people get well?* Paper presented at the Annual Meeting of the North American Primary Care Research Group, Minneapolis.

Shaffir, W. B., Stebbins, R. A., & Turowetz, A. (1980). *Fieldwork experience*. New York: St. Martin's.

Singer, M. (1989). The coming of age of critical medical anthropology. *Social Science and Medicine, 28*, 1193-1203.

Smith, A., & Kleinman, S. (1989). Managing emotions in medical school: Student's contacts with the living and the dead. *Social Psychology Quarterly, 52*, 56-69.

Smith, J. K. (1990). Alternative research paradigms and the problem of criteria. In E. G. Guba (Ed.), *The paradigm dialog* (pp. 167-187). Newbury Park, CA: Sage.

Spradley, J. P. (1979). *The ethnographic interview*. New York: Holt, Rinehart & Winston.

Spradley, J. P. (1980). *Participant observation*. New York: Holt, Rinehart & Winston.

Stange, K. C., & Zyzanski, S. J. (1989). Integrating qualitative and quantitative research methods. *Family Medicine, 21*, 448-451.

Starfield, B., Wray, C., Hess. K., et al. (1981). The influence of patient-practitioner agreement on outcome of care. *American Journal of Public Health, 71*(2), 127-131.

Starosta, W. J. (1984). Qualitative content analysis: A "Burkean" perspective. In W. B. Gudykunst & Y. Y. Kim (Eds.), *Methods for intercultural communication* (pp. 185-194). Beverly Hills, CA: Sage.

Stein, H. F. (1985). *The psychodynamics of medical practice: Unconscious factors in patient care*. Berkeley: University of California Press.

Stein, H. F. (1990). Bridging the gap via context: An ethnographic clinical-training model. In H. F. Stein & M. Apprey (Eds.), *Clinical stories and their translations* (pp. 149-175). Charlottesville: Altheide.

Stein, H. F., & Apprey, M. (1985). *Context and dynamics in clinical knowledge*. Charlottesville: University of Virginia Press.

Stetten, D., Jr. (1981). Coping with blindness. *New England Journal of Medicine, 305*, 458.

Stewart, M., Brown, J. B., & Weston, W. W. (1989). Patient-centred interviewing Part III: Five provocative questions. *Canadian Family Physician, 35*, 159-161.

Stewart, M., & Buck, C. (1977). Physicians' knowledge of and response to patients' problems. *Medical Care, 15*(7), 578-585.

Stiles, W. B. (1986). Development of a taxonomy of verbal response modes. In L. Greenberg & W. Pinsof (Eds.), *The psychotherapeutic process: A research handbook* (pp. 161-199). New York: Guilford.

Strauss, A. L. (1987). *Qualitative analysis for social scientists*. Cambridge, UK: Cambridge University Press.

Strauss, A. L., & Corbin, J. (1990). *Basics of qualitative research: Grounded theory procedures and techniques*. Newbury Park, CA: Sage.

Stubbs, M. (1983). *Discourse analysis: The sociolinguistic analysis of natural language*. Chicago: University of Chicago Press.

Szasz, T. S., & Hollender, M. H. (1955). A contribution to the philosophy of medicine. *Archives of Internal Medicine, 113*, 585-592.

Temkin, O. (1973). *Galenism: Rise and decline of a medical philosophy*. Ithaca, NY: Cornell University Press.

Tesch, R. (1990). *Qualitative research: Analysis types and software tools*. New York: Falmer.

Thomas, J. (Ed.). (1983). The Chicago school (Special issue). *Urban Life, 11*, 908-944.

Thorndike, L. (1955). The true place of astrology in the history of science. *Isis, 46*, 273-278.

Thrower, S. M., Bruce, W. E., & Walton, R. F. (1982). The family circle method for integrating family systems concepts in family medicine. *Journal of Family Practice, 15*, 451-457.

Tinbergen, N. (1951). *The study of instinct*. London: Oxford University Press.

Tudiver, F., Cushman, R. A., Crabtree, B. F., et al. (1991). Combining quantitative and qualitative methodologies in primary care: Some examples. In P. Norton, M. Stewart, F. Tudiver, M. Bass, & E. Dunn (Eds.), *Primary care research: Traditional and innovative approaches* (pp. 159-180). Newbury Park, CA: Sage.

Turner, V. W. (1969). *The ritual process: Structure and anti-structure*. Chicago: Aldine.

Van Dijk, T. A. (Ed.). (1985). *Handtools of discourse analysis* (Vol. 4). London: Academic Press.

Van Kaam, A. L. (1969). *Existential foundations of psychology*. New York: Doubleday.

Ventres, W. B., (1991). *Resuscitative decision making: Ethnographic perspectives*. Unpublished master's thesis, University of Arizona, Tucson.

Vesalius, A. (1543). *De humani corporis fabrica libri septem*. Basilae: Innis Oporini.

Watson, L. C., & Watson-Franke, M. B. (1985). *Interpreting life histories: An anthropological inquiry*. New Brunswick, NJ: Rutgers University Press.

Wax, R. H. (1971). *Doing fieldwork: Warnings and advice*. Chicago: University of Chicago Press.

Weber, M. (1968). *Economy and society*. New York: Bedminster.

Weber, R. P. (1985). *Basic content analysis*. Beverly Hills, CA: Sage.

Weller, S. C., & Romney, K. A. (1988). *Systematic data collection*. Newbury Park, CA: Sage.

Werner, O., & Schoepfle, G. M. (1987a). *Systematic fieldwork: Foundations of ethnography and interviewing*. Newbury Park, CA: Sage.

Werner, O., & Schoepfle, G. M. (1987b). *Systematic fieldwork: Ethnographic analysis and data management*. Newbury Park, CA: Sage.

White, L. (1959). *The evolution of culture*. New York: McGraw-Hill.

White, L. (1978). *Medieval religion and technology: Collected essays*. Berkeley: University of California Press.

White, L., Tursky, B., & Schwartz, G. E. (1985). *Placebo: Theory, research, and mechanisms*. New York: Guilford.

Whitehead, A. N. (1948). *Science and the modern world*. New York: Mentor Books.

Wilber, K. (1983). *Eye to eye: The quest for the new paradigm*. New York: Anchor Books.

Willms, D. G., Best, J. A., Taylor, D. W., et al. (1990). A systematic approach for using qualitative methods in primary prevention research. *Medical Anthropology Quarterly, 4*, 391-409.

Willms, D. G., Kottke, T. E., Solberg, L., & Brekee, M. L. (1986). *Modifiable barriers to the delivery of health promotion advice in family practice medicine: An anthropological perspective*. Unpublished manuscript, University of Minnesota, Department of Medicine.

Wolcott, H. F. (1990). *Writing up qualitative research*. Newbury Park, CA: Sage.

Yin, R. K. (1989). *Case studies research* (rev. ed.). Newbury Park, CA: Sage.

Index

About the Contributors

Richard B. Addison, PhD, is Assistant Clinical Professor in the Department of Family and Community Medicine at the University of California, San Francisco, School of Medicine, and a core faculty member of the Family Practice Residency Program at Community Hospital of Sonoma County in Santa Rosa, California. He leads ongoing support/personal and professional development groups for resident-physicians and other health care workers. He also maintains a private practice as a clinical psychologist specializing in seeing physicians and their families. His research interests include the professional socialization of family physicians, physician stress and impairment, support services for residents, physicians caring for dying patients and their families, and most passionately, interpretive and hermeneutic approaches to naturalistic and other qualitative research. He is co-editor of *Entering the Circle: Hermeneutic Investigation in Psychology.*

Miguel Bedolla, MD, PhD, is Assistant Professor in the Department of Family Practice of the University of Texas Health Science Center at San Antonio. He obtained a BA in history from Saint Mary's University in San Antonio, an MD from the University of Nuevo Leon, and a PhD from Ohio State University. He is actively involved in doing research in medical ethics, the history of medical ethics, and the development of research methods in medicine.

Robert Blake, Jr., MD, is the William C. Allen Professor of Family and Community Medicine at the University of Missouri-Columbia. He received his MD from Washington University and was a Robert Wood Johnson Clinical Scholar at the University of North Carolina. He is Associate Editor of *Family Medicine.* His major research interests involve the effects of social stressors and social supports on health.

Stephen P. Bogdewic, PhD, is Associate Professor and Vice-Chair in the Department of Family Medicine at Indiana University. His scholarly interests include the professional socialization of medical trainees, faculty development, and general methodological issues in qualitative research. His publications have appeared in such journals as *Academic Medicine, Family Medicine,* and *Health Care Management Review.* He received his PhD from the University of North Carolina at Chapel Hill.

Howard Brody, MD, PhD, is Professor of Family Practice and Philosophy, and Director of the Center of Ethics and Humanities in Life Sciences at Michigan State University, East Lansing. His primary areas of research and teaching have been medical ethics and philosophy of medicine.

Benjamin F. Crabtree, PhD, is a medical anthropologist in the Department of Family Medicine at the University of Connecticut and is cofounder of the Qualitative Research Interest Group within the North American Primary Care Research Group. He has contributed a number of methods chapters in books and has published in such journals as the *Journal of Clinical Epidemiology, Medical Care,* and *Family Medicine.*

Larry Culpepper, MD, MPH, is Research Director at Memorial Hospital of Rhode Island/Brown University Department of Family Medicine. He is Past President of the North American Primary Care Research Group and helps direct the International Primary Care Network. He has made frequent contributions to the development of family medicine research over the past 15 years, including publications in the *Journal of the American Medical Association, British Medical Journal, Journal of Family Medicine,* and *Family Practice.*

Valerie J. Gilchrist, MD, is Associate Professor of Family Medicine at Northeastern Ohio University's College of Medicine. A graduate of the University of Toronto Medical School and Family Medicine Residency, she completed a Fellowship in Family Medicine at the University of North Carolina. She has been teaching and practicing in northeast Ohio for more than 10 years. Her writing and research interests are the doctor-patient relationship, health promotion and disease prevention, women's health issues, and feminist theory. She is an Editorial Board Member of the journal *Family Medicine.*

Nancy Arbuthnot Johnson, MA, is currently a Research Coordinator in the Department of Clinical Epidemiology and Biostatistics at McMaster University in Hamilton, Ontario, Canada. Her research interests include participatory research, health policy and planning, and program evaluation. In the past 3 years she has worked on an evaluation of government-funded drug reimbursement programs, local health care needs assessments for seniors and immigrant women, and studies of health professionals' expectations of future physician roles and the psychosocial impacts in populations exposed to solid waste facilities.

Anton J. Kuzel, MD, MHPE, is Associate Professor, Department of Family Practice, at the Medical College of Virginia, Virginia Commonwealth University, Richmond. After completing his undergraduate, graduate, and postgraduate training at the University of Illinois, he served as Associate Director of the Fairfax Family Practice Program in Fairfax, Virginia, and is now Coordinator of Graduate Programs and Faculty Development in the Department of Family Practice at MCV-VCU in Richmond, Virginia. His research interests include the practical application of qualitative inquiry to family medicine research, with particular emphasis on the doctor-patient relationship, preventive care, and chemical dependency.

Ian R. McWhinney, MD, is Professor, Department of Family Medicine at the University of Western Ontario, London, Ontario, Canada. He received his medical degree from Cambridge University in 1949 and spent 14 years in general practice in England before coming to Western in 1968. His interests include the philosophy and history of medicine, the diagnostic process, and the natural history of disease. He has published on these subjects in *Lancet, New England Journal of Medicine, Canadian Medical Association Journal, Proceedings of the Royal Society of Medicine, Journal of Medicine and Philosophy, Journal of Medical Education,* and *Journal of Family Practice.* His textbook of family medicine was published in 1989.

William L. Miller, MD, MA, a Physician-Anthropologist in the Department of Family Medicine at the University of Connecticut, is active in an effort to make qualitative research more accessible to health care researchers. He is co-editor of the quarterly newsletter *The Interpreter,* funded by the North American Primary Care Research Group (NAPCRG) and has contributed book chapters and articles detailing step-by-step applications of qualitative methods. His research interests center on the role of the patient-physician relationship in health care, on physician and patient understanding of pain and pain management, and on hypertension.

David L. Morgan, PhD, is Associate Professor in the Institute on Aging at Portland State University. His research interests center on the role that social networks and personal relationships play in coping with role transitions across the lifecourse. In addition to his book *Focus Groups as Qualitative Research,* his work has appeared in such journals as *American Journal of Sociology, Journal of Health and Social Behavior, Sociology of Health and Illness,* and *The Gerontologist.*

Alfred O. Reid, Jr., PhD, received his PhD in sociology from the University of North Carolina at Chapel Hill in 1992, where he also completed a Fellowship in Applied Medical Sociology. He is a Research Associate in the Department of Family Medicine at the University of North Carolina at Chapel Hill. His research interests center on academic career development. He has studied gender differences in academic careers and the influence of fellowship training on careers in academic medicine.

Moira Stewart, PhD, is Professor in the Centre for Studies in Family Medicine, the Department of Family Medicine at The University of Western Ontario, London, Ontario, Canada. With a PhD in Epidemiology, she has conducted research in the primary care setting for the past 15 years, addressing such topics as research methods, quality of care, doctor-patient communication, and the association of stress with health. She has published papers in *Social Science and Medicine, Journal of the Royal College of General Practitioners, Family Practice: An International Journal, Canadian Medical Association Journal,* and *Medical Care.* She recently edited the books *Communicating with Medical Patients* and *Tools for Primary Care Research.*

Norman A. White, MD, is Professor in the Faculty of Health Sciences at McMaster University, Hamilton, Ontario, Canada. He received his MDCM from McGill University and in 1967 became a Diplomate in Psychiatry at McGill and was admitted by examination as a Fellow to the Royal College of Physicians and Surgeons. He is Director of the Behavioural Medicine Clinic at McMaster. His current research, emphasizing an interdisciplinary approach and combining qualitative and quantitative methods, is in community-based smoking cessation, long-term maintenance of weight loss, post-bypass risk reduction, and psychosocial impacts of environmental contaminants.

Dennis G. Willms, PhD, is Assistant Professor in the Department of Clinical Epidemiology and Biostatistics and an Associate Member of the Department of Anthropology at McMaster University, Hamilton, Ontario, Canada. He is also the Director of the Social Science Program component of the International Clinical Epidemiology Network (INCLEN) at the McMaster Training Centre. His research expertise includes the systematic utilization of qualitative and ethnographic research methods in health science settings and community-based health care programs in Canada and East Africa. He is involved presently in research projects concerned with AIDS prevention (Uganda, Zimbabwe, Canada), supportive cancer care, and the psychosocial impacts of solid waste facilities on populations.

Stephen J. Zyzanski, PhD, is Professor of Family Medicine at Case Western University. His research interests include behavioral medicine and cardiovascular disease epidemiology, primary care and survey research, geriatric and screening studies, and scaling and attitude scale construction. His work has been published in numerous books and journals focusing on primary care and chromic disease research. He also serves as the department's epidemiological, statistical, and computer consultant in the planning of research projects proposed by faculty, fellows, residents, and medical students.